The Complete Idiot's Reference Card

Quick Conversions Chart

This quick chart has handy common measurements that you'll use often.

a pinch = slightly less than $^1/_4$ teaspoon	16 tablespoons = 1 cup
a dash = a few drops	1 tablespoon = $^1/_2$ fluid ounce
1 jigger = 3 tablespoons	1 cup = 8 fluid ounces
3 teaspoons = 1 tablespoon	1 cup = $^1/_2$ pint
4 tablespoons = $^1/_4$ cup	2 cups = 1 pint
$5^1/_2$ tablespoons = $^1/_3$ cup	4 cups = 1 quart
8 tablespoons = $^1/_2$ cup	2 pints = 1 quart
$10^2/_3$ tablespoons = $^2/_3$ cup	4 quarts = 1 gallon
12 tablespoons = $^3/_4$ cup	1 liter = 1.06 quarts

Safe, Effective Home-Brewed Solutions

All-Purpose Cleaner

$^1/_2$ cup vinegar	$^1/_4$ cup baking soda
1 cup clear ammonia	1 gallon warm water

Mix together the ingredients; pour some of it into a spray bottle. Use this to clean all over the house just as you would a commercial spray cleaner such as Fantastic or Formula 409 cleaners.

Heavy-Duty Cleaner

Use this cleaner for really tough jobs such as cleaning grimy ceramic tiles, radiators, air vents, or dirty shower stalls.

1 cup baking soda	1 cup clear ammonia
1 gallon very warm water	1 tablespoon hand-dishwashing soap
1 cup vinegar	

Dissolve the baking soda into the very warm water in a bucket; add the vinegar, ammonia, and liquid soap. Shake or stir to mix the ingredients. Wear rubber gloves, and clean in a well-ventilated area. Rinse with clean water.

Toilet Cleaner

$^1/_4$ cup baking soda	$^1/_4$ cup warm water
$^1/_4$ cup liquid detergent	

Mix together the ingredients. Use a toilet brush to apply the cleaner inside the bowl.

Glass Cleaner

2 cups water	1 tablespoon ammonia
$^1/_2$ cup rubbing alcohol	Blue food coloring (optional)

Mix the water, alcohol, ammonia, and food coloring (if desired) together. Pour the mixture into an empty spray bottle.

continued

alpha
books

Laundry Stain Remover

$^1/_2$ cup ammonia

$^1/_2$ cup white vinegar

$^1/_4$ cup baking soda

2 tablespoons liquid soap

2 quarts water

Mix all ingredients together and pour into a spray bottle. Shake well and then spray the solution on stains; let it soak for a few minutes before washing as usual. Shake the solution before each use.

Car Wash Solution

$^1/_4$ cup hand-dishwashing soap

$^1/_4$ cup baking soda

1 gallon cold or warm (not hot) water

Pour the soap and baking soda into a clean plastic gallon-size jug. Add warm water to fill. To use, shake the container to mix ingredients. Pour 1 cup of the solution into a bucket filled with warm water.

Small Ice Pack

1 cup rubbing alcohol

2 cups water

1 quart-size self-sealing plastic freezer bag

Large Ice Pack

2 cups rubbing alcohol

4 cups water

1 gallon-size self-sealing plastic freezer bag

Mix together the alcohol and the water, and pour into the bag. Zip the bag shut and place it in the freezer. Leave the ice pack in the freezer until you need it. You can re-use these bags many times; after using, simply place back into the freezer for next time. The alcohol and water mixture will not freeze solid; it stays slushy and can be shaped around difficult places such as knees or elbows.

Rough Elbow Softener

1 teaspoon lemon juice

1 teaspoon vegetable oil

1 teaspoon honey

Beat well until thoroughly blended. Rub mixture onto elbows, and massage for a few minutes.

Extra Body Treatment For Hair

2 tablespoons molasses or honey

2 tablespoons unflavored gelatin

1 tablespoon milk

1 tablespoon beer (stale beer is fine)

Combine ingredients in a small bowl. Comb or brush the solution into your hair, then cover your hair with a plastic shower cap and wrap a towel around your head. Leave the conditioner on for 30 minutes. Rinse with warm water, and then shampoo.

Ant Traps

$^1/_4$ cup sugar

$^1/_4$ cup baking yeast

$^1/_2$ cup molasses

3×5-inch small index cards

Mix sugar, yeast, and molasses in a small bowl, and smear a thin layer of the mixture on index cards with a spatula. Place the cards, syrup side up, in areas where ants travel. These are safe and nonpoisonous.

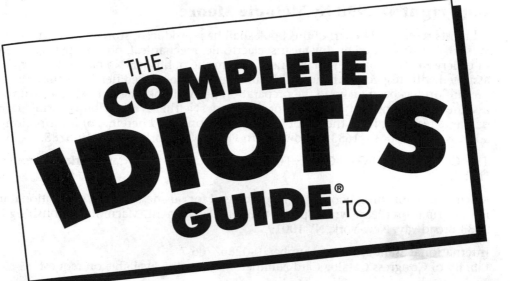

THE COMPLETE IDIOT'S GUIDE® TO

Household Solutions

by Melodie Moore

alpha books

A Division of Macmillan General Reference
A Simon & Schuster Macmillan Company
1633 Broadway, New York, NY 10019-6785

Macmillan Publishing books may be purchased for business or sales promotional use. For information please write: Special Markets Department, Macmillan Publishing USA, 1633 Broadway, New York, NY 10019.

International Standard Book Number: 0-02862706-7
Library of Congress Catalog Card Number: Information available on request

00 99 98   8 7 6 5 4 3 2 1

Interpretation of the printing code: the rightmost number of the first series of numbers is the year of the book's printing; the rightmost number of the second series of numbers is the number of the book's printing. For example, a printing code of 98-1 shows that the first printing occurred in 1998.

Printed in the United States of America

Note: This publication contains the opinions and ideas of its authors. It is intended to provide helpful and informative material on the subject matter covered. It is sold with the understanding that the author and publisher are not engaged in rendering professional services in the book. If the reader requires personal assistance or advice, a competent professional should be consulted.

The authors and publisher specifically disclaim any responsibility for any liability, loss or risk, personal or otherwise, which is incurred as a consequence, directly or indirectly, of the use and application of any of the contents of this book.

Alpha Development Team

Publisher
Kathy Nebenhaus

Editorial Director
Gary M. Krebs

Managing Editor
Bob Shuman

Marketing Brand Manager
Felice Primeau

Senior Editor
Nancy Mikhail

Development Editors
Phil Kitchel
Jennifer Perillo
Amy Zavatto

Assistant Editor
Maureen Horn

Production Team

Development Editor
Carol Hupping

Production Editor
Suzanne Snyder

Copy Editor
Krista Hansing

Cover Designer
Mike Freeland

Photo Editor
Richard H. Fox

Illustrator
Jody P. Schaeffer

Designer
Kevin Spear

Indexer
Sandy Henselmeier
Nadia Ibrahim

Layout/Proofreading
Angela Calvert
Kim Cofer
Mary Hunt

Contents at a Glance

Contents

Part 2: The Clothes Closet   55

4 Durable Duds   57

22 Home Maintenance and Repairs 305

Foreword

Laundry. Mortgage. Mosquito bites.

Dust bunnies. Mildew. Headaches.

Weeds. Rust. Shampoo buildup.

Sexy subjects? Uh uh. But these are facts of life, just some of the hundreds of oh-so-real facts of life that every one of us can use some help with. This book is that help.

Because let's face it: No matter how brilliant, clever, or dexterous we may be, we may still splatter Mom's tomato sauce on our favorite shirt, leave our garden tools out in the rain, lose a sock in the wash, or MAYBE buy a car that's a lemon. And (through no fault of our own, of course) our sink may spring a leak, our paint may begin to chip, and our youngster may get stung by a bee.

No need to worry—or call an emergency hotline. Because in the pages of this book, there's bound to be an easy, practical and smart solution to every one of life's common pesky problems. And there's also—even better—common-sense advice on how to avoid and prevent many of those greasy, grimy, sticky, smelly, caustic and costly household problems next time. And as a result, of course, we can save ourselves a bundle of money, time and headaches. Not bad, hey?

Indeed, come to think of it, *The Complete Idiot's Guide to Household Solutions* is really a bad title. Idiot? You and I may be terribly ignorant about how to fix a leaky faucet or get rid of aphids in the garden, but at least we know that —and we know we can use some help. Which is why we've turned to this book.

Now I call that smart.

Esther Davidowitz, Deputy Editor of *First for women* magazine and a former editor of "The Better Way," *Good Housekeeping* magazine, has had articles published in *Redbook*, *Woman's Day*, *Family Circle*, *Seventeen*, *Parents*, and *Ladies' Home Journal*, among other magazines.

Introduction

When it comes to running a household, we've all felt like an idiot from time to time. There is so much to do and remember, and so many small problems that need to be dealt with every day. How many times have you thought to yourself: "I know there's probably a quick and easy solution to this problem, but I'm just not sure exactly what it is?"

Many of the solutions in this book are not new. They are tried-and-true tips and remedies, proven over time. Our parents and grandparents relied a great deal on common sense and on basic products and tools to get the jobs done because they did not have the gazillion different soaps, gels, sprays, and gadgets that we have now. While we've got a lot more household helpers than generations past, we've still got to wash the dishes after meals, shop and cook, and take care of fixing all the little things that wear out or break down from time to time. If anything, it has gotten more complicated to run a household, because households are more complex than ever.

Think of this book as an owner's manual for your home, be it a small apartment, a large house, or something in between. This book is a comprehensive reference of thousands of time- and money-saving hints, efficient low-cost solutions to everyday household dilemmas, and formulas for homemade alternatives to commercial products. Unlike those you can buy, you'll find few toxic ingredients in the solutions here; they're in only a few formulas as a last resort.

Most of the cleaning ingredients included in this book you'll already have on hand. Vinegar, baking soda, salt, ammonia, and alcohol are inexpensive and very effective when you know how to mix them with what and then use them in the right ways. And they're awfully inexpensive—far less than many brand-name products on the market that have to be priced high to cover the costs of their packaging, ingredients added purely for aesthetics (such as fragrance), and their national advertising campaigns.

Here's my suggestion for getting the most out of this book: Skim through it first so that you have a good idea of what's here and how it can help you. Then put it some place handy—perhaps right in the kitchen—so you can pull it out and look up something at a moment's notice. I bet you'll find yourself reaching for it often.

How to Use this Book

Part 1, Cleaning Solutions Room by Room, provides you with ways to tackle cleaning all around the house. Solutions are included for the kitchen, bathrooms, bedrooms and living rooms—everything from quick and easy ways to clean tubs, toilets and appliances, to removing stains from glassware and carpets.

Part 2, The Clothes Closet, is packed full of ideas to make your clothes last longer. You'll find out how to buy great clothes that you will wear for many years and then the best ways to care for them. Solutions for removing stains and making basic sewing repairs are just a few of the handy hints you'll find in this section.

Part 3, The Lawn, Garden, and Patio, offers ways to make the time you spend working outdoors around the house more enjoyable. Mix up a batch of homemade fertilizer or use one of the home-brew weed killers to make your lawn look beautiful. Find out how to get your garage organized, how to keep your car looking great, and even how to save money when you buy a car.

Part 4, All in the Family, here you'll find solutions for every member of the family, even the four-legged ones. For your children or grandchildren you'll find solutions for diaper rash, how to make homemade baby wipes, and how to entertain the little ones. If you have a family pet, look here for ways to eliminate pet odors and make toys for them. Check out the home remedies section for quick and easy ways to make you feel better. You'll also find tips for the holidays, rainy day projects, beauty tips, and home office solutions.

Part 5, Food, Cooking and Nutrition, gives you good ideas for keeping the refrigerator and pantry stocked and for cooking inexpensive, nutritious meals. You'll learn how to purchase and prepare foods, how long specific foods will keep fresh, and how to save money at the food store. Whether you are a gourmet cook or just cook the basics you'll pick up ideas here.

Part 6, Home Maintenance, has tips for the person who fixes things around the house (don't we all!)—quick and easy ways to keep your house in tip-top condition. You'll also find solutions for eliminating pests and how to save energy around the house.

Extras

Don't overlook all the helpful little boxes throughout; they're filled with useful tidbits of information and more clever ideas to make your life easier. Here's what you'll find in each type of box.

Watch Out!

Take care with these cautions and warnings.

Tightwad Tip

These easy tips are also easy on the pocketbook.

Bet You Didn't Know

Look for these to refresh your memory—or to learn something new. (And you thought you knew it all!)

Smart Solutions

These tips offer a smart or quick and easy way to solve a household problem.

Special Thanks from the Publisher to the Technical Reviewers

Our thanks to the following for reviewing parts of this book and for providing valuable insights and direction:

Susan Crites Price writes on parenting and other lifestyle subjects for numerous magazines, newspapers, and online services. She is the author, with her husband Tom, of *The Working Parents Help Book* (Peterson's, 1996), winner of a Parents' Choice Award.

Heidi Stonehill is a researcher for Rodale Press Garden Books, as well as the editor of the *Organic Gardening Country Calendar and Planning Guide*.

Sarah Hodgson is a dog trainer, ad owner and director of Cooperative Canine, in Bedford Village, NY. She writes a pet care column for the *New York Times* and is the author of *The Complete Idiot's Guide to Choosing, Training, and Raising a Dog*.

Part 1
Cleaning Solutions
Room by Room

Cleaning the house can be hard work. There are so many different things that must be done—and none of us want to spend all weekend cleaning. In the chapters that follow, you'll find helpful hints and solutions that will whip your house into tip-top shape without wearing you out. This section also contains lots of simple formulas for making your own inexpensive cleaning products that are just as effective as those you can buy.

Chapter 1

Doing the Dirty Deed: Cleaning the Kitchen

In This Chapter

➤ Effective, inexpensive cleaning products and how to use them

➤ Doing the dishes, silverware, and pots and pans

➤ Solutions for cleaning kitchen surfaces and large and small appliances

➤ Cleaning stains and those nasty baked-on foods

➤ Preventing clogged drains

➤ Eliminating kitchen odors

Quite some time ago I read an article about an ambitious inventor working on a self-cleaning kitchen. (Not an oven, mind you, but a kitchen!) I thought to myself, what a great idea; maybe I can postpone cleaning my kitchen long enough for him to work out the bugs. But unfortunately, his research was in vain; the self-cleaning kitchen was not to be. So we're all stuck with the inevitable: a dirty kitchen and all its messy contents (dishes, counters, sticky brown gunk on cookie sheets and baking pans, and so on and so forth) that have to be cleaned without the aid of high technology.

But that doesn't necessarily mean cleaning with blood, sweat, and tears. There are lots of ways to make those nasty jobs easier, as you'll discover in the upcoming pages. Read on!

Stick With the Basics First

Solving cleaning problems in the kitchen can be confusing, not to mention hazardous to your wallet. Just take a trip down the cleaning supplies aisle of the grocery store. What do you see? Dozens of jazzy packages of products for all sorts of jobs about the house, tempting you with come-ons like *New, Improved! Deep-Down Cleaning! Kills Germs Dead!*

Do you really need 'em?

You'd be surprised how many you don't. Many cleaning jobs can be done easily and effectively with just a few simple products that cost a fraction of the price of fancy bottles and boxes.

Basic cleaners such as liquid dish detergent, warm water, vinegar, baking soda, household ammonia, and salt will tackle all but the toughest jobs. And these cleaners are not only cheap, but most of them are also easy on your hands, your health, and the environment.

When cleaning any surface, always start with the most gentle cleaning product. If it does a good job, there's no reason to use something more powerful. If the surface to be cleaned can be washed, first try plain old soap and water. I like to take a bucket of warm water and add a squirt of liquid dish detergent; I dip a sponge or cloth into the soap and water and give whatever I'm cleaning a good old wipe-down. If the soap-and-water trick works, I can mark one more job off my cleaning list and quickly move on. If that doesn't quite do it, I've got other good options.

Smart Solution

When cleaning with vinegar, always use white distilled vinegar. Apple cider vinegar usually has a brown color that can actually stain whatever you are trying to clean.

Vinegar: Almost Too Good to Be True

No kitchen should be without the very best cleaner of them all: simple, dirt-cheap white vinegar. Its secret weapon is its acidity, which is just strong enough to cut through dirt and fatty spills without damaging surfaces. Vinegar is the cleaning wizard because it's got so many uses: cleaning windows, removing spots and smells from carpets, cutting grease and grime, and freshening the air.

Baking Soda's Not Just for Baking

That little box of baking soda can pack quite a punch—and it does it just for pennies. Baking soda is a nonpolluting gentle abrasive and grime cutter that you can use to clean counters, pots, pans, and fixtures. It also deodorizes carpets, refrigerators, shoes, and other smelly stuff around the house. Try baking soda instead of harsh scouring powders such as Comet or Ajax. You'll still have to use the strong stuff every once in a while for tough stains, but you can't beat baking soda for light cleaning.

Baking soda is also good for eliminating odors around the house. Most deodorizers work either as a fragrance (for example, a room deodorizer) to mask odors or as an absorbent (such as charcoal, coffee grounds, and salt) to physically entrap the odors.

Fragrances added to lots of household products ("clean lemon scent," "pine fresh,") do not actually eliminate bad odors; they just overpower them with a smell that's more acceptable. And absorbents eventually release back into the air some of the odor they've been containing because they can hold only so much of it for so long.

Bet You Didn't Know

The reason baking soda works so well as a cleaner is that dirt and grease usually contain fatty acids, and these acids are neutralized by the mildly alkaline baking soda. After they're neutralized, the fatty acids (which are normally insoluble) break up, dissolve in water, and can then easily be wiped away.

But baking soda actually neutralizes odors in the air. It deodorizes by chemically reacting to odors and irreversibly converting them to a fresher smell. (You'll find more information on controlling odors later in this chapter.)

Ammonia Packs a Punch

Household ammonia is actually only about 10 percent ammonia; the rest is water. But don't think of it as watered down and weak; it's plenty strong enough for most household jobs. You can buy household ammonia that is clear or slightly cloudy. When the ammonia is cloudy, it contains detergent to boost its cleaning power. Ammonia's powerful smell is sometimes tamed with lemon or pine scent, as indicated on the label. Household ammonia is good for many jobs in the kitchen, including cleaning windows, cutting grease, removing wax from floors, and bringing the sparkle back to your oven.

Salt for Seasoning, and Then Some

No kitchen should be without its salt. Even if you don't season your foods with it, keep some salt handy for cleaning up oven spills and removing burned-on foods from pots and pans. You can mix it with other common ingredients to make a super copper polish (as you'll read about later in this chapter), and you can use it to clean and deodorize your drains and garbage disposal.

When you make a paste of baking soda for cleaning anything, you can add a little salt to give the paste more scrubbing power. The salt granules give it some grit. And because salt absorbs odors, it actually takes some of those bad kitchen smells down the drain with it.

Doing The Dishes

If you've got a dishwasher (and I'm not talking about the kid or the spouse!), use it. It will be easier on you (no dishpan hands, more free time), you'll break fewer pieces because you're not handling soap-slippery dishes, and it'll be easier on your utility bills. Washing dishes by hand uses up to 43 percent more water than washing with a standard automatic dishwasher.

To save energy, stop the washer after the rinse cycle and open it up so that the dishes can air dry. The heat dryer cycle uses quite a bit of electricity.

Of course not everybody has a dishwasher, and even if you do, sometimes you've just got to wash by hand. Here are some tips for doing it easier, better, and even cheaper.

Dish Detergents

As weird as it sounds, soap and detergent are totally different animals. Soap is made from fat and alkali, and detergents have two key ingredients: surfactants and builders. Surfactants work to dissolve dirt, and builders (such as phosphate) soften the water to make the surfactants work better.

Soaps work great in soft water, but are not as effective as detergents in hard water. Detergents, on the other hand, work beautifully in both hard and soft water. That's why you will find only a few soaps and many detergents on the grocery store shelves. Detergents also make more bubbles (suds) than most soaps.

Tightwad Tip

Empty detergent bottle? Don't throw it out quite yet. Add a little water to it when it's almost empty, and you'll be able to get a few more washes out if it.

Stretching Your Detergent

You can cut your costs of dish detergent—without cutting their cleaning power—by diluting them. Save an empty bottle of dish detergent, and when you buy a new one, pour one half of the detergent into the old bottle. Fill both with water. Rotate several times to mix. (Don't shake because shaking creates lots of soap bubbles, which will leave little room for the water and detergent to mix. Then, if you open the bottle quickly after shaking, the bubbles will spill out just like a soda bottle that's been dropped or shaken.)

You'll end up with twice as much detergent by diluting the original product. It may not be as bubbly, but it's not the bubbles that do the cleaning! Those bubbles are mainly there to give you the illusion that the detergent is doing its job. I find that my diluted bottles last just as long as undiluted ones.

Detergent Booster

To boost the power of your detergent when you're washing greasy dishes and pans by hand, add $1/4$ to $1/2$ cup white vinegar to the dishwater.

Glassware and China

China stains. Use a damp cloth dipped in baking soda. To remove tea stains from cups and teapots, add a tablespoon of bleach to lukewarm water.

TLC for delicates. Before you hand-wash china, crystal, or other delicate items, lay a towel at the bottom of your sink to cushion them and prevent them from chipping or breaking.

Glass nicks and chips. You don't have to throw away a glass with a small chip or nick in it. Just smooth out the nick or chip with fine sandpaper or an emery board.

Stuck drinking glasses. To loosen two drinking glasses that seem hopelessly stuck together, fill the inner glass with cold water and stand the glasses in hot water. Expansion and contraction from the temperature difference will often free them.

Smart Solution

If you like to wash dishes and counters with a sponge, but hate the odor the sponge gives off after a while, clean it quick and easy in the dishwasher with a regular load of dishes. You can either put the sponge into the silverware basket or use a clothes pin to attach it to the top rack so that it doesn't drop to the bottom of the dishwasher.

Watch Out!

When you load glassware into the dishwasher, make sure it does not rub against another glass or anything else in the dishwasher. When two glasses rub together, small scratches can form over time.

Smart Solution

You can make homemade glue for broken pieces of china by using flour and the white of an egg. Add enough flour to the white of the egg until you get a consistency similar to white glue. Apply to the break. Secure until dry. This solution is best used for decorative china because the glue will not hold up well when washed in hot soapy water.

Cloudy glassware. When cut glassware gets a thick white film on it, you can apply vinegar to dissolve it. Simply apply full-strength vinegar to the cloudy glassware with an old toothbrush and scrub the cracks and crevices. Rinse with clean water. For regular cleaning that will keep the cloudy residue from returning, use a solution of one part vinegar to three parts water.

Smart Solution

You can use the plastic trays from meat packages to stack between your good china to keep it from scratching or breaking. Wash the trays in warm, soapy water and let them dry. Then cut them into shapes that will cushion your dishes. This is especially helpful when you're packing and moving such breakables.

Plasticware

Oh those little plastic bowls and strange containers, they are so handy to use. Here's some ways to keep yours clean and odor free.

Plastic stain remover. Remove stains from plastic cups and storage dishes by scouring them with baking soda. Sprinkle baking soda on the stains, and scrub with warm water. Repeat if necessary. If you prefer to remove stains without scrubbing, just put the stained plastic item outside in the sun (direct sunlight is best). Even stubborn tomato stains will disappear.

Plastic odor eater. Plastic storage containers can acquire a bad odor that is very hard to remove. Even after washing several times, the odor can remain. To get rid of it, crumple newspaper into wads and stuff them into the containers. Cover the containers tightly and let them sit overnight. The next day, remove the paper and take a deep whiff. Go ahead, don't be afraid. Unless a skunk has been inside your containers, the odor really will be gone.

Knives, Forks, and Spoons

Use these hints to clean and polish your utensils with ease.

Rust relief. You can get rid of the rust on a knife or other utensil by sticking it into an onion and letting it sit for a while. Move the knife or utensil back and forth a few times to let the onion juices work their magic. When the rust is gone, wash the knife with soap and water.

Silverware polish. You can polish silver by adding a tablespoon of baking soda to a quart of water. Pour the water and baking soda mix into a large pot and add the silverware. Bring the water to a boil and let it boil for about three minutes. Let the water cool, and remove the silverware. Dry thoroughly with a soft towel.

For really tough stains that remain after this method, scrub the spots with white toothpaste that contains baking soda. Use an old toothbrush to scrub away the stains. After you remove the stains, keep the silverware spotless by cleaning it regularly in boiling water and baking soda.

Cleaning Pots and Pans

Cleaning stains and those nasty baked-on foods from your pots and pans can be a real chore. Here are some ideas to make the job easier.

Removing Stains

Getting rid of stains is one tough job. Use these tricks of the trade to get the job done.

Nonstick pots and pans. Combine 3 tablespoons of automatic dishwasher detergent and 1 cup of water. Pour the mixture into the pot, and simmer on the stove until the stains disappear. Then wash the pot well, dry it, and coat it with a thin layer of vegetable oil. To apply the vegetable oil, pour one teaspoon of oil onto a paper towel and rub it on the pot or pan. Then take a clean paper towel and wipe out any excess oil.

Watch Out!

The finish on nonstick pans can easily be scratched. Never use any type of sharp utensils (such as knives, forks, or metal pancake flippers) to clean them. Unless you have burned something in the pan, you should be able to clean nonstick pans easily with hot soapy water. You can use a nylon scrubber but not a steel-wool pad.

Smart Solution

When you find that your rubber spatula has become tattered on the edges, don't throw it away. Instead, trim off the rough edges, and it will be as good as new. You can trim off tattered edges again and again, until there's nothing left!

Most nonstick pans should not be washed in the dishwasher. Unless the manufacturer specifically recommends washing in the dishwasher, you should assume that hand-washing is the best way to go.

Stainless pots and pans. Rub the stains with a cut lemon or with a cloth soaked in lemon juice until the stains disappear.

Aluminum pots and pans. Fill the pan almost to the top with water, and add a piece of rhubarb to the pot. Gently boil the rhubarb in the pot until the stains are gone. You'll want to fill the pot as full as you can with water; otherwise, the lower portion will look cleaner than the top, which was not covered with the water/rhubarb solution.

Smart Solution

Make your own copper polish by mixing equal parts of flour, white vinegar, and salt. Rub this solution on your tarnished copper, and then wash it off with hot water.

Tightwad Tip

You can prevent a steel-wool pad from becoming a soapy, rusty mess by putting it in the freezer in a bag or an empty plastic margarine tub. Do this after every use, and you'll be able to use the same pad several times before you need to replace it. Another way to save is to cut the pads in half with kitchen scissors before using them. The smaller pads are easier to use, and your box will last twice as long.

An alternative is to fill the pot with water and boil a lemon in it until the stains disappear. Use half a lemon for a small- to medium-size pot and a whole lemon cut into halves for a large pot. If any stains remain, apply lemon juice directly to the stain and rub with baking soda.

Cream of tartar can clear discoloration on aluminum cookware (and can also remove light stains from porcelain). Simply fill the cookware with hot water, add 2 tablespoons cream of tartar per quart, bring to a boil, and simmer 10 minutes.

Copper-bottomed pots and pans. Mix table salt and white vinegar to form a gritty paste, then apply and work in with a fine (00) steel-wool pad.

You also can use catsup to clean copper-bottom pots and pans and copper utensils. Rub some catsup and sprinkle salt on the copper. Let sit for several hours. Wash in hot soapy water. The copper will look like new: The acid in the catsup dissolves any brown spots on the copper, and the salt granules help scrub away any dirt.

Getting Those Really Tough Pot Stains

To remove stubborn baked-on foods from pots and pans, try these tips:

➤ Pour a few inches of water (enough to cover the baked-on food) into the pot or skillet, and bring it to a boil. Boil for a few minutes, and the baked-on food will scrub out much easier.

➤ Make a paste of baking soda and water, and leave it on the burnt area overnight before scrubbing the pot.

➤ Rinse the pot with cold water, then sprinkle the burnt area with table salt. Allow the salt to remain on the burn for about 10 minutes before you scrub the pot. You may need to repeat the salt application.

➤ Fill the pot halfway with hot water, then add 1/2 cup of white vinegar and 2 tablespoons of baking soda. Bring the mixture to a boil, cover, and simmer for 30 minutes. Then wash the pot.

➤ Pour some tomato juice or tomato sauce into the pot, then wash the pot with hot soapy water.

Cleaning cast iron. Wipe out the grease and any loose pieces of food with a paper towel. Fill the pan with water and detergent, and set it on the stove to simmer. This will loosen most of the burned-on food, but the pan will need to be re-seasoned (see below).

Seasoning cast iron. To prevent foods from sticking to cast-iron skillets and griddles, you need to periodically season them. To do this, wash them in hot, sudsy water, and then rinse and dry. Then cover the inside of the skillet with vegetable oil. Take a paper towel and rub the oil up the interior sides of the pan. Place the pan in the oven pre-heated to the lowest setting (warm) for about 2 hours. After removing the skillet from the oven, let it cool and then wipe out excess oil with paper towels. When you notice that foods are starting to stick, it is time to season the pan again.

Cleaning glass. To remove food stuck or burned on CorningWare and similar glass dishes, add four parts water to one part vinegar, and bring to a gentle boil. When the water cools down, you should be able to gently scrub off the food.

Cleaning baking pans and sheets. To remove cooked-on food from shallow baking pans and cookie sheets, use an expired credit card (or any other similar plastic card). The plastic is hard enough to get under the food and lift it off, but it won't scratch the surface as metal would.

Watch Out!

Never let a cast-iron skillet or pot soak with water in it. Always clean it after use and quickly dry it to keep it from rusting. Cast-iron cookware is a good investment; it cooks evenly and will last a lifetime.

Tightwad Tip

The plastic mesh bags that onions and other produce come in are great for scrubbing carrots and potatoes and pots and pans. Fold the bag over until it's about 3 inches long. Tie it in the middle with a small piece of string or dental floss. Then pouf up the bag and scrub away!

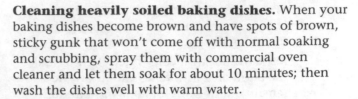

Cleaning heavily soiled baking dishes. When your baking dishes become brown and have spots of brown, sticky gunk that won't come off with normal soaking and scrubbing, spray them with commercial oven cleaner and let them soak for about 10 minutes; then wash the dishes well with warm water.

Cleaning a broiler pan. Remove burned-on food from a broiler pan by sprinkling powdered laundry detergent or dishwasher detergent on the pan while it's still hot. Sprinkle the detergent with water, and place a dampened paper towel on top of the burned food. Leave the paper towel on the spot for 30 minutes, and then use the paper towel to rub the burned food off the broiler pan.

The powdered laundry or dishwasher detergent does a super job on the broiler pan without the harshness and fumes of commercial oven cleaner.

Bet You Didn't Know

You can remove rust from baking sheets and pans by applying scouring powder or baking soda with a cut raw potato. Dip the potato (the cut side) into the scouring powder or baking soda, and use it to scrub away the rust. The moist side of the potato holds the scouring powder, and the starchy potato water aids the soda in removing the rust.

Smart Solution

To brighten up any yellowing appliance, mix together $1/4$ cup bleach, $1/4$ cup baking soda, and 4 cups warm water. Sponge this on the surface and let stand for about 10 minutes. Rinse the appliance with clean water and dry thoroughly.

Don't Sweat The Small Stuff

The small appliances in your kitchen get lots of use, and they can get real grungy before you know it. There are almost as many good tips for cleaning small appliances as there are small appliances!

Always use gentle cleaning products on appliances; a scratch left by harsh scouring powders or a steel-wool pad will last forever. Usually a soft towel or sponge will get the job done.

Electronic Touchpads

Many new appliances (such as microwaves, dishwashers, and ovens) have an electronic touchpad instead of a knob. The keypads may look like they are completely sealed, but water can work its way into the fine breaks in the coating and cause the controls to malfunction. When cleaning the touchpads, wring almost all the water off your sponge or rag before wiping them down. Never spray any type of cleaner (or even water) directly onto the pad. If it's soiled enough to need a cleaner, spray a very small amount on your cloth or sponge instead.

Can Openers

To clean an electric can opener, use an old toothbrush to loosen the dirt, and then run a paper towel through the cutting assembly. Next, spray the metal parts with nonstick vegetable spray to keep them clean longer.

You can wash manual can openers in the dishwasher.

Blenders and Food Processors

To give the plastic container of your blender or food processor a quick clean, here's an easy, time-saving idea: Fill the container half full with warm water, and add a small squirt of dish detergent. Turn the blender on for about 15 seconds. Then pour the soapy water out, rinse with clean water, and let it dry.

Coffeemakers

To eliminate unpleasant lime deposits that can build up and clog your coffeemaker, clean it once a month. Fill the water reservoir with 2 cups white vinegar and 1 cup water; then turn on the brew cycle and let the vinegar water run through. Rinse thoroughly by filling the reservoir with clean water and "brewing" it again, and then once again. You will be surprised how much better your morning coffee will taste! You can also pour the vinegar water used to clean your coffeemaker on your rubber drain board to remove soap scum and lime deposits.

Toasters

Always unplug the toaster before you clean it. Then remove the crumbs in the bottom. If your toaster has a crumb tray, pull it out and shake or brush the crumbs out. If not, then turn the toaster upside down and shake out the crumbs into the sink or a garbage pail. It is important to remove the crumbs often because they will attract unwanted company (perhaps ants, roaches, and other nasty pests!).

Wipe the outside of the toaster with a cloth dipped in warm water and baking soda to clean the metal and give it a nice shine. If plastic has melted onto the toaster (from a plastic bread bag that got too close, for example) wipe it off with a little nail-polish remover.

Microwave Ovens

You can clean your microwave and eliminate odors with vinegar. Pour $1/4$ cup white vinegar and 1 cup water in a small glass or ceramic bowl, and then microwave on high for 5 minutes. The steam from the vinegar water will remove any odors and will soften baked-on splatters. Open the oven door and allow some of the steam to escape before you start to wipe down the walls. After the vinegar water cools down, dip a sponge or cloth into the water and use it to wipe off the inside surfaces of the microwave and around the door seals.

The Big Ones

Cleaning a large appliance does not have to be a big job. Here are some tips to get the job done without too much time or elbow grease.

Dishwashers

To remove stubborn stains, white film, or just plain crud from the inside of your dishwasher (and from glassware and dishes) run a cup of vinegar through the whole dishwasher cycle once a month. The vinegar will also reduce the soap buildup inside the pipes. You can also do this by pouring vinegar into a coffee cup or small bowl and sitting it upright in the top rack with a full load of dishes.

When your dishwasher smells less than fresh, sprinkle some baking soda in the bottom of it and let it sit a few hours or overnight before you run the machine (full of dishes, of course) through a normal cycle. The odors will be washed away with the baking soda during the wash cycle.

Watch Out!

Be sure to unplug the refrigerator before giving it a major cleaning.

Smart Solution

To make defrosting your freezer a snap, turn off the freezer and use a hair dryer to melt the ice. Loosen large ice pieces with a wooden or plastic pancake flipper (not metal—it can scratch). Wipe clean with soap and water, then spray the clean interior freezer surfaces with an edible nonstick spray such as Pam. Next time, the ice will slide right off when you defrost it.

Refrigerators and Freezers

A mild cleaner is all you should need to clean the outside of your refrigerator and freezer. An all-purpose spray cleaner, vinegar and water, or baking soda sprinkled on a damp sponge or cloth should all do a good job of it.

Mildew control. To prevent mildew from building up on the inside of your refrigerator, clean it with a solution of half water and half white vinegar. Then wipe down the whole inside (including the shelves) with full-strength white vinegar. If you still have a problem with mildew, check your temperature setting. Some refrigerators have an energy saver setting that may cause some extra moisture to accumulate inside, inviting mildew.

Gaskets. To clean the gasket (the white rubber around the door of the refrigerator that keeps the seal tight), wipe it with rubbing alcohol. To keep the gasket from cracking, give it a light coat of mineral oil. Wipe off any excess with a paper towel.

Freezer interior. To clean occasional food spills and sometimes even ice formation in the freezer section of a frost-free refrigerator, dip a clean sponge into a solution of 1 quart warm water to 1/4 cup baking soda. The baking soda not only cleans, disinfects, and deodorizes, but it also keeps the sponge from freezing on and sticking to the surface of the freezer.

Tip-top refrigerator cleaner. The best way to remove that stubborn dirt and grime on top of your refrigerator is to make this home-brew cleaner: Mix 1 part ammonia to 10 parts hot water. Let the solution soak on the muck to break down the grease; then wipe it all off with a cloth or towel.

To make the cleaning job easier next time, you can do one of two things:

➤ Apply a thin layer of appliance wax on the clean, dry surface; or

➤ Cover the just-cleaned top with plastic wrap. The wrap will cling and create a nonslip surface. The wrap collects grease and dirt as it protects the surface from scratches. When it's dirty, just peel off the plastic wrap, throw it away, and put down more plastic wrap.

Coils. In addition to cleaning the inside and outside of the refrigerator, you also need to clean the coils. This is a very important step because if the coils get very dirty, the refrigerator won't cool foods properly. And dirty coils make the fridge work much harder, using significantly more electricity.

To clean the coils, remove the louvered base grill or kick plate on the bottom of your fridge. Because the coils are usually hard to reach, here's an easy way to get to them: Take a yardstick and attach an old sock to the end with a rubber band. Use the yardstick to wipe the dirt and grime off the coils. If you don't find the coils under the front of your fridge, you'll find them in the back. You will need to pull the refrigerator away from the wall to get to them.

Tightwad Tip

When doing any cleaning job, don't use too much soap. Not only is it wasteful, but you'll just have that much more to rinse off.

Washing Machines

Clean the outside of the washing machine with baking soda and warm water. Dip a clean cloth or sponge into warm water, and sprinkle some baking soda on it. Wipe down the outside with the baking soda and water, then rinse by wiping down with clean water.

To clean the inside of your washing machine (yes, it really does need cleaning!) run the washing machine through a rinse cycle with 2 cups of white vinegar. The vinegar will not only clean the inside of the machine, it will also remove soap scum from the inside of pipes.

If You Can't Stand the Heat: Cleaning Ovens and Stoves

Lucky you if you've got a self-cleaning oven. But if not, you don't have to resort to those very nasty commercial oven cleaners. There are other options.

Watch Out!

If you have a self-cleaning oven, never use a commercial oven cleaner on it because the harsh cleaner will damage or destroy the interior finish.

Tightwad Tip

Use a paste of baking soda to clean the chrome and glass doors of ovens. Baking soda, by the way, is a good cleaner for any chrome appliance.

Salt the Spill

To clean up large messy spills in the oven, sprinkle them immediately with table salt; it will absorb much or all of the overflowing custard, gravy mess, or whatever else made it to the oven floor. When the oven has cooled, brush away the burned-on food with a damp sponge. The salt will make the spill much easier to clean up. This method saves time and work because you won't have to clean the whole oven as often!

After a small spill in the oven, soak a cloth in ammonia and leave it on the burnt area for about an hour. The ammonia will loosen the food enough so you will be able to scrape off the spot with a plastic pancake turner without scratching the enamel inside your oven.

Whole-Oven Cleaning

A cheap and effective way to clean a dirty oven is with plain old household ammonia. Pour 1 cup of ammonia in a glass bowl and place it in the oven. Close the oven and let it sit overnight. In the morning, pour the ammonia into a pail of warm water, and use this solution to wash down the inside of the oven. Open a window when you wash down the oven because the fumes will be very strong for a few minutes before they dissipate.

Range Hood Cleaner Without Elbow Grease

To clean your range hood filter, place it into your dishwasher and wash on a normal cycle right along with the dishes. It will come out clean and looking like new.

If you don't have a dishwasher, buy (or borrow) some automatic dish-washing detergent, and place the filter in a container large enough to submerge it. Fill the container with very hot water and add 6 tablespoons of the dish detergent and mix well. Now put in the filter and let it soak overnight. In the morning, swish the filter around for a few minutes. Rinse, shake dry, and put the filter back in the hood.

Range Rings

The chrome rings (and burner liners) on your range can be almost impossible to clean once gunk gets burned on them. If you want to keep them from getting gross-looking without going to the trouble of covering them with aluminum foil, there's a quick and easy solution.

Start with clean burner liners. You can buy replacement burner liners at a discount store such as WalMart or K Mart. Then keep them clean by washing them once a week in your dishwasher (with a full load of dishes, of course). Hot water will loosen grease that's too hard to remove with a cloth, and there will be no buildup of hard-to-remove stains. The key is to do this often.

The Kitchen Sink

You can save time in the kitchen by rinsing the kitchen sink with hot, soapy water after each use. But from time to time you'll need to give it a deep cleaning.

Stainless Steel Sinks

The best way to clean a stainless steel sink is with club soda (or seltzer) or white vinegar. Use a soft cloth to wipe the sink clean with the club soda or vinegar. If the sink has some grease or other grime in it, sprinkle baking soda on the sink beforehand.

You can also make small scratches in stainless steel sinks disappear by rubbing over the scratches in the direction of the grain of the steel with fine steel wool. Buff with a soft cloth after removing the scratches.

Porcelain Sinks

You can remove stains from a porcelain sink by filling the sink with warm water and adding a few tablespoons of chlorine bleach. Let the bleach solution sit for an hour or two before draining the water and rinsing the sink. If the spots still remain

Tightwad Tip

Don't throw away club soda (or seltzer) or other clear soft drink such as Sprite or 7-Up that is too flat to drink. Instead, use it to clean your stainless steel sink. Even without its original carbonation, the clear soda will make your sink sparkle.

Watch Out!

When cleaning a stainless steel sink, do not use a heavy abrasive cleaner or steel-wool pads because they will scratch the surface. If you have a very tough stain and must scrub with a steel-wool pad or a heavy abrasive, be sure to scour *with* the grain of the sink, not against it, to somewhat camouflage the small scratches you may make!

Bet You Didn't Know

A damp sponge or damp newspapers dipped in baking soda makes the perfect scrubber for all kinds of sinks.

17

Watch Out!

Don't get wood floors too wet when cleaning. The excess water can work its way into small cracks in the wood flooring, causing the wood to swell and crack.

Watch Out!

Too-frequent washing of linoleum floors can make them brittle—and brittle floors may crack.

Bet You Didn't Know

Soap residue can make the surface of wood floors dull. To make them shine again, damp-mop with $1/2$ cup vinegar and 2 tablespoons furniture polish in a gallon of warm water.

after this process, drench some paper towels in the bleach and use them to cover the spots overnight.

Cleaning Underfoot

The kitchen floor gets dirty fast. The best defense is to sweep or dry-mop it often to pick up any dust and dirt before it gets tracked all over the house. A quick sponge mop with warm water is great for sopping up spills and giving the floor a quick freshening up between washings.

Hardwood Floors

For a quick cleanup, damp-mop a small area at a time using warm water, and wipe dry before continuing.

For a more thorough cleaning, use vinegar and water. Add 1 cup white vinegar to a bucket of warm water, dip a mop into the vinegar water, and ring out as much water as possible.

Linoleum Floors

Use a broom or dry mop on linoleum floors often to keep dirt and dust off the surface. When needed, wash with warm soapy water and dry each section promptly. Remove marks by rubbing gently with baking soda sprinkled on a damp soft cloth.

Tile Floors

Sweep and damp-mop as necessary. Use a mild detergent rather than alkaline cleaners such as ammonia or borax, which will dull the surface. You'll also want to avoid abrasive cleaners such as scouring powders because they will scratch the surface.

Painted Floors

I've found the best way to handle painted floors is to wax them because this makes them easier to clean.

Damp-mop painted floors with a mild detergent and water solution. Wring most of the water out of the mop before washing the floors. Rub stubborn spots gently with baking soda.

Counters and Cabinets

Once again, vinegar comes to the rescue. Keep a bottle of vinegar within easy reach. When your stove, counters, walls, or anything else becomes spattered with grease, pour about 1/4 cup vinegar on the surface and wipe with a clean dry rag. Vinegar cuts the grease and leaves a nice shine.

Stain Remover

To remove stains from plastic laminate counters such as Formica, take 1 tablespoon of baking soda and add water, drop by drop, until you have a paste. Apply the paste to the stain, leave it on for a minute or two, and then wipe it off.

You can also clean counter stains with lemon juice and baking soda. Just pour some lemon juice on the spot and sprinkle baking soda over it. Then watch it fizz the counter clean. Let the solution soak on the counter for 5 to 10 minutes before scrubbing. Wash with water. This will clean even the toughest stains.

Tile Backsplash

If you have a tile backsplash. you'll want to wash it often with hot, soapy water. If you do this, you won't have to scrub the grout very often. When the grout gets so dirty or stained that hot soapy water won't get it clean, use the heavy-duty grout cleaner, in Chapter 2, "Sparkling Bathrooms." I save an old toothbrush to scrub the grout when needed.

In extreme cases, you may need to mix a little bleach and water to remove really tough stains from grout. Always be very careful when working with bleach. Make sure you have adequate ventilation—open a nearby window. Don't mix the bleach and water solution with any other cleaning product you are using in the kitchen. Quickly wash the bleach and water off the grout with clean water.

Watch Out!

Don't let any of the bleach water get on carpet, towels, or your clothes. It will bleach the color out and can eat a hole through fabric.

Cabinet Door Cleaner

Clean wooden doors on kitchen cabinets with a solution of 1 part ammonia and 10 parts water. When dry, apply a thin coat of wax.

Down the Drain

Keep sink drains free of grease and odors by pouring hot salt water through them once or twice a week. You can create extra pressure with the water—which can help in flushing your pipes—by stopping up the sink first. Fill it right up to the top with hot water, then release the stopper.

Salt eats through small amounts of grease stuck to pipes. Salt is also a natural odor neutralizer that will eliminate most odors in your pipes. So, to open a slow-moving or stopped-up drain, try this simple idea before using a chemical product: Pour $1/2$ cup of salt down the drain, followed by 3 cups or more of boiling water. Continue to flush the drain with very hot tap water until the clog breaks.

Watch Out!

Though garbage disposals do a miraculous job getting rid of most foods, there are some things that you should never put into them. Onion skins, celery stalks, flower stems, and leaves can get stuck between the blades and stop up the system.

Garbage Disposals

Always run plenty of cold water when you use the garbage disposal. Using too little can result in jammed blades. It is important to use cold water when using the garbage disposal because warm or hot water makes any grease that slips in more likely to stick to the disposal interior than be flushed away.

Preventing Clogged Drains

Follow these simple rules to keep your drains running freely in kitchen sinks and elsewhere in the house:

➤ If your sink isn't fitted with a garbage disposal, scrape food and grease off dirty dishes into the trash so that they don't go down the drain. Grease can clog up pipes even if you've got a garbage disposal, so always put it in the trash.

➤ Fatty liquids left over from cooking should be allowed to cool so that solidified fat can be lifted off and discarded rather than rinsed down the drain.

➤ If the hose from your washing machine drains water into a plastic pipe, you can easily prevent dirt and lint from washing down the drain. Simply slip the foot part from one half of an old pair of pantyhose over the end of the hose, and use a rubber band to secure the pantyhose in place. You'll want to clean or replace the pantyhose periodically to keep it from getting full of dirt and lint. You'll be surprised how much stuff has been going down the drain!

➤ All sinks used for washing hair should have their drains protected with a screen. Clean out the hair often. Hair is one of the biggest culprits when it comes to clogging drains.

Oh, the Odor!

A lot goes on in the kitchen, so there are bound to be unpleasant odors there sometimes, no matter how clean you keep it.

Sweet-smelling garbage disposals. Freshen your garbage disposal with citrus rinds. Just drop the rind of an orange, lemon, lime, or grapefruit into the disposal and run cold water while the rinds get chopped up. The odors will vanish with the rinds!

You can also keep your garbage disposal clean and fresh-smelling with vinegar ice cubes. Mix one cup of vinegar in enough water to fill an ice cube tray, freeze the mixture, then grind the cubes through the disposal. Rinse with cold water. (The vinegar gives you a bonus: it'll also clean and deodorize the plastic ice cube trays. For extra cleaning and deodorizing, pour full-strength white vinegar in the trays for several hours before freezing.)

Room Deodorizers

For an inexpensive room deodorizer, place a small open cup half full of vinegar in the kitchen. It will absorb even the strongest odors, such as cabbage, for just pennies! When finished, pour the used vinegar down the sink drain or garbage disposal.

After cooking fish, cabbage, or any other smelly item, boil cinnamon and cloves in water on the back of the stove to freshen the air. Alternatively, you can place a whole, unpeeled lemon in a 300°F oven for about 15 minutes, leaving the door slightly open. Turn off the oven and let the lemon cool before removing it.

Cutting Boards

Rub cutting boards with a paste of baking soda and water, then rinse well. For really strong odors such as garlic or onions, you may want to leave the paste on for 15 to 30 minutes before rinsing.

You can also get rid of the smell of onions, garlic, or other really tough odors on your cutting board by rubbing lemon or lime juice on the board after you have washed it in hot soapy water.

Refrigerators

There are a number of ways to keep your refrigerator smelling sweet:

➤ *Baking soda.* Leave an open box of baking soda on a shelf inside the refrigerator. Buy a new box of baking soda to replace the old one every three months, or sooner if you notice odors again.

➤ *Charcoal.* Keep a small plastic container (a margarine container works great) with charcoal briquettes in it. You can either leave the lid off or punch holes into the lid. Every three months, remove the briquettes and heat them up in a pan on the stove. The briquettes will continue to absorb odors for years!

➤ *Vanilla.* Keep a few cotton balls dipped in vanilla extract on the shelf. One or two cotton balls will keep odors away for several weeks.

➤ *Coffee grounds.* Leave an open can of ground coffee inside the refrigerator to eliminate odors. Coffee grounds will keep the refrigerator smelling nice for several months. The downside is that you will need to discard the coffee grounds instead of brewing them. All the absorbed odors will give the coffee grounds an off taste.

➤ *Lemon.* Cut a lemon in half and leave one or both halves, cut side up, inside the refrigerator.

➤ *Citrus and salt.* Make a homemade air freshener by cutting an orange, grapefruit, or other citrus fruit in half, removing the pulp, and filling the inside of the peel with salt. This will provide a pleasant aromatic scent inside the refrigerator for a couple of weeks. Sit the citrus air freshener inside a bowl to keep the salt inside the orange instead of all over the refrigerator. The citrus fruit provides a nice smell, and the salt absorbs odors.

The Least You Need to Know

➤ Most kitchen cleaning problems can be solved with basic cleaners such as liquid soap, detergent, vinegar, and baking soda.

➤ Stains and baked-on foods can be removed from pots and pans, often quite easily, with a homemade cleaner. Sometimes soaking is the "special hidden ingredient."

➤ Prevent clogged drains by using your sink only as a sink, and not also as a trash can. If you can keep food particles, grease, hair, lint, and other foreign objects out of the drain pipes, you can save yourself some major headaches.

➤ When cleaning kitchen floors, go easy on the water. Excess water can actually harm floors. Frequent sweeping and dust-mopping will reduce the number of times you'll need to do a major floor cleaning.

➤ Baking soda, vinegar, citrus fruit, and charcoal are just a few of the natural deodorizers that can be used to keep kitchen odors under control.

Chapter 2

Sparkling Bathrooms

> ### In This Chapter
>
> ➤ General bathroom cleaning tips and how to tackle the job
>
> ➤ Sparkling bathtubs, toilet bowls, and showers
>
> ➤ Shiny sinks and clear, fresh-smelling drains
>
> ➤ Clean bathroom floors, walls, fixtures, and mirrors

The bathroom is quite literally the most used room in the house, so cleaning it can seem like a never-ending job. As soon as you're finished cleaning it, someone's in there using it again!

Ready, Set, Clean!

You won't have to give the bathroom a heavy-duty cleaning job very often at all if you do a light cleaning every week. Let's get started.

First, pick up the bath mat (or rug), and remove it so you can shake out the dirt and toss it into the washing machine. Next, use a broom to sweep up any dirt, dust, and hair off the floor. Then dampen a paper towel (or even a piece of toilet tissue), and use it to wipe down the baseboards and corners. This will get rid of the dirt and hair that the broom couldn't reach.

Instead of using a broom, you may prefer to use a vacuum cleaner. You can quickly vacuum the floor to pick up dirt, dust, and hair. Make sure the floor is dry, and adjust your vacuum so the brush is close to the floor. Try the lowest setting on your vacuum if it does not have a specific setting for bare floors.

Dampen a piece of toilet paper or a paper towel, and use it to wipe out the sink and bathtub. This will pick up the few strands of hair always lurking in the sink or tub.

With these jobs done, you're ready for an all-purpose bathroom cleaner. The next section's formula for homemade bath cleaner works great for light cleaning and, when used often (about once a week), it will keep your bathroom sparkling without a lot of effort.

Homemade All-Purpose Bath Cleaner

To clean the bathroom, you can buy a zillion different products and spend a small fortune. This cleaning formula works on most everything in the bathroom except the mirrors. Use it on the tub, sinks, tile, floor, walls, toilet, and cabinets.

> $1/2$ cup vinegar
>
> 1 cup clear ammonia
>
> $1/4$ cup baking soda
>
> 1 gallon warm water

If you use a plastic trash can in the bathroom, it can double as a cleaning bucket. Empty the trash can and rinse it out with warm water, then mix up the all-purpose bath cleaner in it. That way you don't need a separate bucket, and you get a bonus: The trash can gets cleaned in the process!

Before you get started using the cleaner, pour some of it into a spray bottle. This bottle of spray cleaner will come in handy in the bathroom and the kitchen. Use it to spray one surface at a time, and wipe with a damp cloth. You can quickly clean up a small mess before it becomes a big one.

Bet You Didn't Know

Most household detergents are highly concentrated. Experiment with your favorite brand: you can usually use $1/2$–$3/4$ of the suggested amount and still do the job right.

A Good Once-Over

Dip a sponge or cloth into the all-purpose bath cleaner and wipe down the walls of the shower stall or tub walls. Next, use it to wipe down the tub or the floor of the shower. Don't forget the faucets, soap dishes, and everything else inside the shower stall or tub enclosure. Use a clean sponge or cloth and water to rinse off the cleaning solution. On the walls and the sides of the tub, you can use a large plastic cup full of water to rinse the cleaning solution away, or you can use the flexible hose shower spray, if you've got one.

Use the same homemade all-purpose cleaning solution to wipe down the sinks, toilets, counters, faucets, and vanities. Rinse with clean water.

Home-Brewed, Heavy-Duty Cleaner

For really tough jobs that require more than a light cleaning, you'll need a rough and tough cleaning solution. This formula really packs a punch. It is good for jobs such as cleaning neglected ceramic tiles, radiators, air vents, and dirty shower stalls.

> 1 cup baking soda
>
> 1 gallon very warm water
>
> 1 cup vinegar
>
> 1 cup clear household ammonia
>
> 1 tablespoon liquid detergent

Tightwad Tip

Cleanser (scouring powder) is often wasted because the containers have too many or too large holes. To keep the cleanser from coming out too fast, cover half of the holes with tape. You will find that you use less cleanser to do the job. This especially works great when the children clean their own bathrooms!

Dissolve the baking soda into the very warm water in a bucket; add the vinegar, clear ammonia, and liquid detergent. Shake or stir to mix the ingredients. Wear rubber gloves and clean in a well-ventilated area. Rinse with clean water.

Home-Brewed Disinfectant

After you have cleaned the bathroom, it is always a good idea to use a disinfectant (especially during cold and flu season, or any time a member of the family has been sick). But no need to buy an expensive commercial product when this home-brewed formula is quick to make and easy to use.

> $1/2$ cup borax
>
> 1 gallon of warm water

Mix together the borax and water. Use a sponge to wipe down the tub, shower walls, sinks, counters, floor, and toilet. Do not rinse.

Rub Dub Dub: Cleaning the Tub

Scrub porcelain enamel bath tubs and sinks with the home-brewed all-purpose bath cleaner, or a solution of hot water and a few drops of liquid dishwashing detergent. Both mixtures will easily clean the fixtures without scratching the shiny finish.

Always rinse the tub after taking a bath. If you can somehow coax, bribe, or threaten your family to do likewise, the chore of cleaning the bathtub will be much easier, and you won't have to do it as often.

Tightwad Tip

To get nasty soap scum and dirt off your tub or shower, put a little baby oil in a spray bottle and add water. Spray the mixture on a section and wipe off with a sponge. I've never found a cleaner at any price that gets soap scum off easier. When I'm done, I just go over once with a disinfectant to make sure all the germs are killed. This saves money (baby oil is cheap), and it saves time, too!

Watch Out!

Though bubble baths will help keep the tub clean, bath oils can be a royal pain to clean out. The slimy, greasy mess left behind is worse than the dry skin! When possible, avoid using bath oils. Instead, rub baby oil on your skin *after* bathing. The oil will stay on your skin longer, and you won't find yourself down on your hands and knees scrubbing the oil out of the tub!

Plastic and Acrylic Tubs

If you have a new bathtub, it may be plastic or acrylic. You need to be extra careful when cleaning these types of tubs. Always use a mild cleaner, such as the all-purpose bath cleaner or a dishwashing liquid (but not dishwasher soap!). Avoid using a scouring powder cleaner because it can permanently scratch the surface. Rub any scratches with a little silver polish, then buff with a soft cloth.

Remove tough stains from a plastic or acrylic tub with a lemon cut in half. Simply run the lemon over the stain until it disappears.

"Automatic" Tub Cleaner

A great way to help keep the bathtub clean is to frequently use bubble bath when you or the kids take a bath. I've found that most any type of liquid soap (even dishwashing liquid) does a good job of making bubbles and cleaning the tub at the same time. Just don't tell the kids that they are helping to clean the tub; let them think you are doing them a big favor by letting them take a bubble bath.

Soggy Soap Solution

To keep your soap bars from melting into a soggy mess that you'll have to clean up, place a sponge under the bar of soap. Then use the sponge to wash yourself or clean the inside of the tub. This will help keep the area neat, and you will actually use most of the melted soap instead of washing the soapy mess down the drain.

Bathtub Ring

You can get rid of a stubborn bathtub ring with a paste of cream of tartar and hydrogen peroxide. Take 2 tablespoons of cream of tartar and add hydrogen peroxide drop by drop until you have a paste. Apply the paste to the ring and let it dry. When you come back to wipe off the paste, the ugly bathtub ring will disappear, too.

Sticky Decals

Bath decals can be a real bear to remove from a tub, especially if they've been stuck on for many years. It's as if the glue on the back has actually melted into the enamel of the tub. To remove them, first try full-strength white vinegar. Pour the white vinegar around the edges of the decal, and let it soak for 30 minutes. This should loosen the decals so you can pull them off. You may want to heat the vinegar up in the microwave first. The heat combined with the vinegar will melt away some of the old glue.

If the vinegar does not work, try nail polish remover. Apply it around the edge of the decals, and pull them up. Use a little more nail polish remover or vinegar to clean off any remaining sticky residue. Be sure to rinse away the nail polish remover or vinegar with soapy water, followed by clean water.

Tightwad Tip

Don't throw away those old pantyhose or nylon stockings—they work wonders cleaning the bathtub and sinks. Roll the stockings into a ball and tie the ends together. You now have a scrub pad that won't scratch. When you're done cleaning, you can toss the stockings into the wash, and they're ready for the next cleaning project.

Shower Power

To clean the shower walls and floor, use a bucket of the all-purpose bath cleaner or the heavy-duty cleaner. I like to take a cleaning brush and dip it into the cleaning solution. Then brush down the wet shower walls and floor with the cleaner. Leave it on the walls and floor for a few minutes before rinsing off with clean water.

Smart Solution

Use an expired credit card to scrape off the decals and glue remaining on the tub. The credit card can't scratch the surface like a razor blade can.

Shower Door Solutions

The metal frames of shower doors can get water spots on them that seem impossible to remove. Lemon oil removes those tough water spots. Apply a little oil to a rag, and rub over the metal. Use a dry cloth to buff the metal to a shine. The oil will help repel water and will make it tougher for new water spots to form.

Glass shower doors will sparkle and stay clean if you wipe them down once a week with a sponge dipped into full-strength white vinegar.

You can also clean out shower door tracks with a toothbrush or cotton swab dipped into a solution of bleach and water.

Heads Up!

Shower heads clog up quickly with mineral deposits if you have hard water. To get rid of the deposits, take the shower head apart and clean it from the inside. Unscrew the head, and scrub it with an old toothbrush or nail brush. Then take a toothpick and poke it through the holes to clear out the mineral deposits.

To clean mineral deposits off shower heads that cannot be removed, you'll need a little plastic bag and some white vinegar. Take the bag and fill it half full of white vinegar. Tape the bag on your shower head so that the shower head is completely immersed in the white vinegar. Wait a half hour to an hour, depending on how bad the buildup is. Then wipe off the shower head, and it should be as clean as new.

Curtain Call

You may be tempted to replace the shower curtain when it gets too dirty—most people think these are very hard to clean. But I have good news: There's an easy way to wash a shower curtain that does not include scrubbing. To get a shower curtain really clean, wash it in the washing machine. Here's how:

Fill the washing machine with warm water and two or three dirty towels (we all have plenty). Add $1/2$ cup of laundry detergent and $1/2$ cup of baking soda. Then wash, adding 1 cup white vinegar to the rinse cycle. Pull the shower curtain out after the rinse cycle, then let the towels continue through the spin dry cycle. Hang the shower curtain back up immediately, and the wrinkles will disappear as the curtain dries. This is so easy, and you won't be tempted to throw away the curtain when it gets dirty.

Tightwad Tip

You can easily repair the ring holes in your shower curtain when they tear. All you need is plain old duct tape or heavy-duty clear plastic tape. Just tear off a small square for each side of the shower curtain and place them over the hole. Use a paper hole punch to cut out a new hole in the tape. The tape will hold practically forever!

Mold and Mildew

Prevent mildew on a plastic shower curtain by soaking it in warm salt water before hanging. You can eliminate mildew (at least for a while) by spraying your clean shower curtains with a disinfectant.

To remove mold and mildew from shower curtains, spray a solution of half vinegar and half water on the curtains, and let soak a few minutes.

Mold and mildew at the bottom of the shower curtain is real tough to get off, so don't even try. Just take a pair of scissors and cut off about an inch of the curtain. This will remove the hem at the bottom that catches water and works as a mildew factory.

Bath Mat Cleaner

A rubber or vinyl bathtub mat can be cleaned by tossing it into the washer with a few bath towels. The terry cloth scrubs the mat, and the whole wash comes out clean. Take the mat out of the washer and place back into the tub.

Ceramic Tile

The best advice I can give you on ceramic tile is to stay on top of it. A light cleaning is easy—but once you get some major gunk and mildew stains built up, it can be very time-consuming and tedious to remove the stains.

Watch Out!

Don't put a rubber, vinyl, or plastic shower curtain or tub mat into the dryer. The heat can melt these items and make a real big mess.

Home-Brewed Ceramic Cleaner

You can make your own ceramic tile cleaner. Here's how:

$1/4$ cup of baking soda

$1/2$ cup of white vinegar

1 cup of household ammonia

1 gallon of warm water

Mix the first three ingredients in a bucket. Add the water, stirring until the baking soda dissolves. Wearing rubber glues, apply the mixture with a sponge or scrub brush. Rinse with clean water. Mix a fresh batch for each cleaning.

Heavy-Duty Grout Cleaner

This homemade grout cleaner will clean between ceramic bathroom tiles.

3 cups baking soda

1 cup warm water

Put the soda and water into a large bowl and mix into a smooth paste. Scrub this paste into the grout with an old toothbrush or sponge. Rinse well with clean water.

Mildew Stains on Grout

Mildew stains, which can be difficult to remove, make your bathroom look old and dirty. Try these ideas to eliminate the mildew stains in your bathroom.

Cleaning with vinegar. You can remove most mildew stains and tough dirt from the white grout between ceramic tiles by rubbing them with a toothbrush or a nail brush (reserved only for this purpose) dipped into full-strength vinegar. Rinse with cool water after cleaning.

Watch Out!

Don't use abrasive powders or steel-wool pads on ceramic tile or the grout. Both can—and—will scratch the tiles.

If you still have some spots after you use vinegar, the best thing to do is try to hide them. You can buy a product called X-14 that more or less paints the grout white—it comes in a bottle that looks like white shoe polish. You can even use plain old white liquid shoe polish for the same purpose. If you get some of the polish on the tiles, simply let it dry, and then you'll be able to wipe it off with a rag.

Cleaning with alcohol. You can also use rubbing alcohol to clean grout. It's great at removing mildew and other stains from grout and the silicone caulking around the tub.

Cleaning Sinks

Wipe sinks frequently with the all-purpose cleaner or any type of nonabrasive cleaner, then rinse and dry with a towel. The frequent wiping will keep sinks clean without having to resort to harsh cleaning products. Never use abrasive cleaners on sinks because they can scratch and damage the surface.

For a shiny porcelain-white sink, cover the sink with paper towels saturated in white vinegar. Let stand for 30 minutes; then rinse thoroughly with cool water. The white vinegar will also remove many stubborn stains without scrubbing.

Pain in the Drain

Got a slow drain in the sink or tub? Well, it isn't a pretty job to clean it out, but it is necessary. Here's what you need to do. You first need to get the hair and other gunk out of the drain. Twist the stopper and pull. Clean out the hair and slime, and replace the stopper. Now the water will drain out much faster.

Drain cleaner. Clean scum and water residue from tub and sink drains with this drain cleaner. First pour about 3 to 5 cups of boiling water down the drain. Then pour down 1/4 cup baking soda, and follow it with 2 ounces of white vinegar. Let the mixture stay in the drain for 30 minutes before rinsing with cold water. This drain cleaner will help eliminate clogs and keep the drain smelling fresh.

The Most Used Seat in the House

I doubt cleaning the toilet would be at the top of anyone's favorite things to do list but it really doesn't have to be a nasty job. Here are some easy ways to keep the toilets sparkling clean.

Home-Brewed Toilet Cleaner

Here's a solution for cleaning the toilet bowl that will remove all but the toughest stains.

$1/4$ cup baking soda

$1/4$ cup liquid detergent

$1/4$ cup warm water

Mix together the baking soda, liquid detergent, and water in a bowl. Use a toilet brush to apply the cleaner inside the bowl. You can let the solution soak inside the bowl for as long as you like, or you can immediately swish it around with the toilet brush before flushing. If the bowl is especially soiled or has a ring, let the cleaner soak overnight. In the morning, use a toilet brush to help remove the dirt or ring.

Automatic Bowl Cleaner

Denture cleanser tablets can be used to clean the toilet bowl. Just drop one in the bowl, and let it bubble away the stains. If you have a buildup, you will need to swish a toilet brush around to loosen the grime—but if you do this regularly, you won't even have to scrub. It is much cheaper than buying those blue toilet bowl cleaners than go into the tank.

Hard-Water Stains

Brush the toilet bowl daily to prevent mineral buildup. A daily brushing will help prevent toilet bowl rings that are caused by hard-water deposits. Keep a toilet brush near every toilet in the house. If you don't have to drag it from one toilet to another, you'll be more likely to brush daily.

You can remove stubborn hard-water rings in the toilet bowl with cola—whether flat or fresh and bubbly, it makes no difference. Pour the cola into the toilet bowl, and leave it for one

Tightwad Tip

To make a container for your toilet brush, cut half of a plastic half-gallon milk container. You can even leave the handle on it to make it easy to carry.

hour or overnight. The soft drink will actually remove stains inside the toilet bowl. After about an hour, or in the morning, use a toilet brush inside the bowl and flush—your toilet will be sparkling clean. You can use any brand of cola, but it must be cola, not lemon-lime or any other soda flavor.

Lime stain remover. Instead of buying expensive lime removers for the toilet and other bathroom fixtures, try hydrogen peroxide first. It can do the job for a fraction of the price.

Rust Stain Remover

Rust stains under a toilet bowl rim can many times be removed with laundry bleach. Pour 1 cup bleach into the bowl. Use a toilet brush to swish the bleach around before flushing. Always use caution and wear rubber gloves when cleaning with bleach.

If the bleach does not work, rub the toilet ring gently with a pumice stone. Make sure the pumice stone is wet so you won't scratch the surface.

Watch Out!

Don't spill hydrogen peroxide on carpet, towels, rugs, or any other fabric. It will leave white spots and can even eat through the fabric, just like laundry bleach.

Toilet Brush Cleaner

Now that you have the toilet cleaned, you need to clean the toilet brush. It's not as bad as it sounds. Rinse the toilet brush in a fresh flush of water after cleaning the toilet, and occasionally wash it in hot water and disinfectant. Keep the brush free of mildew by letting it dry completely before putting it away.

Watch Out!

Never combine bleach with toilet bowl cleaners; the mix can release a really smelly or even toxic gas. Chemical toilet bowl cleaners should never be used to clean the bathtub or sink. The chemicals designed to clean the toilet can ruin the finish on a bathtub or sink.

Spic 'n' Span Floors

Most bathroom floors are either linoleum or tile, and they can be washed with plain old soap and water. Take a bucket of warm water and add a squirt of liquid soap. Use a mop to wash the floor. Wash the mop with clean water, and go over the floor again to remove any soap residue.

Cleaning Painted Walls and Washable Wallpaper

You don't have to clean the bathroom walls every week, but when you do need to tackle the job, here are some ways to make the work easier.

Always wipe off anything you see on the walls as soon as possible. Fingerprints and SUOs (small unidentified objects!) will usually come off easily when they are fresh. But let those babies sit there for days on end, and you have a job ahead of you.

From the Top Down

When cleaning the walls, always start with a fresh batch of all-purpose cleaner and a clean sponge or cloth. You don't want to transfer the dirt from the last cleaning job onto your walls. Your natural instinct may be to start cleaning walls from the top down, but this is a no-no. When you clean from the top down, water will drip down the walls. This dirty water can be tough to wash off. The solution to the problem is to start at the bottom and work your way up.

Watch Out!

Too-frequent washing of linoleum floors makes them brittle. To preserve your floor and still get it clean, use a broom or vacuum to remove dust, dirt, and hair. If the floors are not real dirty, you may be able to get away with a quick spit-shine. Just spot-clean the dirty areas with a damp cloth instead of mopping the entire floor.

First, wipe down the baseboard. Then wipe a small section of the wall above the baseboard. Continue working your way up a little at a time until you reach the ceiling.

Faucets and Fixtures

The fastest way to clean shiny faucets such as chrome or polished brass is to apply baking soda or even flour to the surface with a dry cloth. The baking soda or flour will remove smudges, water marks, fingerprints, and even sticky residue. The good news is you don't have to rinse the baking soda or flour off because there's no paste or filmy residue left behind. Unless your faucets are really caked with grime or soap scum, this method will work.

When the faucets or fixtures require more than a light cleaning, use rubbing alcohol (70 percent isopropyl) in a spray bottle. Spray the solution on, and wipe off with a clean, dry cloth. Rubbing alcohol cleans perfectly with no abrasive action, and it's a natural cleaner that will not build up on fixtures.

Wood Cleaner

Treat wooden towel racks, toilet seats, or shelves with an occasional application of furniture polish to bring out the shine and give the wood a protective coating. You can make your own furniture polish by mixing one part lemon juice with two parts olive oil.

Mirror, Mirror

Spray on home-brewed window and mirror cleaner. Then use a dry towel or paper towels to clean and wipe dry. Of course, you can buy window cleaner at the store, but it is so easy and economical to make that I prefer to make my own.

Home-Brewed Window and Mirror Cleaner

Here's my recipe:

2 cups water

$1/2$ cup rubbing alcohol

1 tablespoon ammonia

blue food coloring (optional)

Mix the water, alcohol, ammonia, and food coloring (if desired) together. Pour the mixture into an empty spray bottle. This cleaner works great on windows and glass-top tables, too.

Scratch Remedy

To remove small scratches in mirrors, all you need is white toothpaste. Take your finger and rub some of the toothpaste into the scratch; then use a soft cloth to buff the scratch away.

Help, I'm in a Fog!

There are a number of ways to keep mirrors fog-free; pick the one that works best for you.

➤ Rub a bit of moistened soap onto the mirror, then wipe it off with a towel . You can use bar soap lather or creamy soft soap to do the trick. The area where soap was applied will stay fog-free for several weeks, no matter how steamy the bathroom gets.

➤ Apply a thin coat of shaving cream on the dry mirror. Rub the shaving cream in with a dry towel until the shaving cream disappears. Do not rinse off.

➤ When taking a bath, you can keep the mirrors from fogging up by running some cold water (about an inch or two) into the tub before adding hot water.

➤ If you burn candles while taking a bath or shower, this will also help keep the mirror from fogging up. (But when your partner walks in and sees the candles, the mirrors may get fogged up anyway!)

➤ If you find yourself in a bathroom with a fogged-up mirror and need a quick fix, use a hairdryer to dry off enough of the mirror so you can see. (Make sure you're not touching any water at the time, or you'll get zapped!)

The Least You Need to Know

➤ You don't have to buy a bunch of different cleaners for the bathroom. An all-purpose cleaner and a glass and mirror cleaner will clean almost everything.

➤ Use gentle cleaners on bathtubs and sinks. Newer tubs and sinks can be scratched when you use abrasive scouring powders.

➤ The easiest way to wash shower curtains and rubber or vinyl tub mats is in the washing machine. Toss them in with several towels, but don't put them in the dryer.

➤ If you've got hard water, brush your toilet bowl daily to prevent mineral buildup and other stains.

➤ Keeping the grout between your tiles clean is easier than removing the stains once you get them. Clean and wash them regularly with soap and water to keep them that way.

➤ Soap, shaving cream, cold water, and even candles are just a few things that can be used to keep your bathroom mirrors from fogging up.

Chapter 3

Spotless Bedrooms, Dining, and Living Rooms

In This Chapter

➤ Dusting tips, eliminating dust in nooks and crannies

➤ Cleaning pillows, blankets, and mattresses

➤ Keeping floors clean

➤ Carpets and carpet stains

➤ Windows, blinds, and walls

Although cleaning the bedrooms and living and dining rooms may not require as much time and effort as the kitchen and bathrooms, there still are a lot of shortcuts and smart solutions you can take advantage of to save time and money.

Start at the Beginning

When cleaning the bedrooms, first start by picking up all the dirty clothes and tossing them into a laundry basket. Then pick up anything on the floor and return it to where it belongs. If some things belong in other rooms, don't run around like crazy putting everything in its place right now. Instead, put a basket outside the door so that you can place things in it as you collect them, to return items to their homes when you are finished. You'll save yourself steps by grouping items together later. Next clean off all the junk on top of the dressers. Throw away anything that is trash, and put everything else in its rightful place. Now you are ready to dust the furniture.

Down with Dust Bunnies

Always dust a room before you vacuum it. Some of the dust will fall to the floor, and you can pick it up later with the vacuum cleaner. Work from high to low because dust falls down. You can speed up dusting by using a feather duster or one of the new-fangled dusters that have a long handle to reach ceilings and high places.

Remove dust from a feather duster frequently while dusting by twirling it around by the handle in a brown paper bag, or take the duster outside and shake it like crazy.

When dusting, I like to take a large piece of cotton, and fold it in half once and then in half again. This will leave you with several sides of the cloth to clean with. When one side gets dirty, you can turn it over for a clean side.

Dusting Tight Spots, Nooks, and Crannies

Having trouble removing the dust when a piece of furniture is close to the wall? It can be difficult to dust tight spaces and hard-to-reach places.

Tight spaces. Place a thin sock or pantyhose over a straightened wire coat hanger, a fly swatter, a yardstick, or a flattened gift-wrap cardboard tube. Then slide it between the wall and the furniture. Use this trick in the kitchen to remove dust between appliances and under the refrigerator.

Hard-to-reach places. Here's how to dust a high place or remove cobwebs from ceilings: Wrap a towel, sock, T-shirt, or old pantyhose over a broom, dust mop, or yardstick, and fasten it in place with a rubber band. Use this long handle to extend your reach. If your ceilings are really high, you should be able to reach if you stand on a chair.

The impossible dust. Carved furniture, corners of picture frames, pleated tops of draperies, pleated lampshades, and chandelier chains are just a few of the items that can be tough to dust. To handle these and many other intricate items, use a natural-bristle paintbrush—it works like a charm.

The Dust is Flying

Dusting can be, well, dusty. To prevent your dusting cloth from scattering dust instead of picking it up, try these tips:

➤ Dip dusting cloths in a solution of 2 cups water and $1/4$ cup lemon oil, and allow them to dry before using.

➤ Put the dusting cloth into a jar with a little turpentine. To make sure the turpentine gets all over the dusting rag, roll the jar around to cover the entire interior of the jar before inserting the cloth. Leave the cloth in the jar for a few days before using it to dust. After dusting, shake out the cloth and then put it back in the jar. Next time you're ready to dust, the cloth will be waiting for you.

➤ Spray the dusting cloth with a commercial product, such as Endust, and keep it in a covered jar for 24 hours before using it for the first time.

Bedtime

After you finish dusting the bedroom, it's time to move on to the bed. Take the sheets off the bed and toss them into the washer. Wash your sheets once a week; wash the mattress pad, dust ruffle, blankets, and comforter once a month, or more often as needed.

Mattress Matters

Unless your mattress label specifically states not to turn it, to extend the life of your mattress, you'll need to turn it (flip it) once a month. Turn the mattress over head to foot one month and the next month turn it over side to side.

Vacuum your mattress with the upholstery attachment of the vacuum cleaner, or brush with a whisk broom once a month. This will keep your mattress clean and fresh-smelling.

Remove any stains on the mattress with a solution of 1 cup white vinegar, 1 tablespoon liquid detergent, and 1 cup water. Rinse with clean water and use a fan or hair dryer to dry the area.

Bet You Didn't Know

Knowing the size of your mattress can help when moving a bed into a new house or different room. Some smaller bedrooms simply will not accommodate a queen- or king-size bed. Mattress measurements are usually standard: twin—38 x 75 inches, full—53 x 75 inches, queen—60 x 80 inches, and king—76 x 80 inches.

Oh, the Odor!

Neutralize urine odor by dampening the spot with water and sprinkling borax over it. Rub the borax into the area and let dry. Then brush or vacuum to remove the dry borax. You can also sponge the area with white vinegar, then rinse with clean water.

Freshen a stale-smelling mattress by sprinkling baking soda over it. Leave the baking soda on for a couple of hours, or all day, and then vacuum or sweep it up.

A Place to Lay My Head

Fluff pillows daily and air them out at least once a month outdoors or by an open window. Fresh air puffs them up and helps eliminate odors. If possible, pick a breezy day to hang them outside, but keep them out of direct sunlight. Tumble them occasionally in the clothes dryer on an air setting for a minute or two.

Most pillows can be washed. Feather, foam, down, and polyester pillows can be hand-washed with a liquid detergent or machine-washed on a short, delicate cycle. Feather, down, and polyester pillows can be machine-dried on low heat, but you should hang foam pillows out to air-dry. Feather pillows can take a long time to dry. You may have to dry them through 2 or 3 cycles on low heat to get them completely dry, or if you have time let them air dry outside in the hot sun, shaking frequently until completely dry.

Bundle Up

Most all blankets that you can buy today are machine-washable. Only older wool blankets can't be thrown into the wash.

When washing blankets, don't overload the washer. Make sure there's enough room for the blankets to move freely. The best way to wash blankets to keep them from pilling and make them last longer is to let them soak in the wash water (with the detergent) for about 10 minutes before washing them on the shortest cycle.

Be sure to add some fabric softener to the load when washing blankets. You can hang blankets to dry or toss them in the dryer. Some blankets will become very stiff when hung outside to dry. To make them softer, toss them into the dryer and fluff them up for about five minutes.

Smart Solution

When the weather is nice, the quickest and easiest way to clean lampshades is to blow-dry them clean. Remove the shades from the lamps and take them outside. Plug in your blow dryer and blow off the dust using the lowest (coolest) setting.

Made in the Shade

Dust lampshades regularly, using the dusting attachment of your vacuum cleaner, a baby's brush, or a clean feather duster. Keeping the dust off lampshades will usually eliminate the need for further cleaning.

If the dust is really stuck to the shade, take a clean sponge and dip it into water, then wring out as much of the water as possible. Use this almost-dry sponge to wipe off the dirt and dust.

While you have the shades off the lamp, use a dry or just slightly damp cloth to wipe the light bulbs clean. This will keep the dust there from falling onto the floor, and you'll get more light from your bulbs.

Cleaning Down Under

Now you are ready to start working on the floors. To clean tile, linoleum, and ceramic floors, make one of these basic floor solutions.

Basic Floor Cleaner

> 1 cup white vinegar
>
> 1 gallon water

Mix the ingredients together and use them to mop the floor. You don't have to rinse off this solution because the vinegar won't leave a film on the floor. If this doesn't do the trick, try the heavy-duty floor cleaner.

Heavy-Duty Floor Cleaner

> $3/4$ cup household ammonia
>
> 1 gallon of warm water

You don't have to rinse this solution off, either. This formula works best on heavily soiled floors.

Wood Floors

Clean wood floors once a week with a dust mop, a soft attachment of the vacuum, or a broom with the leg of old pantyhose over the bristles. Sweep with the grain of the wood.

When more of a cleaning is needed (probably about two to three times a month), mix up the basic floor cleaner (1 cup white vinegar into a gallon of cold water) and wipe with a well-wrung mop or soft cloth.

Watch Out!

Never use plain water to wash wood floors.

Water spots. You can remove water spots on finished wood floors by rubbing gently with a cloth moistened with rubbing alcohol, then wiping with a cloth slightly dampened with vegetable oil. Use a dry cloth to buff the vegetable oil.

Dustpan Solutions

Tired of dust and dirt sticking to your dust pan? First, wash the dustpan in hot, soapy water and dry thoroughly. Then spray with furniture polish and buff with a soft cloth. Next time you use this baby, the dust will slide right off.

Can't find your dustpan? Here's a couple of quick substitutes:

➤ Cut a paper plate or aluminum pie plate in half, and moisten the edge.

➤ Take a sheet of newspaper and dampen 1 to 2 inches of the cut side. Press the dampened edge to the floor, and sweep up the dust.

➤ Dampen a paper towel or napkin, and scoop up the dust.

Caring for Carpets

Frequent vacuuming will actually make carpets last longer. When the carpet is dirty, tiny particles of dust and dirt get ground into the carpet and actually cut the fibers. These cuts make the carpet wear out much faster.

High-Traffic Areas

Vacuum carpets and rugs once a week, or as necessary. If you notice some dirt on high-traffic areas, make a quick pass with the vacuum just over these areas.

As you vacuum each week, it is not necessary to vacuum every single inch of carpet. You can skip areas that don't get dirt ground into it. Vacuum under the bed, sofas, chairs, and other areas that you don't walk on about once a month instead of each week, and use the time you save on the high-traffic areas.

Make It Easy on Yourself

A long extension cord on the vacuum cleaner will save time and make the job easier. You'll be able to move from room to room without having to stop and unplug the cord.

If you have a two-story house, one of the best investments you can make is to have a vacuum cleaner for each floor. You won't have to lug the thing up the steps, and you'll keep from beating up your walls and steps when dragging it up and down each flight.

Keep a rug by every door in the house. A welcome mat outside the door and another rug just inside it will catch tons of dirt that would otherwise have made it to your carpet and floors. Shake off the welcome mats, and shake or wash the other rugs often. Encourage your family members to wipe their feet before coming in the house. Getting your family to take their shoes off before walking around the house is another great idea to keep carpets clean.

Stairs

When vacuuming stairs, start from the top and work your way down. Stairs get a lot of traffic, so they will need frequent vacuuming. I like to use one of the little hand-held vacuums for cleaning stairs. Put a long cord on it (or use a cordless one), and—zip—you're done before you know it.

Fluffing Up Indented Carpet

When you move furniture, you end up with smushed areas in the carpet. Here's a couple of ways to get rid of that dent:

➤ Place an ice cube on each indention, and let them sit and melt overnight. In the morning, blot up any moisture with paper towels and fluff up the carpet fibers carefully with a stiff brush.

➤ Brush the carpet back into place with a stiff brush that's been moistened slightly with water.

➤ Hold a steam iron over the area for a few seconds, being very careful not to touch the carpet with the iron. Then brush the nap with a stiff brush, or work it up gently with a coin. Repeat the process several times, if needed.

Smelly Carpet Odors?

If your carpet smells, try one of these solutions:

➤ If your carpet has a stale odor to it but really doesn't need a deep cleaning, sprinkle a box of baking soda on the carpet and let it sit for at least an hour before vacuuming it.

➤ Use borax to freshen the carpet if you have any cats or dogs inside the house. Borax also kills any fleas in the carpet. (The easiest way to spread baking soda or borax on the carpet is to use a flour sifter. Or you can break up any clumps with your finger or the back of a spoon.)

➤ Sponge the smelly area with white vinegar, rinse with clear water, and let dry.

➤ Put a few drops of oil of peppermint on a tissue. Vacuum up the tissue right before you vacuum the smelly carpet.

➤ When you change the vacuum cleaner bag, add a few cloves. The cloves will keep the vacuum smelling nice and will make the carpet smell good.

Homemade Dry Carpet Cleaner

Use this handy dry carpet cleaner for light cleaning and to freshen your carpet.

2 cups baking soda

$1/3$ cup cornstarch

5 bay leaves (crumbled)

1 tablespoon ground cloves

Bet You Didn't Know

To eliminate static electricity in carpets, mix $1/2$ cup liquid fabric softener with 1 quart water in a spray bottle. Spray on the area where you want to eliminate static electricity, then let it dry. It will remain static free for several months.

Mix the ingredients together and store in a glass jar or other container with a tight-fitting lid. Shake the cleaner to mix the ingredients, then sprinkle liberally all over the carpet and leave on overnight. The next day, vacuum it up.

At first, you'll think you're making a mess, but be brave—you'll like the results. Close the doors to the rooms that you are cleaning so pets or children won't get on the carpet.

Carpet Stains

Here are some basic stain-removal tricks. Always test a stain removal technique on a small area of carpet that's in an out-of-the-way place to make sure the method works and gives you the desired results. Try one of these to get rid of spots:

Smart Solution

White vinegar not only removes odors and stains from carpet, but it also brightens the color of your carpet. Once in a while, take a white cloth dipped into white vinegar and quickly wipe the top of your carpet after it has been vacuumed. You'll be amazed at how much brighter the color will look. This works well on regular carpets, but test it on wool carpeting or expensive area rugs first.

➤ Pour a little club soda on the stain, allow it to sit for a few seconds, then blot up with a cloth.

➤ Combine $1/4$ cup white vinegar and $1/4$ cup water, and apply to the stain with a white cloth. Rinse well with clear water.

➤ Spray shaving cream on the stain, and allow it to sit for a few seconds before rinsing it off with a damp cloth. Always use a white, foamy shaving cream. Some of the gel-type shave creams—and even some foamy ones—are blue or green, and the color can stain your carpet worse than whatever you are trying to remove.

➤ Rub cornstarch into lightly soiled spots before vacuuming. The cornstarch will clean the spot and freshen the carpet at the same time.

Greasy spills. Cover the spill immediately with an absorbent powder, such as baking soda, cornmeal, cornstarch, talcum powder, or baby powder. Lightly brush it into the carpet and leave overnight. In the morning, vacuum. If the carpet is dark-colored, you will need to take a damp rag to remove the light traces of the powdery residue.

Nongreasy spills. Blot up as much of the liquid as possible with white paper towels, white napkins, or any other type of white absorbent cloth. Don't rub—rubbing works to force the stain deeper into the carpet fibers. Blot and lift. Pour a little club soda over the stain and let it sit for a few seconds, then blot the spill up with the white cloth. Repeat until no more of the spill seems to be coming up. Club soda is especially effective on food and beverage spills.

Bet You Didn't Know

When cleaning up spills on carpets, you always should use a clean, white cloth because a cloth's color can bleed and make the stain worse.

Dropped java. Blot spilled coffee quickly, and use clean water on a white cloth. Rinse out the cloth often, and get the area quite wet to coax out stubborn stains. Place a dry, white towel over the area, and weight it down with a book to absorb the water.

Carpet Stain Remover

This spot remover works best on nongreasy spills.

$1/2$ teaspoon mild dishwashing liquid

1 tablespoon white vinegar

1 cup warm water

Mix together the ingredients in a small bowl. After blotting up as much liquid from the stain as possible, gently apply the carpet stain remover to the stain. Do not rub. Rinse with clear water, using a white cloth. Repeat the process, if necessary, until the spot disappears.

Rx for Carpets

Paint drips. Dried paint drips on carpet can be very difficult to remove. I've found the best solution is to snip off the paint drip. This method will work as long as the carpet is not a very close weave. Use a small pair of scissors (fingernail scissors are perfect), and slide them under the paint drop. Then simply snip off the fibers that have paint on them. You probably won't even be able to tell where you cut the carpet, and you won't have to look at the paint drip anymore.

Carpet tears. Place a strip of carpet tape under the tear and press down. You may be able to sew the backing of the carpet together with a needle and thread. Pick a color thread that's close to the color of the carpet so it won't show.

Glue. Dip a cloth into full-strength white vinegar, and blot the spot if the glue is fresh. If the glue has dried, pour a little white vinegar directly on the glue and work it into the area. Leave the vinegar on the area for 30 minutes, then use a cloth to rub the glue out.

Carpet burns. Cut out the burned section with a small pair of scissors, then cut some strands from a matching carpet scrap or a hidden area of the carpet, and glue them over the hole with fabric glue. Place a piece of paper over the mended spot, weight it down with a heavy book or two, then allow the glue to dry. While this is not a perfect solution, it looks better than the burned spot.

Blood. Cover the spot immediately with cornstarch mixed with cold water to form a paste. Spread the paste thickly on the stain, let it dry, then brush it off. Repeat, if necessary, until the stain is gone. Always use cold water when working on a blood stain.

Pet accidents. Blot the stain quickly with paper towels or an old white towel to absorb all the moisture. Then do one of the following:

➤ Rub the spot in a circular motion with a terry-cloth towel dipped in white vinegar. When dry, fluff up the area with your hand or a soft brush.

➤ Blot the area with club soda, then cover with a dry white towel and weight it down with some heavy books so the towel can absorb the moisture from the rug. If the towel becomes damp, replace it with a dry one.

After the carpet has dried, sprinkle baking soda over the area to get rid of any lingering smell. Apply it to the area and leave it for at least 24 hours, then vacuum it up. The smell should be gone.

A Room With A View

You can use many different solutions to clean windows. Here are a few that I think work the best.

➤ Mix 2 tablespoons ammonia with 2 tablespoons white vinegar, or with 2 tablespoons borax for each quart of warm water.

➤ Mix 1/4 cup rubbing alcohol per quart of water.

➤ Mix 1 tablespoon borax and 1 tablespoon ammonia per quart of water.

➤ Mix 2 ounces rubbing alcohol, 2 ounces nonsudsing ammonia, and 12 ounces water. This makes enough to fill a 16-ounce spray bottle.

➤ Use full-strength white vinegar to remove stubborn hard-water spots and to clean really dirty windows.

➤ Use 1/2 cup nonsudsing ammonia per quart of water for really dirty windows.

➤ Use cola to remove grease marks and fingerprints from windows. Saturate a sponge or cloth with the soda, and wipe clean. Flat cola works just as good as fresh.

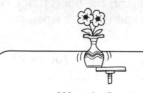

Watch Out!

Avoid using ammonia to clean up pet accidents on carpets. It will remove the problem but leave behind its own smell—like urine.

Washing Windows

Now that you've got the cleaning solution, it's time to get down and do those windows:

➤ *Crumpled-up newspaper.* Dip newspaper into white vinegar or any of the cleaning solutions above, and wipe the glass until almost dry. Then finish off with a cloth or a dry newspaper. Old newspapers work best for cleaning windows because they're soft and work more like a soft cloth than like paper. Dig to the bottom of the recycling pile and get the oldest ones you have, or save some just for this purpose. Many people swear by newspapers for cleaning windows because they give windows a beautiful shine that is hard to duplicate with paper towels or a cloth.

➤ *A chamois.* This is a soft leather type cleaning cloth. Wet the chamois and then dip it into the window cleaner. Wring it out thoroughly and wipe the window until almost dry.

➤ *A pump spray bottle.* Spray on the cleaning solution, then wipe dry with a lint-free cloth, a paper towel, or a newspaper.

➤ *A sponge, an old diaper, or a soft cloth.* Apply the cleaning solution with the sponge, diaper, or cloth and then dry with a lint-free cloth, paper towel, or newspaper.

➤ *A squeegee.* Apply the cleaning solution to the window with the sponge side of a squeegee. Or, dip a sponge into the cleaning solution and wash the windows, then use the squeegee blade. Wipe the blade with a damp cloth to help it slide easily over the window, and wipe it with a dry cloth after each stroke. Work from top to bottom by pulling the squeegee across the window at an angle and down the side.

Smart Solution

Use horizontal strokes when washing outside and vertical strokes when washing inside. This way you'll be able to tell if any streaks you see are inside or out.

After washing windows, use a clean chalkboard eraser to give them an extra shine.

Cleaning Window Frames

Wash out the window grooves with a narrow paint brush or a sock wrapped around a piece of wood. If the window frame isn't too dirty, you can use the crack and crevice attachment of the vacuum cleaner to remove dust and small amounts of dirt. Use a cotton swab dipped in window cleaner to get the corners clean.

Blind Date

Dust mini blinds or venetian blinds with a feather duster, a clean 2-inch paint brush, or the dusting attachment of the vacuum cleaner. Close the blinds completely, dust one side, then close them in the opposite direction and dust the other side. After dusting, rub each side with a soft cloth to make sure all the dust and dirt is removed.

If after dusting, the blinds are still dirty, you'll need to do more cleaning. For light cleaning, I like to put an old sock or even an old pair of cotton gloves on my hand and spray it with window cleaner. Then I close the blinds and, starting at the top, go over them from one side to the other. When I finish the first side, I close them in the opposite direction and clean the other side.

To do a real thorough cleaning job on the blinds, you'll need to take them down and scrub them outside. Lay the blinds on the driveway or sidewalk and hose them off. Then clean the blinds with an all-purpose cleaner, or make a solution of 1/2 cup ammonia to 1 quart warm water. Scrub the slats using a soft-bristle brush or an old towel. Turn the blind over and clean the other side. Hang the blind on a ladder or clothesline, and rinse with the garden hose. Shake off the excess water and let air-dry.

White cords to mini blinds or venetian blinds can get nasty looking, but they are real easy to get clean. Soak the cords in a solution of 1/2 cup water and 1/4 cup chlorine bleach in a jar or small bowl for about 1 minute. Check after a minute to see if they are white; if not, keep the cords in the bleach solution for a little while longer. Rinse in a clean container of water, then blot dry with a towel.

Watch Out!

Be very careful if you are cleaning the cords while they are hanging over a carpeted room. One drip of the bleach solution will leave you with a white spot in the carpet. Put down several thicknesses of newspaper if you clean the cords while they're hanging up. You can also take the blinds down and do this job outside.

Watch Out!

If you are not sure whether your wallpaper is washable, test a little of the all-purpose cleaner on an inconspicuous spot before you go crazy cleaning.

Climbing the Walls

When cleaning painted walls and washable wallpaper, always start with a fresh batch of all-purpose cleaner (see the next section) and a clean sponge or cloth. You don't want to transfer the dirt from the last cleaning job onto your walls. Though your natural instinct may be to start cleaning walls from the top down, this is a no-no, as you may recall from Chapter 2, "Sparkling Bathrooms." When you clean from the top down, water will drip down the walls. This dirty water can be tough to wash off. The solution to the problem is to start at the bottom and work your way up.

First, wipe down the baseboard. Then wipe a small section of the wall above the baseboard. Continue working your way up a little at a time until you reach the ceiling.

All-Purpose Cleaner

Mix up a batch of this all-purpose cleaner and keep it handy. Use it just like you would a commercial brand such as Formula 409.

> $1/2$ cup vinegar
>
> 1 cup clear ammonia
>
> $1/4$ cup baking soda
>
> 1 gallon warm water

Mix ingredients together in a bucket, and pour some of the solution into a spray bottle before you get started.

Crayon Marks

To remove crayon marks from walls, try one of these:

➤ Rub them lightly with a damp rag sprinkled with baking soda.

➤ Use undiluted liquid dishwashing detergent. Rinse with clean water.

➤ Squirt a little white toothpaste on a sponge or cloth, and wipe your worries away. (I think this works the best for this job. But only use the white toothpaste; the colored gels will stain your wall. A baking soda toothpaste doubles the punch.)

Spots On Nonwashable Wallpaper

For light spots, take a stale slice of bread, roll it into a few little balls, and use the bread balls to lift off the spot.

To remove grease stains, put blotting paper over the stain and press with a warm (not hot) iron. Do not use steam.

Remove grease spots and crayon marks with a thick paste of baking soda or corn starch. Let the paste dry, then brush off. You may have to repeat the procedure a couple of times to remove all the stain or marks. Let's hope Junior didn't color a really big picture!

Install jumbo-size light switch covers to keep fingerprints and dirt off the wallpaper. You can find these large covers at some hardware and home improvement stores. They are not very expensive and will save lots of cleaning time.

Ring a Ding Ding

Clean around the push buttons or the dial and the crevices of a telephone with a cotton swab dipped in rubbing alcohol. Then clean the rest of the phone and the cord with a paper towel or a clean cloth dipped into alcohol. Not only will the alcohol clean the telephone, but it will also kill the germs. If anyone in your family has a cold, clean the phone with alcohol after he or she uses it.

The Boob Tube

Wipe the television screen clean with a little rubbing alcohol on a cloth, or use a fabric softener sheet. The fabric softener sheet will also remove any static on the television screen and repel dust.

Watch Out!

Never put anything wet (such as a drinking glass that could sweat or a live plant without a saucer underneath) on top of the television because it can leave rings. When cleaning, do not spray a wet cleaner directly onto the set. Always spray it on a cloth before using it on the television. Excessive moisture can warp and bubble older TV cases made of pressed wood.

Bet You Didn't Know

After cleaning a room, you may want to give it a nice aroma. The easiest way to do this is to put a dab of perfume or aromatic oil on a cool light bulb. Later, when you turn on the light, the bulb will release the scent as it heats up. When you have guests, find out what their favorite fragrance is and use it on the bulbs. They'll love the pleasant surprise.

Mildew in the Closet

To prevent mildew from growing in closets, tie several pieces of blackboard chalk together and hang them up inside the closet; they'll absorb moisture and reduce dampness. Replace the chalk every couple of months.

If you've already got mildew, here's how you can get it off the walls: Dissolve $1/4$ cup borax in 2 cups hot water and mix thoroughly. Saturate a sponge or cloth with the mixture, and wash the mildewed areas. Leave the solution on for a couple of hours or overnight and then rinse well. If the mildew has penetrated deeply into the walls, you can leave the solution on for a number of days until it is completely dry. Then sweep or vacuum up the powder.

If you have a continuing problem with mildew in closets, a fan may be the answer to your prayers. After you have removed the mildew, plug in a small fan and let it run a few hours each day to keep mildew from forming. Fans don't use much electricity, so leave it on as long as necessary.

The Lazy Way to Clean a Chandelier

Make sure the chandelier lights are off and the bulbs are tight in their sockets and cool. Take a large umbrella and hang it open, upside down from the bottom of the chandelier to keep the cleaning solution from dripping on the floor or the table beneath. If you don't have an umbrella, cover the table or floor beneath with plastic or towels covered with several thicknesses of newspaper before starting the cleaning process.

Cover each light bulb with a small plastic bag after you have made sure they are completely cool. The plastic bags that home-delivered newspapers often come in work great for this job. Use a twist-tie or piece of string to hold the plastic bags over the light bulbs.

Mix a solution of 2 cups warm water and 2 tablespoons rubbing alcohol. Pour the mixture into a spray bottle. Stand on a chair and start spraying the fixture with your alcohol solution at the top and work your way down. Let the fixture drip dry. The alcohol solution will not leave very many water spots. If you see a few spots you can't live with after it's dry, take a soft cloth dipped into full-strength rubbing alcohol and wipe them away.

The Least You Need to Know

➤ Vacuum a room only after you have dusted it so you don't get dust on a freshly vacuumed floor.

➤ A simple solution of vinegar and water will clean most floors in the house.

➤ To make carpet last longer, vacuum dirt off the high-traffic areas as often as needed.

➤ When something is spilled on the carpet, blot it up as soon as possible with a clean, white cloth.

Part 2
The Clothes Closet

We spend hours shopping for clothes, then plunk down big bucks to pay for them. But there are bargains to be had, if you know where and how to look for them. Durable, great-looking clothes don't have to be expensive, take it from me. And how you care for them once you've got them can a big difference in how long clothes stay looking like new, how great they look on you, and how good they make you feel.

Chapter 4

Durable Duds

In This Chapter

➤ How to tell if it's well-made

➤ Where to find the best clothing buys

➤ Clothing labels translated

➤ Storing seasonal clothes

➤ Making clothes last and look better longer

Clothes can put a sizable dent in your budget. So, to get the most for your money, you need to be a smart shopper and make the clothes that you already own last longer.

Quality Assurance

Well-made clothing will last through many seasons of wear. Unless you're a trendy dresser and you only wear your clothes for a year or two anyway, in the long run, it's more economical to spend a little more and get better-made clothing. That will last you longer. You pretty much get what you pay for, and cheap clothing is often poorly constructed from less durable fabrics. Here's what to look for when buying new or used clothes to get the most for your money:

Smart Solution

Patterns that can be matched (plaids, stripes, checks) should match at the seams. Armhole and crotch cross-seams should match up. If they do not match, it is a sure sign of poor quality.

➤ *Good stitching.* Small, close stitching usually means a garment will hold up well to washing and wearing. Stitches should be neat, straight, and even. Lots of strings hanging down from the garment indicates poor quality and workmanship.

➤ *No gathers or puckering at the seams or darts.* All seams should be flat; even slight puckering at the seams should be avoided.

➤ *Evenly woven fabric with no flaws.* Some natural fibers have small flaws that do not detract from the garment. Other flaws (especially in manmade fibers) should be avoided.

➤ *Flat pockets.* Pockets should be flat with reinforced corners and should be large enough to use comfortably.

➤ *Secure ornaments.* Trim items, such as snaps, buttons, and buckles should be neatly secured with enough thread to keep them from falling off.

➤ *Flat zippers.* Zippers should be sewn in straight, lie flat, and be dyed to match the fabric of the garment.

➤ *Reinforced buttonholes.* Ones that are sewn through both sides of the fabric hold up especially well.

➤ *Hidden hems.* Hems should be straight, and stitches should not be visible on the outside of the garment.

Clothing on the Cheap

When shopping for clothing, there is no magic formula for getting the best bargains every time. Sometimes you can find good buys in the most unlikely places. But knowing when and where to look can increase your chances of getting top-notch clothing for bargain basement prices. Here's what you can expect to find at the different types of stores.

Specialty Shops

Specialty shops usually limit their inventory to one type of merchandise, such as lingerie, handbags and accessories, children's clothing, sportswear, and so on.

You can expect the regular prices to be higher at specialty shops. But you can also find some really terrific bargains when they clear out merchandise two or three times a year. If you like the merchandise but the prices are high, ask when they will take the final markdowns. Many of these stores have a set schedule for marking down merchandise, and the final markdown can be as much as 75 to 80 percent off.

Department Stores

Department stores offer a large selection of clothing and typically carry a wide range of quality and prices. Frequently, the better (upscale) department stores will surprise you with prices that are comparable to or even lower than those offered by discount or chain stores.

Look for end-of-season sales at the best (and most expensive) department stores. They like to quickly liquidate this merchandise to make room for the next season, so they drastically mark down clothing to move it out of the store.

Discount and Chain Stores

Prices in discount and chain stores tend to be less than the prices at discount and department stores, but the quality of clothing is also usually less. Frequent problems are poor construction (pull a string and the whole garment falls apart) or fading (wash the item three to four times and it looks worn out).

Generally, the best buys at discount and chain stores are socks, underwear, pajamas, sweatshirts and sweat pants, and jeans (look for a name brand).

Factory Outlets

At one time (years ago), factory outlets just sold overstocks, overruns, display goods, samples, seconds, and irregulars— and most items were bargain-priced. Today, factory outlets still exist—and they do carry some discontinued merchandise, overstocks and flawed merchandise—but now they supplement the inventory with first-quality new clothing at retail prices.

The best buys at a factory outlet generally are seconds and marked-down merchandise. First-quality merchandise may or may not be cheaper than the exact same item at a department store. Don't be taken by the price tags that often show an inflated retail price. In the example below, keep in mind that no one actually paid $24.99 or $22.99 for the item. Also note that you may be able to find the same shirt on sale at a department store for $9.99. To be sure you're getting the lowest prices, you've got to do some comparison shopping.

Factory Outlet Tag	
Retail Price	$24.99
Discount Price	$22.99
Our Low Factory Outlet Price	$10.99

Label Lingo

Confused about the different types of merchandise for sale at factory outlet stores? Clothing experts say that about 80 percent of outlet merchandise is first-quality, but some of the best buys are slightly flawed. Here's what the labels mean.

➤ *Irregular.* Items will have tiny imperfections but no serious flaws. For example, the tiny imperfections in irregular panty hose cannot be seen when someone is wearing them.

➤ *Seconds.* This is flawed merchandise. Generally, it is wearable, but you need to carefully inspect it to make sure you won't find any unacceptable surprises when you get it home.

➤ *Samples.* These items have been on display and can be shopworn. The colors may not exactly match in coordinating pieces. Sizes and colors will be limited.

➤ *Past season.* Last year's styles are this year's best buys. As long as it's still in style, past season merchandise can be some of the best bargains.

➤ *Discontinued.* These items will no longer be manufactured, so stores are getting rid of the last pieces. They're usually first quality, but sizes and colors will usually be limited.

Life Expectancy of Clothes

According to the clothes manufacturers, you can expect frequently worn clothes to last this long. With proper care, cleaning and stain removal you can probably stretch the life of garments significantly.

Wool or wool-blend suit	4 years
Lightweight suit	2 years
Cloth coat	3 years
Leather coat	4 years
Cotton or cotton-blend shirt	2 to 3 years
Sweater	4 years
Daytime dress	2 years
Evening dress	3 years

The Second Time Around

You can find some incredible bargains on used clothing. A friend of mine bought her beautiful wedding gown for $5, and I bought a tailor-made tuxedo for my husband for $35. When shopping for second-hand clothing, the selection will be limited, but the prices will be low.

There are several ways to get second-hand clothing. The cheapest way is as hand-me-downs (from another family member, a friend, or a relative). You can also find used clothing at yard sales, church bazaars, flea markets, consignment shops, and thrift stores.

When shopping for used clothing, look for items that are well-made. Instead of shopping for a specific item (such as a blue blazer with gold buttons), look at what's there in your size and style, and try to find pieces that will go with clothing you already own.

Examine the clothing carefully before buying. If a shirt has a stain that is noticeable, assume that you will not be able to get it out. On the other hand, if it needs a little repair work (maybe stitches are missing along a seam), you probably can quickly fix that problem when you get home.

Consignment Shops

Most consignment shops carry women or children's clothing. A few stores also have a limited selection of men's clothing. These shops generally carry high-quality and barely worn clothing. The styles will usually be up-to-date or classic fashions that never go out of style.

Articles accepted for consignment must look almost new. As a shopper, you can find good-looking clothing at a fraction of what it would cost new. Some of the best buys in consignment shops are special-occasion clothing (formal dresses for proms, weddings, or parties) and business wear, such as jackets and suits.

Castaway Cash. Consignment shops are also an easy way to make some extra money when you clean out your closet. Simply take your clothing (clean and on hangers) to the owner or manager of a consignment shop. (Such shops may have a certain time or day of the week that new items will be accepted, so it's best to ask before dropping off clothing.) The shop owner or manager will set the price and, generally, if the item sells, the owner splits the sales price 50/50 with you.

Smart Solution

Consigning clothing truly is a win/win situation. The shop owner wins by making a commission on the clothes she sells. And the consignee (person who owns the clothing) wins by making some money from clothing that would either end up being discarded, donated, or sold at a garage sale for a lower price. The consumer wins by getting quality used clothing at a low price.

Tightwad Tip

Shop thrift stores and consignment shops near upscale neighborhoods. You'll find the best merchandise because people with higher incomes tend to buy high-quality clothes and replace them often.

Thrift Stores

Thrift stores may carry a wide assortment of merchandise—everything from old records to furniture. But you can bet that most of the store will be filled with clothing. Thrift stores are sponsored by the Salvation Army, Goodwill, American Veterans, and other charitable or nonprofit organizations. The items they sell are collected through donations.

The quality of merchandise at thrift stores will vary tremendously. You can find items that look like new at bargain prices. But other clothing can be shabby and out of style, so look carefully. Thrift stores may or may not have a dressing room. Some offer discounts to seniors and even run special mark-down sales from time to time.

It's in the Mail

Shopping in the comfort of your home by mail is very convenient, and in some cases you can save quite a bit of money. Here are a few tips to help you get the best deal.

➤ Comparison shop. Compare prices at local retail or discount stores with similar items in mail-order catalogs. And compare one catalog's prices to those in another; just as with retail stores, some have good buys and others will be overpriced.

➤ Keep in mind shipping, handling, and sales tax charges. The shipping and handling charges added to the cost of your purchase may turn bargain into pricey. Then again, if you buy from a different state, you may not be required to pay sales tax, which can turn an average price into a bargain (see the following chart).

➤ Keep the catalog until your order arrives so you can call the company if your order does not come when promised. If you pay by check, write the phone number of the company on your check. Check your order for errors or missing items promptly when it arrives. Notify the company immediately if there is a mistake or damage.

➤ Stick to buying items that you are familiar with. It's easy to get a perfect fit for basic clothing items such as pantyhose and slips. Stay away from ordering catalog clothing such as bathing suits and bras that you probably need to try on to get the correct size.

➤ Don't be afraid to return an item that does not fit or that doesn't meet your expectations. Most mail-order companies are willing to refund your money or at least exchange the item for a different size or style. Before placing your first order with a particular company, ask if satisfaction is guaranteed and who pays for the postage if an item has to be returned.

Mail–Order Cost Comparison

Price	Sales Tax	Shipping	Total cost
T-shirt (local purchase): $6.99	$0.49	$0.00	$7.48
T-shirt (mail-order): $5.99	$0.00	$3.00	$8.99
Difference/Savings: $1.00	$0.49	-$3.00	-$1.51

You can see from the calculations in this table that even though the T-shirt here is priced $1 less in the catalog, you'll save $1.51 buying the shirt locally.

Designer Labels

Ever wondered if a designer label means better quality clothing? Well, the answer is, for the most part, "No." There are a few very high-priced designer clothing lines that are of exceptional quality. But in most cases, the designer has simply allowed his or her name to be placed on the garments, with no direct control over the quality of them.

Typically, a designer or celebrity will sell the rights to his name to a manufacturer. The manufacturer then pays that person a certain amount of money for each piece of clothing sold. The clothing may not even be unique. Some manufacturers put different labels on the same exact articles of clothing. The only difference will be the price, and that difference can be considerable.

Smart Solution

To make clothes last longer between cleanings, brush them with a natural-bristle clothes brush after wearing them and hang them to air out overnight. By doing this, you should be able to get another day's wear out of the outfit before having to clean it. This trick works as long as you didn't spill any food on the clothes, and as long as there are no perspiration stains.

Tightwad Tip

It's staggering to think about how much money we women spend each year on pantyhose. You can cut costs dramatically by ordering pantyhose through the mail. Showcase of Savings sells pantyhose, lingerie, socks, T-shirts, and other items at drastically reduced prices. The pantyhose are imperfect or seconds from the factory, but don't worry—you won't be able to find the flaws. Satisfaction is guaranteed. Call for a free catalog: One Hanes Place—800-522-9567.

Label Lookout

Always read the label when buying clothes, and be on the lookout for dry-clean-only tags. Even if the price is right, having to dry clean an item many times over its life can add up to a pretty penny. Dry cleaning a basic skirt can cost up to $5, and if it has pleats, you can pay much more.

Clothes that can be machine- or hand-washed cost only pennies to clean. Business clothing such as blazers or suits will understandably have to be sent to the dry cleaners, but there's no need to buy casual clothing that must be dry cleaned. In the long run, you may find yourself spending more money on dry cleaning than you paid for the clothing in the first place!

Take It Back

If you discover that clothing you've bought is defective or poorly constructed, don't just push it to the back of the closet. By all means, march it right back to the store. The sooner you return the merchandise, the more likely you will get a full refund or exchange.

Even if you did not save your receipt, it is still worth your time to talk to the store manager and try to get a replacement. But not all clothing is returnable: Some outlet stores have a no-return policy, and final markdowns at department stores are generally not returnable either. But first-quality merchandise that is defective should be returnable.

Just Say No to Runs and Snags

Want to make your pantyhose last longer? Try these tips:

➤ Add a drop or two of fabric softener to the final rinse. It lubricates the fibers and adds life to your hose.

➤ Buy pantyhose with reinforced toes because they are less vulnerable to snags and holes in toes, an area of stress.

➤ Buy the largest size that will fit properly. The less stretch and stress on the fabric, the longer they will last.

➤ Support pantyhose will save you money even though they cost more to start with. The fabric is much more durable and will stand up to more washings and everyday wear than regular pantyhose.

➤ Remove jewelry, and make sure your hands are smooth (apply lotion, if needed) before you put on your pantyhose. Rings and long fingernails can snag or run them.

➤ Soak pantyhose in salt water before washing. Salt will coat the fibers and make them stronger. Add about a half cup of salt for each quart of water. Soak pantyhose for a half hour or longer; then wash as usual.

Frugal Formal Wear

You don't have to break your budget to outfit yourself for your next formal event. There are several ways to look terrific without spending big bucks:

➤ If you are lucky enough to have a close friend or relative that wears the same dress size, you can borrow and exchange formal dresses and accessories.

➤ Consignment shops and thrift stores almost always have a large selection of formal dresses. But shop early for holiday or prom dresses because the best dresses will fly off the racks when the occasion draws near.

Tightwad Tip

Buy several pairs of the same brand and color of pantyhose. When you get a run in one leg, cut off the bad leg just below the panty. Do the same with the next pair when it gets a run. Then, you can wear the two panty tops with the good legs for a "free" pair.

Tightwad Tip

For men that have to attend formal events, it's cheaper to buy a basic black tuxedo than rent one each time. Even if you attend just one or two formal events per year, a tuxedo will quickly pay for itself. Consignment shops frequently have men's tuxedos for less than the price of one rental. You can buy used tuxedo shoes, shirts, bow ties, and cummerbunds from a tuxedo rental shop for less than half the original cost.

Watch Out!

Don't starch clothes to be stored—starch can attract silverfish and other bugs.

Bet You Didn't Know

If you don't like the smell of moth balls or cedar, here's another way to keep moths from eating small holes in your clothes: Scatter dried bay leaves in the boxes and between layers of the clothing you're packing up. The bay leaves will keep the moths away without leaving an overpowering odor.

➤ Rent a dress instead of buying it. You can rent a very expensive dress or gown for much less than the cost of buying one. Look in the *Yellow Pages* under "formal wear" to find stores that rent women's formal gowns and dresses.

Pack It Up

A few precautions will help to ensure than clothing looks as good after being stored for many months as it did the day you packed it away. Before storing any garment when the season is over, first wash or dry clean it. Make sure clothes are completely dry before packing them away. Damp clothes encourage mildew, and mildew stains can become permanent.

To prevent moth damage to wool clothes, store them in a cedar chest, if you have one. If not, use inexpensive cedar chips (you can buy a small bag marketed for hamsters and gerbils in a pet store). Take an old pair of pantyhose and pour a cup of cedar chips into one leg. Place the hose filled with cedar with your clothes to be stored.

After you take your stored clothing out of the cedar chest, re-scent it. Do this by rubbing the inside of the chest with fine sandpaper. Then vacuum up the dust particles. This will revive the wood's scent, which will help keep moths out of your clothes next time you use it.

The Least You Need to Know

➤ It's cheaper in the long run to spend a little more money and buy well-made clothing.

➤ You can find great clothing bargains in thrift stores, consignment shops, and even flea markets.

➤ Do you really need a dry-clean-only item? Over its life, the cleaning costs can exceed its purchase price.

➤ When mail-order shopping, comparison shop between catalogs, and always factor in the shipping, handling, and sales tax costs before you order.

➤ Save on formal wear by renting, borrowing, or buying at consignment shops.

➤ Always make sure seasonal clothing is clean and dry before packing it away.

Chapter 5

Wash and Wear: Laundry Solutions

In This Chapter

➤ Saving time and money when washing clothes

➤ Ways to avoid and eliminate lint

➤ Removing tough clothing stains

➤ Cutting the high cost of dry cleaning

➤ Smooth ironing tips

➤ Sewing repairs simplified

Chances are you have a mountain of laundry waiting on you right now. But before you toss another load into the washer, take a look at these tips for making the job easier and a little cheaper, and for making your clothes last longer.

Wash and Wear

Separate white and colored items. If you wash your whites with colored clothes, over time they will take on a gray tinge. Lint from light clothing also will stick like glue to your dark clothes.

You'll want to sort out delicate items, too. A thin nightgown can be torn to shreds by a zipper on a pair of jeans. Wash delicate items on the delicate cycle or by hand.

To make your clothes last longer, wash clothes with care. Never overload the washing machine; clothes that are stuffed too tightly into the washer tend to rub together and cause pilling. To prevent snags, close all zippers and fasteners before washing. Turn pockets inside out to make sure they are empty; one ball point pen left in a pocket can ruin a whole load of clothes.

Remove the wash as soon as it's done, and either hang it up to dry or put it into the dryer.

Presoaking and Prewashing

If clothes need presoaking, put clothes, soap, and water in the washing machine, let it stand for several minutes, then turn on the washer. You're saving time, water, and soap by not using a separate pre-wash cycle first.

Treat stains with a prewash spray (see the recipe for super-duper stain remover, later), or squirt a little liquid detergent on them. For tough stains, see Out, Out, D… Spot!, later in this chapter.

Mix small and large items in each load to circulate and distribute the load evenly around the wash basket.

Bet You Didn't Know

You can do your hand washing in your washing machine. Just start the tub and add a little laundry detergent. Then use this soapy water for your hand washing—as the water is still flowing into the tub, rinse the wash under it. By the time the tub is full, you should be finished with your hand washing, and you can add a load of regular laundry to the water.

Soap Solutions

Most laundry detergents are highly concentrated. Experiment with the brand that you use. Many times, you can use about $1/2$ to $3/4$ of the recommended amount and still get your clothes just as clean. If you have an extra-large-capacity washer or very hard water, you may need to use a little extra detergent to get clothes clean.

If you use a powdered detergent that comes with a measuring scoop, make sure you are not using more than the recommended amount. Some scoops are made to fill all the way to the top, while others have a "fill to" line much lower. Don't use more detergent than you need.

Smart Solution

Instead of buying an expensive all-color bleach product, try adding either $1/2$ cup of white vinegar or $1/2$ cup baking soda to the wash load. Either one will help clean and brighten clothes—and both are priced right!

Before adding detergent, read the label on the package. You want to use enough detergent to make a few suds, but making a mountain of suds will not get your clothes any cleaner. Usually, you'll need to add $1/2$ cup or a scoop of powdered detergent, or one capful of the liquid detergent for a full load.

Water

Use warm water for sheets and for white and colorfast items that won't shrink. Use cold wash for all other items. Always use cold-water rinse cycles.

Always read the care label of clothing to determine what temperature to wash it in. In general here are the guidelines for what temperature to use:

➤ Hot water (130° to 150°F) should be used for clothes with heavy dirt and for greasy clothes, diapers, whites (especially when you are bleaching them), and other white or light-colored cottons.

➤ Warm water (100° to 110°F) is recommended for light to moderately soiled permanent press clothing, dark-colored clothing and knit synthetics.

➤ Cold water (80° to 110°F) can be used for any lightly soiled wash, bright-colored clothes, delicates, and any colors that might bleed. Note: The water should not be ice cold but rather about 80°F.

Always use a cold water rinse. It saves energy and makes ironing easier since it helps prevent permanent press clothing from wrinkling.

Bleach

When you need to bleach clothes, add 1 cup chlorine bleach diluted in 1 quart of water to the machine a few minutes after it has been running. This will allow the detergent some time to do its job and ensure that the bleach gets evenly distributed quickly.

If the machine has an automatic bleach dispenser, follow the manufacturer's directions. To give bleach more time to do its job, let the machine run for a few more minutes after adding it, then turn off the machine and let the clothes soak for 10 minutes. Start the machine again and let it finish the wash cycle.

Smart Solution

To cut down on pilling, wash synthetic fibers separately from terry cloth and other fabrics that tend to rub. When possible, line–dry items that are likely to pill.

Smart Solution

Wash your delicate clothes in a pillow case instead of buying a special lingerie bag. Place the clothes in the pillow case (an old, thin one works best), and tie a knot in the end. Run your washing machine on the delicate setting or the shortest washing cycle.

Smart Solution

To eliminate static electricity, add 1 tablespoon white vinegar to the final rinse water if you choose not to use a fabric softener.

71

Lint Hints

Most problems can be eliminated or avoided with proper laundering. Lint is usually caused by one of these five problems:

➤ Overfilling the washing machine

➤ Not using enough laundry detergent to hold lint in suspension

➤ Using a dirty lint filter (lint trap)

➤ Using too much bleach

➤ Washing light and dark clothes in the same load

To avoid lint, follow these guidelines:

➤ Fill the washing machine no more than about two-thirds full.

➤ Always measure out the amount of detergent for each load. Look on the box or bottle to see how much is needed.

➤ Clean the dryer's lint filter after each use. A clogged filter will restrict air flow, and your dryer will use more energy to get the clothes dry. Keep a small trash can near the dryer so you can quickly remove and dispose of the lint.

➤ When using bleach for a load of laundry, don't go crazy. One cup of bleach per load of laundry is plenty to get the job done. The old saying "If a little is good, then a lot must be great" does not hold true here.

➤ Sort laundry before washing. Wash light-colored clothes separately from dark-colored ones.

➤ Turn dark-colored garments inside out before washing so light colored lint won't show if it gets on the dark clothing. When you turn it right side out any traces of lint will be on the inside.

Tightwad Tip

Instead of throwing away a clothing article that has pilled, try gently rubbing it with a pumice stone or carefully cut off the pills with scissors.

Smart Solution

Fabric softener dryer sheets are convenient, but they also can be expensive. Instead of buying fabric softener sheets, dip a sponge in diluted liquid fabric softener (mix half water with half liquid fabric softener) and then squeeze it so it's almost dry. Then simply toss the squeezed-out sponge in the dryer with your load of clothes to be dried. The sponge will work just like a fabric softener sheet for a fraction of the price. You can use the same sponge over and over for this purpose.

Removing Stains

When removing stains from clothing, the most important thing to remember is that speed counts.

Take immediate action. The longer a stain remains on the fabric, the more difficult it will be to remove. Always treat stains before laundering. Once a stain has been washed and dried, it becomes extremely difficult to remove.

When treating a stain, it's best to work from the underside of the garment to avoid grinding the stain through the fabric. And always use white towels and cloths to treat stains. The color can bleed from one fabric to another when you are trying to remove a stain.

There are many different stain-removal products you can buy at a premium price, but most stains can be treated with simple, inexpensive products you already have on hand. If one method of stain removal doesn't work, try another one. You can never really be sure exactly what will work on individual stains. Persistence can pay off.

Super Duper Stain Remover

You may never have to buy pretreating stain remover again! Try this formula:

$^1/_2$ cup ammonia

$^1/_2$ cup white vinegar

$^1/_4$ cup baking soda

2 tablespoons liquid soap

2 quarts water

Mix all ingredients together and pour into a spray bottle. Spray the solution on the stain and let it soak for a few minutes before washing as usual. Shake the solution before each use.

Out, Out D... Spot!

Here are some common stain-removal techniques for washable fabrics:

Alcoholic beverage. Soak immediately in cold water, then wash in warm, sudsy water. Rinse. If the stain remains, you can soak silk, wool, or colored items for 30 minutes in 2 tablespoons hydrogen peroxide mixed in a gallon of water. Launder. White linen, rayon, and cotton can be soaked in 1 tablespoon liquid chlorine bleach to each quart of water. Launder.

Barbecue sauce. Sponge with a 1 to 1 water-vinegar solution. Wash in warm water. Don't use hot water or place the garment into the dryer until the stain is removed because heat will set in the stain.

> ### Watch Out!
>
> After treating a stain and washing the item, check it carefully before drying it. If the spot's not completely gone, treat it again while it's still wet. Once dry, the stain may be impossible to remove.

Blood. Keep the spot wet, if possible, and treat it as soon as you can. Dried blood stains can be very difficult to remove. Soak the garment in cold salt water (add 1 cup of salt). Wash in cold water and add ammonia for really tough blood stains. If the stains remain, apply some super-duper stain remover and soak in lukewarm water for 30 more minutes; then launder.

Chocolate. Soak in cool water for half an hour. Then work full-strength detergent or soap into the stain. If the stain also contains milk, soak in warm water and an enzyme laundry product such as Wisk, then launder.

Coffee. Try soaking or dabbing with a solution of 1 tablespoon ammonia, $1/4$ teaspoon soap, and $1/2$ cup water. Then flush with hot water.

Crayon. First apply some homemade stain remover, then machine-wash in hot water using laundry soap and 1 cup baking soda. If the crayon mark remains, launder again in the hottest water that is safe for the fabric. If the fabric can be bleached, add 1 cup bleach to a hot water wash.

Deodorant. Rub the stain with full-strength liquid laundry detergent, then wash in the hottest water that's safe for the fabric.

Fruit or berry stains. Sponge the stain with a solution of $1/2$ tablespoon salt and 2 cups cold water. If safe for the fabric, pour boiling water through the stain. Apply soap or detergent directly to the stained area, and launder.

Grass. Sponge the stain with warm water, followed by rubbing alcohol. Wash in warm water.

Grease. Rub some talcum powder or baking soda into the spot and let a heavy coating sit on the spot overnight. The next morning, a stiff brush will usually remove the entire problem without a costly trip to the cleaners!

Gum. Put the garment in a plastic bag in the freezer. When frozen, scrape off the hard gum. You can also soak the garment in white vinegar, or rub the gum with egg white before washing.

Ink. Spray hair spray liberally on the stain, and rub with a clean, dry cloth. This works especially well on polyesters. On cotton fabrics, apply rubbing alcohol to the spot before washing.

Lipstick. Wash immediately with cold salt water or a mixture of half white vinegar and half water. For tougher stains, try blotting with denatured alcohol or hydrogen peroxide. Then wash in an enzyme laundry product.

Mildew. Brush off as much as possible. Rub stain with liquid laundry detergent, then launder. If stain remains, launder using a bleach that is safe for the fabric. Sometimes serious or old mildew stains can cause permanent damage to the clothing fibers, making it impossible to remove the stains.

Milk. Soak in cold water. Rub full-strength detergent or soap directly onto the stain. Launder as usual.

Red wine. On a fresh stain, sprinkle liberally with table salt, then dunk in cold water. Rub the spot under cold water until the stain washes away, and wash the garment as soon as possible.

Collar rings. To remove "ring around the collar" stains, use inexpensive shampoo. Ordinary hair shampoo dissolves body oils. Using a small paint brush or sponge, paint a small amount of shampoo on the stain, and let it soak overnight before washing.

Shoe polish. Sponge with rubbing alcohol, then launder in hot water.

Suntan oil. Soak up excess oil with cornmeal for several hours or overnight. Brush off dry cornmeal. Apply liquid laundry detergent or laundry pretreat, smear with petroleum jelly, and wash in warm water. Suntan oil should be treated quickly because the oil tends to attract more dirt.

Sweat. Soak for an hour or more in warm salt water to remove perspiration stains and odors. (Add 1 cup of salt to the warm water.) Be sure to wash well before drying, because heat will set perspiration stains and make them difficult, if not impossible, to remove. To avoid getting stains on your clothes, never get dressed until all antiperspirants, perfumes, and lotions are dry. These often show up later as mystery stains on clothing.

Drying

Shake the clothes before you put them into the dryer. This will separate them and speed up drying time. And don't over-dry clothes; this makes fabric stiff and wrinkled and shortens its life. Remove clothes as soon as they are dry, and hang them up immediately.

Save Loads on Laundry Costs

The cost of cleaning clothes can add up. Here are some tips on keeping those costs down.

One is Cheaper Than Two

When washing clothes, you'll save energy by doing one large load instead of two small or medium loads. Some newer washing machines are considered large-capacity machines. These enable you to wash bigger loads and save energy. They may cost slightly more when you buy them, but if you do a lot of laundry frequently, they'll save you money in energy consumption in the long run.

Water-Heating Savings

When washing clothes, conserving hot water is the key to saving. Studies show that 90 percent of the cost of washing clothes is attributable to water-heating expense.

If you have an electric hot water heater, you can save up to $230 per year by washing in cold water (see the chart below). With a gas water heater, you can save up to $60 per year if you switch to cold water.

Use hot water only for heavily soiled clothes that have been presoaked. Always rinse with cold water. Remember that the temperature of the rinse cycle does not affect cleaning. A cold-water rinse for laundry not only saves energy, but it reduces wrinkles, too!

Turn down the thermostat on your water heater. Most water heaters are preset at 140° F. A setting of 120° F. is adequate for most household needs. When you reduce your hot water temperature, you will save money washing in warm and hot water. A lower thermostat temperature also reduces the risk of a family member getting burned by hot water.

The Annual Energy Cost of Washing Clothes

Wash/Rinse cycle	Cost per load	Annual cost	Cost per load	Annual cost
Electric water heater set at 140° F			**Gas water heater set at 140° F**	
Hot/Hot	66¢	$240.90	20¢	$73.00
Hot/Warm	50¢	$182.50	15¢	$54.75
Hot/Cold	34¢	$124.10	10¢	$36.50
Warm/Warm	34¢	$124.10	10¢	$36.50
Warm/Cold	18¢	$65.70	5¢	$18.25
Cold/Cold	3¢	$10.95	3¢	$10.95
Electric water heater set at 120° F			**Gas water heater set at 120° F**	
Hot/Hot	52¢	$189.80	15¢	$54.75
Hot/Warm	39¢	$142.35	10¢	$36.50
Hot/Cold	27¢	$98.55	7¢	$25.55
Warm/Warm	27¢	$98.55	7¢	$25.55

Wash/Rinse cycle	Cost per load	Annual cost	Cost per load	Annual cost
Warm/Cold	15¢	$54.75	4¢	$14.60
Cold/Cold	3¢	$10.95	3¢	$10.95

Note: Electric estimates are based on 8 cents per kWh. Gas estimates are based on 60 cents per therm. Annual costs based on 365 loads per year.

Save on Drying

A gas clothes dryer usually costs about $50 more to buy than a similar electric model, but you'll quickly start saving money because a gas dryer is much cheaper to operate. As you can see in the following chart, the annual cost for a gas dryer is less than half the cost of running an electric model.

Electric vs. Gas Dryer Cost Comparison

Annual cost to operate	Average existing appliance	New energy-efficient appliance
Clothes dryer (electric)	$75	$59
Clothes dryer (gas)	$30	$25
Savings per year	$45	$34

Note: Table assumes electricity price of 8 cents per kWh and a gas price of 60 cents per therm. Dryers purchased after 1986 are energy-efficient.

More Ways to Save

Throw a dry towel in the dryer with especially damp or bulky clothes. The dry towel will speed up the drying time and save energy.

You can also save energy by doing several loads of laundry at a time. When you dry two or more loads in a row, you take advantage of the heat still in the dryer after the first load.

Tightwad Tip

To save the most, use a clothesline. When the weather is not suitable, hang clothes to dry in the garage or basement. If you have an older electric dryer, you can save about $75 per year by using a clothesline, and about $25 per year if you have a newer-model gas dryer.

Smart Solution

Before you spend a fortune to dry clean curtains, check to see if they actually need to be professionally cleaned. Many times, the curtains are just dusty. If this is the case, toss them in the dryer for a few minutes on air fluff to get the dust and loose dirt off.

Watch Out!

Sometimes the main part of a garment is washable but the lining and interfacing are not. Be sure to test these areas carefully, too.

Label Lookout

Always read the label when buying clothes, and be on the lookout for dry-clean-only tags. Manufacturers usually only have room for one recommended cleaning method for the garment. If the tag says "dry-clean only," it means just that. But if it just says "dry-clean," other methods, such as hand-washing, are often safe.

Before hand-washing any garment marked "dry clean," be sure to do a washing test on an inconspicuous area first. Take a clean, white cloth and dip it into cold water with a little liquid laundry detergent. Then rub the cloth on a hidden area of the garment. If the color does not bleed onto the white cloth, you probably will be able to hand-wash the item. Let the spot you have tested dry before you hand-wash it.

Hand-washing Sweaters

Most hand-washed sweaters will have a better feel to them if you add a little fabric softener to the final rinse.

After hand-washing a sweater, don't just lay it flat to dry. To make it really look nice, you'll need a rolling pin. Wash and squeeze out the excess water, then lay the damp sweater on a clean towel and use the rolling pin to shape and flatten all the seams and openings (such as the neck and the sleeves). This will prevent the puckering that can make a sweater look old and worn.

How to Save on Dry Cleaning

If the three little words "dry clean only" make you want to scream, here are some tips to keep the high cost of dry cleaning under control.

➤ Wash delicate clothes by hand, or use the gentle cycle of the washing machine. Chances are, many of the shirts, blouses, and dresses that you're dry cleaning are probably hand-washable. Cotton, nylon, silk, ramie, and polyester can be washed by hand as long as they are colorfast.

➤ To test for colorfastness (the capability of holding dyes without running), blot a white rag dipped in hot water on an inside, unexposed seam of the garment. If the color comes off onto the white rag, you'll have to have it dry cleaned. Some materials (such as acetate and viscose rayon), no matter what their color, will shrink substantially, so they need to be dry-cleaned, too.

➤ Dry clean less frequently. After each wearing, remove any soil from jackets or coats by brushing with a soft bristled brush. Let wrinkles smooth out by allowing them to hang for a few days. Many times, a skirt or pants may not need to be dry cleaned; they just need the wrinkles ironed out.

➤ Always dry clean the entire suit. Don't be tempted to just have the pants or skirt cleaned and wait until next time to clean the jacket. Dry cleaning can slightly change (or fade) the color of your garments, so over time both pieces of your suit may not be the exact color.

➤ Point out any stains, and let your cleaner know exactly what the stain is. Dry cleaners are very proficient at removing stains, but once the garment is cleaned, the stain will be harder to remove—and may even be permanent.

Tightwad Tip

Buy clothes from the dry cleaner. Once a year many dry cleaners will sell off the clothes that have not been picked up. Most will sell them for the price of the cleaning!

Iron It Out

Let's face it, I doubt you can find anyone who actually likes to iron clothes. I think the best strategy is to do as little ironing as possible. Always pull clothes out of the dryer as soon as they are dry. Fold or hang them up immediately to avoid having to iron them later.

If you didn't get to the dryer in time and the clothes inside are wrinkled, add a large wet or damp bath towel and turn the dryer back on. The dampness from the towel and the heat from the dryer will remove the wrinkles.

You can also hang wrinkled clothes in a steamy bathroom. The heat and steam will make many of the wrinkles fall out. This strategy works especially well on knits.

When you are packing clothes for a trip, roll them instead of folding. When you get to your destination, hang up the items that are prone to wrinkle as quickly as possible.

Many times, you can take a piece of clothing straight out of the dryer (while it is still warm) and lay it flat on a counter or ironing board and quickly smooth out the wrinkles with your hands.

Bet You Didn't Know

You may think that pressing and ironing are the same procedure, but actually there is a difference. Pressing means lifting and lowering the iron on the fabric. Ironing means that you glide the iron over the fabric.

Watch Out!

Never iron over a stain because the heat will set it and make it almost impossible to remove.

Iron-Clad Advice

When you do have to iron, be smart about it:

➤ Always test the iron first to see if it sticks to the fabric, jerks, or produces a glaze on the material. If any of these happen, you will need to clean the iron (see the cleaning instructions that follow).

➤ Don't iron dirty or sweaty clothes. You'll set the stain and make it almost impossible to remove.

➤ Don't iron over zippers, buttons, or other decorative items. Always check pockets before ironing over them (there may be something inside that will melt when the iron goes over it).

➤ Use only a cool iron on synthetic fibers. Don't iron stretch clothing, rubber, or ultrasuede.

➤ If your iron is more than a few years old, consider buying a new one. Shop the sales and discount stores, and you won't have to pay big money for one. The new features and temperature settings will save time and make the job easier.

➤ Knits, wools and other delicate fabrics should be pressed rather than ironed.

➤ To steam very delicate items such as silk ties, wrap a steam iron with a damp cloth and hold it near—not on—the garment until wrinkles are eased out.

➤ Before using a steam-burst feature, be sure the fabric you're ironing won't spot. Silks are especially prone to water spots.

A Pressing Cloth

Use a pressing cloth when ironing fragile fabrics. The extra layer of light cloth will keep the garment clean and prevent scorching. A pressing cloth is also handy when ironing a dark piece of clothing. The cloth will keep the dark material from shining. A pressing cloth is simply a piece of cloth laid between the iron and the garment. Any lightweight cotton cloth, such as a clean tea towel or an old pillowcase, will do the trick. Because starch may come off the garment onto the pressing cloth, always wash the cloth after you've used it.

Homemade Spray Starch

Here's how to make your own inexpensive spray starch for ironing clothes.

> 1 tablespoon cornstarch
>
> 2 cups water

Mix well and pour into a clean spray bottle. If you prefer a heavier starch, add 2 or 3 tablespoons of starch. Shake the mixture before each use. Spray directly on clothing just as you would a can of aerosol spray starch.

Rinse the spray nozzle after each use to prevent clogging. You can add ¹/₂ cup cold black tea to stain the starch when starching dark clothes to prevent any light-colored residue on the fabric.

Bet You Didn't Know

It isn't necessary to buy distilled water for steam irons to prevent the steam vents from clogging with minerals. Most iron manufacturers today say that unless you have extremely hard water (more than 180 ppm dissolved minerals), go ahead and use plain old tap water. (Softened hard water still has minerals in it that will clog the vents.)

Right Side Out or Inside Out?

When ironing clothing, many times you'll get the best results by turning the item inside out. Cotton (except for chintz), silky rayon, or net can be ironed right side out. Polyester and polyester-cotton blend fabrics can be ironed right side out or inside out. Iron dark fabrics, acetate, acrylic, crepe, corduroy, flock fabric, cotton lace, linen, satin, silk, rayons, mat rayon, and wool garments inside out to prevent shiny patches from developing.

Smart Solution

Spray starch on the inside of the garments to eliminate starch buildup on the ironing board and on the outside of the clothing items.

Keeping Your Iron in Tip-Top Shape

Always rub a clean cloth over the iron before you turn it on. This should remove any light dirt or dust on the iron. In addition to this quick wipe before each use, you'll need to give your iron a more thorough cleaning from time to time, depending on how often it is used:

➤ Rub scratches and stains gently with a piece of fine steel wool when the iron is cold.

➤ If your iron has a tendency to build up deposits, you probably have hard water. Try using distilled or filtered water instead of your tap water, and see if the problem disappears.

➤ Clean irons that have nonstick bottom plates with a cotton cloth or diaper dipped in warm water and detergent or baking soda. Never use an abrasive cleaner (such as scouring powder); it will scratch the plate.

➤ An iron without a nonstick finish can be cleaned on a hot, nonsteam setting. Run the hot iron over some table salt sprinkled on a large brown paper grocery bag. When the iron is cool, wipe it down with a cotton cloth dipped in white vinegar.

➤ If you prefer to clean an iron that doesn't have a nonstick finish while it is cool, use some laundry prewash (stain remover) sprayed on a damp cotton cloth. After using the prewash, wipe the iron with a clean damp cloth to remove all the soap.

Emergency Clothing Repairs

We have all been there: You're at work or another public place when a seam rips in your clothing. Here are a few tips to get you through the day until you can go home and do some repair work.

Hems. If your skirt or pants hem becomes unstitched at an inconvenient time, you can use safety pins or even your desktop stapler to hold the hem in place until you get home. Staple from inside out so the staples will not catch on your pantyhose and snag them. When you get home, use a staple remover to pull out the staples. If you are not careful, the staples will snag or tear the fabric. On some fabrics, you can use clear or masking tape to temporarily hold the hem in place.

Buttons. When buttons with shanks on them fall off, you can easily use safety pins to hold them on until you can get home and sew them back on. If you have a button that keeps falling off, try sewing it on with dental floss or clear nylon fishing line instead of using thread. Both are tough as nails and should not pull off. This works great for heavy-duty items such as coats and jeans.

To keep buttons from falling off, put a drop of super glue or a dab of clear nail polish on the top of the button (over the thread). Do this first thing, even before you wear the garment.

Smart Solution

If you end up with a stain on one of your favorite shirts or jeans that will not come out, consider sewing an appliqué or some type of fabric trim over the stain.

A Stitch in Time

Most of us don't take the time to sew, but you need to have some basic sewing supplies for simple mending jobs. A basic sewing kit will save the day many times over. To be safe, you might want to keep one sewing kit at home and one in the car. If you have a clothing emergency while you are at work or just out and about, you can grab the sewing kit and make a quick repair—hopefully without too much embarrassment.

Emergency Sewing Kit

1 spool white thread

1 spool black thread

1 spool clear (invisible) thread

1 packet of needles

1 needle threader (if desired)

2 or 3 white shirt buttons

Iron-on patches

Pair of small scissors

Thimble (if desired)

Safety pins (large and small)

Place these and any other items you think you'll need in a small plastic box or refrigerator container. Label it and keep it someplace handy.

A Hot Solution: Iron-On Patches

Iron-on patches are one of the handiest mending supplies you can buy. We tend to think of these patches just for the knees of kids' jeans, but they can be handy for quite a few jobs around the house. When you find a small tear in your sheets, use an iron-on patch to keep the tear from growing. Even rips in shirts and other garments can many times be fixed with an iron-on patch.

You can find patches in department or discount stores in the notions or sewing departments. Packages of patches will usually contain several different colors and sizes. For sheets or shirts, buy lightweight (thin) patches. To patch blue jean knees, buy the heavier (thicker) denim ones.

Cut the patch slightly bigger than the tear you are repairing, and place it sticky-side down on the underside of the rip. Then use the heat of the iron to melt the glue on its back to the fabric. More detailed directions will be on the package, but you get the general idea. It's a quick fix that requires no sewing.

The Least You Need to Know

➤ Do full washer loads to save time and energy, but don't be tempted to overload your machine.

➤ To avoid lint, sort your clothes, clean the lint trap, don't add too much detergent or bleach, and don't overload the washer.

➤ Treat stains and spills on clothing immediately to increase your chances of removing the spots.

➤ Never iron or dry a piece of clothing with a stain. The heat will set the stain.

➤ Keep a simple sewing repair kit handy for emergencies, and make sure it includes an assortment of iron-on patches.

Accessorize Your Life

Variety is said to be the spice of life. And accessories such as jewelry, shoes, and eyewear are the spice of our wardrobes. Here's some tips for buying, maintaining, and repairing them.

If the Shoe Fits...

Shoes can be one of the most expensive items in your closet, so it makes sense to buy shoes than fit well and are made to last. Here's some tips on getting the best fit.

Try on shoes late in the day, when your feet may be slightly swollen. Wear the same type of hosiery or socks that you plan to wear with the new shoes. The thickness of socks can make a big difference in fit.

Take your time in the store, and always try on both the right and left shoes. Walk around for a few minutes to make sure they feel comfortable. Walk on hard surfaces, not just carpeted ones. If they aren't comfortable, don't buy them; they may never be comfortable. You shouldn't have to "break in" new shoes for them to feel right.

Fit, Not Size

Sizing varies from one manufacturer to another. Even different styles by the same manufacturer may fit differently, so time spent trying on shoes is time well spent.

Chances are that both your feet are not the exact same size. Always fit your larger foot. If needed, you can add a half-sole in the front of the shoe for your smaller foot.

Shoes should be wide enough for you to wiggle your toes comfortably. The front of the shoe should not pinch or squeeze your toes. The back of the shoe should be tight enough to grip your heel and not slip when you walk.

Style Right

Avoid extremely high heels. The most comfortable heel height is $1/2$ inch to 2 inches high. If you wear very high heels long enough, not only will your feet suffer but you can develop painful (and expensive) back problems.

When buying sandals, open-toe shoes, or sling-back shoes, make sure that neither your toe nor your heel hangs over the sole.

To get the most for your money, look for classic styles of shoes such as pumps, loafers, docksiders, and wing tips that never go out of style.

Poor Fit? Take 'em Back!

Buying shoes can be tricky. The pair of shoes that seems to fit perfectly can end up being torture on your feet. Instead of pushing the toe-crunching shoes to the back of the closet, take them back to the store. Most stores are very customer service–oriented and will be willing to refund your money or exchange merchandise, even if you have used the item slightly.

If you did not save the cash register receipt, most stores will offer you a store credit without a hassle. Large chain stores and department stores have come to realize that writing off a few items is worth it to keep customers happy—and to keep them coming back. You may have more trouble returning slightly used items to small stores that are individually owned, but it's worth a try.

Next time you buy a new pair of shoes, save the box and sales receipt. If possible, wear the shoes inside the house on carpet for a few hours before wearing them outside. You may find that after a few minutes the shoes are not comfortable. If they're not, take them back.

Too Tight?

To stretch shoes that are too tight, saturate a cotton ball with rubbing alcohol and rub inside the shoes at the tight spot. Then put the shoes on and walk around for a while.

Or put plastic bags in the shoes, then fill the bags with water. Seal the bags, then put the shoes with the bags of water in a large plastic bag and freeze. When the water expands, it will stretch the leather.

Loosey Goosey

To shrink shoes that are slightly large, soak from the inside with a wet sponge, then let the shoes sit outside in the warm sun to dry.

The Shoe Doctor

You can save real money by replacing heels and even the soles on your old leather shoes instead of buying a new pair. While getting shoes repaired, ask what preventive steps you can take to keep your shoes from wearing down and wearing out.

Broken heel. To repair a scraped or wrinkled heel, press a warm iron gently against the scraped area. The warmth of the iron will remove wrinkles so that you can smooth the leather back out and glue it into place.

Shoelaces

When shoelace ends get frayed and hard to lace, try one of these tips:

➤ Twist the ends tightly (you may have to dampen them a bit), dip them into clear nail polish, and let dry. Your laces will be like new again. And to keep the tips on new shoes from breaking off, dip them in clear nail polish and let dry before you wear them.

➤ Dip the ends into glue; twist to a point and allow them to dry.

➤ Wind transparent tape around the ends a few times.

Polish It Off

It's amazing what a little spit shine can do for a pair of shoes. Don't worry if you don't have a shoe shine kit—you can still get your shoes in tip-top shape with these solutions.

If you find you're out of polish, you can apply olive oil to leather shoes of any color and buff with a soft cloth. This works well for a quick fix when you don't have many new scuff marks that need to be covered.

You can shine your leather or imitation leather shoes with a banana peel. Simply rub the inside

Smart Solution

To make shoe polish that's hardened usable again, heat it in its metal or plastic container in a bowl of hot water, or moisten it with a little turpentine.

of the banana peel on the shoe and buff to a high shine with a soft cloth. Oils in the banana peel will soak into your leather shoes and actually make them last longer. This trick works great for dress shoes and leather athletic or casual shoes.

Liquid shoe polish is best for covering scuffs, while paste wax gives shoes the best shine.

White Shoes

These are especially hard to keep looking clean. You can make white shoes look nice longer if you rub wax paper over them after they have been polished. Be sure the polish is completely dry before you rub them. Or you can spray them with hair spray after the polish is dry.

Your white shoe polish will go on evenly if you rub the shoes with a raw potato or rubbing alcohol before applying the polish. The moisture softens them slightly and the polish seems to go on easier.

Polishing shoes regularly will help prevent scuffs and stains. Even a quick coat of polish will offer some protection.

Smart Solution

To keep your shoes looking new longer, keep a pair of old slip-ons in the car to change into. This will eliminate the scraped heels and ugly scuff marks you get on your shoes while driving.

Give Shoes a Rest

Change shoes frequently to allow them to completely dry out. Try not to wear the same shoe all day long, and never wear them two days in a row. Just like your feet, shoes need to rest.

One-liter plastic soda bottles make excellent boot trees to help keep leather boots in shape.

Scuff Stuff

Scuffs are a fact of life but are still a pain to deal with. When you can't simply remove the scuff, you're forced to hide it.

Cleaning Off Scuff Marks

To remove or hide scuff marks on light-colored shoes, try one of these solutions:

➤ Rub the scuff mark lightly with nail polish remover or lighter fluid.

➤ White toothpaste will remove scuffs from white, light-colored, silver, or gold shoes.

Covering Scuff Marks

If all else falls, cover up those dark marks one of these ways:

> ➤ Scrub the scuff marks vigorously with a prewash (laundry) spray.

> ➤ Use a matching color in acrylic paint, indelible felt marker or crayon to cover the scuff marks after you have cleaned the area.

> ➤ Cover scuff marks on white shoes with white-out correction fluid, then polish.

Suede Shoes

Here's some helpful advice for keeping suede shoes looking great.

First, if it looks like rain, choose a different shoe today. Nothing makes suede look worse than getting wet.

Suede shoes can be kept looking fresh by rubbing with a dry sponge after each wearing.

Use fine sandpaper to remove scuff marks or water stains from suede shoes.

To steam-clean suede shoes at home, use a soft dry brush and a pan of boiling water. Gently brush the shoe, then hold it over the pan until the steam has raised the nap of the suede. Lightly brush again in one direction.

Leather Shoes and Boots

Leather shoes and boots are a great investment because they will last many years with proper care. Here are some tips to keep these babies beautiful.

Treating Wet Shoes

When your leather shoes or boots get wet, coat them with saddle soap and buff, then stuff them with paper to hold their shape. Avoid placing them near a heat source when drying. You want them to dry slowly and evenly. When placed near a heat source one side may dry faster than the other and actually shrink more.

When dry, rub the shoes with castor oil or even vegetable oil if you didn't initially coat them with saddle soap. This will soften and recondition the leather. Now you are ready to give them a good polish—and a promise to avoid that big water puddle.

Tightwad Tip

Got more shoes than closet space? You can make your own and double your shoe storage space with supplies you probably already have around the house. Suspend a piece of board on two shoe boxes, a stack of bricks, or books. Put your shoes under and on the board to save space in the closet. You can even add another layer on the top if you need more shoe space and your clothes don't hang down too low.

Remove water stains on leather shoes or boots by rubbing with a cloth wrung out in a solution of half water and half white vinegar.

Vinegar and water will also take care of salt stains on leather shoes or boots from winter streets. Dab a half-and-half mixture gently on the salt stain. Be careful not to saturate the leather, or you might wind up with a water ring.

Oh, Shiny Feet: Patent Leather Shoes

To clean patent leather shoes, rub a dab of petroleum jelly or castor oil over the shoes and buff, or spray glass cleaner on them and buff.

Smart Solutions

Coat the eyelets of athletic shoes with clear nail polish to prevent discoloration of the laces and tongues while washing.

Athletic Shoes

To keep canvas tennis shoes looking new longer, spray them with a light coating of starch (the regular spray starch used for ironing) before wearing them. The starch will give them a protective coating that helps them stay clean longer. After washing your tennis shoes, apply another coat of spray starch to them as soon as they are dry. If you apply spray starch to your shoes after each washing, you will find that you do not need to wash them as often—which will make them last longer.

Cleaning

When washing tennis shoes in the washing machine, put them inside an old pillow case. The pillow case will help protect them from zippers or anything sharp and will keep the shoe strings from wrapping around the other clothes in the dryer and making a fun mess for you to pull apart.

You can clean and deodorize athletic or canvas shoes by hand, too. Mix 1 1/2 cups baking soda and 4 cups water in a container. Scrub the mixture onto the shoes thoroughly and use an old toothbrush to get the crevices clean. Remove and scrub the insoles, if possible. Let the mixture stand for 10 minutes, then rinse well. Repeat if the shoes are really dirty or smelly. Then stuff the toes with paper towels or newspaper and let them air-dry.

Or, you can spray them with carpet cleaner. Scrub with a toothbrush, let dry, then brush with a dry brush.

Remove grease spots by sprinkling the spot with baking soda or cornstarch. Leave the absorbent on the grease for several minutes, then brush it off.

High and Dry

Here's an easy way to dry wet tennis shoes: Place the shoes on the floor in front of the refrigerator by the grille overnight. The movement from the fan inside will thoroughly dry them out. Shoes dried this way will keep their shape better than if dried in the clothes dryer. This method is also quieter and requires no extra electricity.

Smelly Shoe Solutions

To remove odor in shoes, place crumpled newspapers or paper towels inside to absorb the moisture. You'll be amazed how much odor the paper absorbs.

Sprinkle the inside of smelly shoes liberally with baking soda, and let the shoes sit overnight. In the morning, shake out the excess baking soda before wearing them.

Don't Be Cruel to Your Jewels

You love your jewelry, right? Then treat it right. Keep the pieces clean and store them carefully, and they'll stay beautiful for years to come.

Storage Solutions

Keep your expensive and frequently worn pieces of jewelry in a lined jewelry box. The box will keep the jewelry protected from dust and scratches.

Earrings. If you have lots of earrings or other small pieces of jewelry, plastic ice cube trays or Styrofoam egg cartons make perfect containers. Stack the ice cube trays and close the top of the egg cartons to keep out dust.

Line a small drawer or box with a piece of Styrofoam. Store pierced earrings by poking them into the foam. Keep a small box handy for storing the earring backs.

Necklaces. Install small hooks (the kind you hang cups and mugs on) inside your closet door. Hang beaded necklaces, bracelets, and other

Bet You Didn't Know

To increase the life of your workout shoes, wear them only for exercise. If they get wet, stuff them with rolled-up newspapers or paper towels to help absorb the moisture. When shoes are left wet, they lose some of their shape and the moisture speeds up the breakdown of shoe materials.

Smart Solution

Chains, necklaces, and bracelets can be almost impossible to get apart once they become tangled. To avoid having to untangle them, use this simple storage trick: Cut a plastic drinking straw a little shorter than half the length of the necklace (or bracelet). Then slip the chain into the straw and clasp the two ends together.

jewelry there. Things won't get tangled up together, and you'll quickly be able to see what you have to coordinate with your clothes.

All That Glitters: Cleaning Jewelry

It's a good idea to have your expensive pieces of jewelry cleaned and checked once a year. A professional can make sure the settings, strings, clasps, and pins are in good shape. Most jewelry stores will be happy to do this for you (often free of charge). They know that when you bring your jewelry in, you'll look at all their goodies—and you may just walk out with a new purchase.

Clean your jewelry often, especially the good stuff. You wear jewelry so close to your body that it can collect body oils, lotions, and even tiny particles of skin. This will not only dull the sparkle, but accumulated grime can settle into the prongs and cause the setting to become loose.

Watch Out!

Cleaning jewelry in the sink is quick and convenient, but be sure to close the drain before you start cleaning. You'll also want to lay a soft washcloth in the bottom of the sink to prevent the jewelry from getting scratched.

Watch Out!

Don't soak pearls in any type of homemade or store-bought jewelry cleaner that contains alcohol or ammonia. It may take off the finish, so don't chance it.

Home-Brewed Jewelry Cleaner

$1/2$ cup clear or sudsy ammonia

1 cup warm water

Mix ammonia and water together. Soak jewelry in the solution for 10 to 15 minutes. Rub gently with a cloth or soft brush, and allow to dry. Do not use this solution on pearls.

Caring for Pearls

Pearls require special care. To keep yours looking dazzling, here's some advice.

It's best not to soak a pearl necklace in water or any type of liquid because the string can get soaked, which can cause the necklace to stretch, weaken, and possibly break. Instead, wash pearls with a soft cloth dipped in soapy water. Gently wipe them clean, then lay them on a clean towel to dry.

You can soak pearl rings or pins in a mild soapy water solution. Rinse with clean water and pat dry.

After cleaning your pearls, you can make them shine by wiping with a tiny drop of vegetable oil. Use a clean soft cloth to buff the oil to a high luster.

Gold Jewelry

Gold chains should be soaked clean in a solution of 1 cup water and $1/2$ cup sudsy ammonia. Soak the chains one at a time for about 10 to 15 minutes. If you haven't cleaned the chain in a while, you may see quite a bit of dirt in the cleaning solution. Swish the chain around, being careful not to bend or tangle it. Rinse in cold water and pat dry.

Silver Jewelry

Silver jewelry requires more care than gold jewelry. It needs to be lightly buffed with a soft cloth after wearing. Be sure to remove any fingerprints, as they can discolor the silver.

Clean silver jewelry with a silver cloth, or lightly rub with silver polish. You can also use white toothpaste to clean silver. Just brush it on and rinse with water. Toothpaste works great when you have some major cleaning to do. Make sure that you thoroughly dry the silver after cleaning. To keep your silver jewelry looking nice, you can store it in a pouch designed to protect silver tableware.

Baking soda can also be used to clean silver. Simply rub gently with dry baking soda on a soft cloth.

Precious Stones

Diamonds. These gems should be soaked in a solution of warm water and sudsy ammonia. Gently brush the diamond with a soft toothbrush to remove the dirt and grime. Take care to clean near the prongs, because this is where the most dirt collects. Always look at the prongs closely when cleaning a diamond. If any are bent or the diamond is loose, take it to a jeweler for repair.

Sapphires. Soak these in water and ammonia, then brush lightly with a toothbrush, rinse, and pat dry.

Watchbands

Because most people wear a watch every day, after a while it can really get nasty-looking. To clean the band, it's best to remove gold or stainless steel trim, if possible. Once removed, soak the band in a solution of 1 cup warm water and $1/2$ cup sudsy ammonia. If you cannot remove the watchband from the watch, dip a cloth into the ammonia solution and wipe the dirt off.

Clean leather watchbands with saddle soap or a leather cleaner, or use the banana peel trick. Rub the inside of a banana peel on the watchband, and buff off with a soft cloth.

Jewelry Repairs

When a necklace pops or gets a tangle or knot in it, you have to be the emergency technician on call. Here's how to save your valuables.

Re-stringing necklaces. Use the smallest (thinnest) fishing line you can find to re-string a broken necklace. The line is firm enough that you won't have to use a needle, but it's soft enough to hand-string the beads easily.

When re-stringing beads of graduated sizes, you can save yourself some major time and headaches with a little prep work. Take a strip of tape and tape it down (sticky side up) with more tape onto a smooth surface. Arrange the beads in order on the piece of tape before re-stringing.

Eliminating knots. If a necklace chain is knotted, put a drop or two of vegetable oil on a piece of waxed paper, lay the knot on the oil and undo it by using two straight pins. This should make it easy to get the knot out.

Smart Solution

You can use vodka to clean eye-glasses. Put a drop on a piece of soft, clean cloth and polish clean.

Jeepers Peepers: Cleaning Eyeglasses

Here are a few tips for cleaning eyeglasses:

Avoid using tissue or paper towels on plastic lenses. They will scratch the surface. Instead, use a soft, lint-free cloth. An old diaper or scrap of T-shirt works perfectly.

Put a drop of white vinegar or rubbing alcohol on a piece of soft, clean cloth and polish the glasses clean.

Wet your glasses under hot running water, then rub a drop of mild dishwashing or liquid soap on the lenses with your fingers. Rinse under hot running water and dry with a soft, clean lint-free cloth.

Four Eyes Emergency Repairs

Don't have a tiny eyeglass screwdriver? Use a pencil eraser to tighten a screw. Press it against the screw to hold it in place, and turn. Once the screw is set, you can keep it in place with a dab of clear nail polish; this will prevent it from working loose again.

For a temporary repair, replace a missing screw with a stud-type earring or a bit of wire from a bread or garbage bag twist tie.

The Least You Need to Know

➤ When it comes to shoes, fit and comfort are everything. If the shoes aren't comfortable, don't buy them; they should not have to be "broken in."

➤ A frequent polish will protect your shoes and make them last longer.

➤ Store your jewelry carefully so it doesn't get tangled, scratched, or lost in the drawer. Also clean it regularly.

➤ You can make your eyeglasses sparkle with vinegar, rubbing alcohol, or even vodka.

Part 3
The Great Outdoors

For proud homeowners, there's little more satisfying than enjoying your own beautiful yard or garden. Getting yours in shape need not wear you out or cost you a small fortune. It can be fun, and quite rewarding!

Need to organize your garage or basement? You'll find solutions to make space you didn't even know you had.

Can you think of a much worse way to spend your time than using it to haggle with a salesperson over the car you want to buy? If it's not that, then maybe it's the time (and money) spent maintaining your car. Chapter 9, "Savings on Wheels," comes to the rescue with advice about buying new and used cars, finding auto insurance, and keeping your car in good shape.

Chapter 7

The Lawn and Garden

> ## In This Chapter
>
> ➤ Lawn mowing made easier
>
> ➤ Low-maintenance means less work and less money
>
> ➤ Natural weed and pest control
>
> ➤ The ultimate in recycling: garden composting
>
> ➤ Container gardening for limited spaces

When spring rolls around, the lawn and garden demand attention. These shortcuts will save you time and money as you create an attractive and useful landscape.

Cutting The Lawn

Summertime means lawn-mowing season. Use these tricks of the trade to make the job easier and save money.

Keep lawn mower blades sharp. Check them several times during the mowing season, and sharpen at least once a year. Dull mower blades can tear grass instead of making a nice sharp cut; the tears leave grass more prone to weeds and disease.

Don't cut your lawn too short. Setting your mower blades to leave grass a little higher will encourage strong, deep roots that help keep moisture without having to be watered as often. But don't let grass get too tall between mowings. Infrequent mowings are a shock to the grass, and you'll end up with more weeds in your lawn.

Never remove more than half of the height of the lawn in a single mowing. If rain or an extended vacation has turned your yard into a jungle, adjust the mower blade to cut about half of the height, and then wait a couple days to cut it to the desired height (this also saves wear and tear on your mower).

Bet You Didn't Know

Take it easy when watering. Not only is water expensive, but a lawn that gets too much water will have more weed problems.

Smart Solution

No sense taking chances with a grass seed not suited to your lawn. Always buy a seed that's specifically recommended for your particular area and conditions. Farm supply stores and home improvement centers usually sell seed for less than small nurseries and hardware stores.

Maybe A Manual Mower?

Manual mowers are less expensive than gas or electric mowers, and they require less maintenance and no electricity, oil, or gasoline. If you have a small yard, it won't take much longer to mow with a manual mower—and you get the added benefit of more exercise!

Apply vegetable oil or spray a nonstick cooking spray to the blades of a hand mower when the ground is damp and you have to mow. The oil will make the blades slick so that the grass doesn't stick to them.

Low-Maintenance, Low-Cost

When it comes to gardens, low maintenance also means low cost. If you plant your yard and landscape so that you need less water, fewer tools, and less fertilizer and other accessories you'll save a significant amount of time, energy, and money. Try some of these low-maintenance landscape ideas.

Plants You Can Count On

Shop for disease-resistant or disease-tolerant varieties of trees, flowers, and shrubs.

While some annuals are expensive and last for just a season, many perennials are just as beautiful and don't die off—they multiply each year.

Daisy, daisy. The classic white Shasta daisies are a bargain for the price. In two seasons, an inexpensive 2- or 3-inch plant will grow to fill a square foot of your flower garden with lots of beautiful flowers.

Daffodils. Buy daffodil bulbs instead of tulip bulbs. While tulips will wither and die off in a few years, daffodils will multiply over time.

Fruit trees. Consider planting fruit trees instead of ordinary shade trees. You'll still get the shade to keep things cooler in hot weather, plus you'll get a beautiful fruit-bearing tree that can grow in a small space without much care for years. Dwarf apple trees are low-cost and low-maintenance and produce lots of apples.

Bargain Plants

The biggest plant sales are at the end of the season. When fall is in the air, you often can find drastic markdowns because many retailers want to clear out their entire growing stock before the winter months. If you have a place where you can protect plants until they can safely be planted next year, you can save a bundle buying at the end of the season. Also look for end-of-season markdowns on lawn and garden supplies and tools. You may be able to find just what you've been looking for at a very low price.

Go native. Choose plants, trees, and shrubs that are native to your area. They will thrive during the seasonal weather changes, and you won't have to pay a premium for more unusual types and varieties.

Small can save. If you're looking to keep landscaping costs down, buy the smallest size tree or shrubs you can use. Smaller is almost always cheaper.

Bargain shop. Shop garage sales and flea markets for plants and garden tools. You may also be able to find low-cost flower pots and other accessories.

Tightwad Tip

Trade cuttings and seeds with neighbors and friends. Many people are happy to share plant divisions with you in exchange for your extras.

Smart Solution

Buy slow-growing trees and bushes. These will not have to be pruned or fertilized as often.

Smart Solution

Don't throw away used coffee grounds. Instead, sprinkle them in your garden or flower bed around acid-loving plants such as azaleas and rhododendrons. Coffee grounds add acid to the soil.

Fertilizer Hints

Better to see you with. When using dry fertilizer on lawns, mix some flour with it before you spread it. The white flour will help you see exactly where you've fertilized and where you haven't.

Bet You Didn't Know

Egg shells will help the plant growth in your garden or flower bed. The shells don't decompose easily by themselves, so crush them first and then sprinkle them around plants or flowers. Use your fingers or a trowel to work them into the soil.

Bet You Didn't Know

If you've got golf shoes, wear them when fertilizing the lawn or working in the garden. The cleats go into the ground and aerate the lawn.

Watch Out!

Avoid a heavy dose of fertilizer for your lawn in the middle of the summer; doing so can stimulate the weeds. Also, always apply fertilizer to damp, never dry, soil.

Veggie scraps. Banana peels and most all fruit and vegetable scraps can be used to enrich the soil. Chop them into small pieces and bury them around shrubs and perennials, as well as in the vegetable garden. Just be careful not to damage plant roots when burying them.

Fish water. Recycle the water from your aquarium or fish bowl to water vegetable plants or roses. This water is loaded with minerals.

Ashes. Fireplace ashes make a no-cost fertilizer rich in potash. Make sure the ashes are completely cooled before spreading on the ground around bushes and trees. Because potash is alkaline, avoid sprinkling near acid-loving plants.

Test Your Soil

Get an inexpensive (or maybe even free) soil test from your local agricultural agent or state cooperative extension service. By testing your soil, you'll find out exactly what it lacks, and you won't waste money on useless additives. Test results most often come with suggestions on what your soil needs, but if not, ask your agent. He has all sorts of useful free information—and it's often just a phone call away.

Homemade Lawn Fertilizer

Before you go out and buy bags of fertilizer for your lawn, try a low-cost home brew. You'll save money, and the results can be dramatic.

1 cup Epsom salts

1 cup household ammonia

Combine ingredients in a clean jar. To use, mix 2 tablespoons of the mixture with 2 gallons of water in a watering can, and sprinkle over 150 to 200 square feet of turf. Or, if you prefer to use a hose sprayer, mix the entire batch with enough water to make a quart of liquid. Pour the liquid into the sprayer. A quart of diluted fertilizer will cover about 2,500 square feet of grass.

Snuff Out Those Weeds!

If you can't seem to get rid of the weeds in your driveway cracks or keep grass from growing between bricks in a sidewalk, try any of these tips:

➤ Pour full-strength white vinegar on the weeds to kill them.

➤ Pour boiling water with a little salt on the weeds, or sprinkle salt into the cracks. Replace the salt a couple of times during the year, especially after a hard rain.

➤ Sprinkle borax in the cracks in the early spring to help prevent weeds from sprouting.

➤ Pour chlorine bleach in the cracks. The vegetation dies and can be easily pulled out. The bleach also prevents the weeds from growing back.

➤ Sprinkle baking soda in the cracks to kill weeds and prevent them from sprouting again.

Caution: These methods to kill weeds are very effective but can kill more than weeds. Use salt, borax, baking soda, and bleach with caution near your property line because the runoff may end up in your neighbor's yard. When using any of these techniques for killing weeds use the products sparingly. Try to use just enough to kill the weeds and apply the product directly on the weeds. Salt, borax, baking soda, and bleach can also kill grass and other nearby plants.

Poison Ivy Remedy

To get rid of poison ivy without letting it get the best of you, try this formula:

> 2 gallons warm water
>
> 2 tablespoons liquid soap
>
> 2 pounds salt

Mix the water, soap, and salt together in a bucket. Spray or pour the solution on the poison ivy. The salt kills the leaves and the plant, while the soap helps with absorption of the salt. With repeated applications, over time you can kill the plant and the roots. Spray the plant again after some of it dies and then again next year early when new growth starts.

Bet You Didn't Know

If you're allergic to poison ivy and you realize that you've touched a plant, act fast—you may be able to avoid an irritating rash. Quickly wash the area with lots of soap and warm water. If you can get all the poison off quick enough, you won't break out.

Kitchen Garden Savings

A backyard garden can be a frugal person's dream come true. If you've got the time, energy, and garden space, you can turn some inexpensive packets of seed into an abundance of fresh, healthy food. Planned right, a vegetable garden can provide a steady supply of vegetables from late spring right through fall. It's not necessary to have a large garden to save money. Start small and work your way into it. Gardening is a fun hobby—and unlike other hobbies, instead of costing you money, this one can actually save you some. To get the most from your garden, try some of these tips and ideas.

If your time and space is limited, concentrate on growing foods your family likes, those that are easy to grow, and those that are expensive to buy in the grocery store. A good list to start with is tomatoes, green peppers, broccoli, lettuce, radishes, strawberries, green beans, and raspberries.

Get Only What You Need

You'll need some garden tools, but not too many. Garden supply stores and catalogs are full of gadgets and supplies that won't improve your yield or reduce your labor. The basics—a shovel, a hoe, a rake, and a trowel—will get the job done. Shop garage sales and flea markets for used garden tools, too. A good tool, if well cared for, should last a lifetime.

Weed Control

Weeds rob your plants of water and nutrients, so weed often. You can keep most weeds under control by covering the ground around them with a 3-inch layer of hay or leaves or a layer of newspapers. Any of these materials will also help retain moisture in the soil.

Tomatoes

Staking. Use old pantyhose or strips of old sheeting tied loosely in the shape of an "8" around the tomato stake and vine to tie up tomato plants. Either is better than string because they won't cut into the delicate vines.

Planting. When you plant tomatoes, first mix some fireplace ashes, dried manure, or compost into the soil before planting. Then take a medium- to large-sized metal can (such as a vegetable can or coffee can) and remove both the top and the bottom. Place the can around the new tomato plant. The can will help protect the plant as it starts to grow. Once the plant reaches the top of the can, remove it and save it for next year.

Watering

If you don't get enough rain, water your garden in the morning so there is plenty of time for the ground to dry before dark. If the soil stays damp too long, plants and vegetables are more susceptible to fungus. During dry spells, give your garden a thorough soaking once a week instead of a little water more often. A thorough weekly soaking encourages root growth, which makes for healthier plants.

Smart Solution

Rather than one large planting, make several different plantings of the same vegetable, spaced several days or weeks apart, throughout the vegetable's planting season. This will assure you fresh vegetables over a longer period of time.

Get right to the roots. Use plastic gallon milk or water jugs to drip-irrigate your vegetables. Simply poke a few small holes in the bottom of the containers and sink them up to their neck in the middle of the bed. Fill the containers with water, which will seep through the ground to the thirsty roots. Not a drop of the water will be lost to evaporation. Overall, you'll use less water than using an overhead hose or sprinkler, and you'll get better results.

Garden Hose Hints

Your garden hose is one of your most valuable players in the garden. If you take good care of it, your hose will last for many seasons. Uncoil the garden hose while the water is still running through it to keep it from getting kinks as you pull it to the bed. Also, turn the water on before pulling the hose to the flower bed or garden area. The water inside keeps it from wrapping over itself and cutting off the water supply.

An inexpensive garden hose hanger is a worthwhile investment. It will make your hose last longer by preventing the hose from crimping and cracking.

Repairing leaks. You can repair a hole in your garden hose with a rubber patch. Rub very fine sandpaper on the hose around the hole. Then apply contact cement to both the hose and a rubber patch. Allow the cement to dry, then firmly press the patch over the hole and wrap the patched area with black electrical tape or silver duct tape.

Drip, drip. Make a low-cost drip-irrigation system for your garden out of an old, leaky garden hose. With an ice pick or a nail, poke more holes in the hose. Plug up the open end of the hose with a cork or hose plug. Then lay the hose between the rows in your garden. Turn the water on low so that it will slowly drip out through the holes into the ground.

Preventing Gardener's Hands

Your hands can take a beating when working in the yard and garden. Here are two ideas to keep them clean and soft:

Rub a thin coat of petroleum jelly on your hands before starting a messy job, such as repotting plants. Be sure to rub the petroleum jelly in good and wipe off any excess on a paper towel so your hands won't be greasy.

Scrape your fingernails over a bar of soap before you begin gardening. This will make cleaning your nails easier after the job is done.

To clean your hands after working outside, try these tips:

➤ Add a little sugar to the soapy lather when you wash up. The mild abrasiveness of the sugar granules will gently rub your hands clean.

➤ Pour a little cooking oil in your hands, add a little sugar, and rub hands well, then wash with soap and warm water. The oil and sugar will help work the dirt out of your skin without drying it out.

➤ Moisten a couple tablespoons of dry oatmeal with milk or water, and vigorously massage into your hands, then rinse. This will leave hands smooth and remove dirt and stains.

➤ Sprinkle some baking soda on your damp hands, and rub them together before washing with soap and water. Baking soda is a mild abrasive.

Hand Cleaner

3 tablespoons cornmeal

1 tablespoon water

1 tablespoon vinegar

Mix together cornmeal, water, and vinegar. Rub the paste into your hands until they are clean, then rinse with water. This cleaner will get your hands clean without drying them out.

Kneeling Pad

When working in the garden, a kneeling pad really comes in handy. You don't have to buy one; you can make your own.

Take an old pillow or a piece of foam rubber or Styrofoam, and wrap in plastic or place in a plastic bag. You can use a trash bag, a department store bag, or the plastic that dry cleaners use to cover clothes. Tape the plastic around the pillow with duct tape.

Natural Insect Control

Here are some natural, nontoxic alternatives to garden chemicals.

Herbal Insect Repellents

Herbs are wonderful for cooking, and many gardeners have had luck in using them as natural pest repellents. They may not always work for everyone, but unlike chemical insecticides, they are not harmful to people or the environment. Plant a variety of them in your garden.

Basil. Planted near tomatoes, basil will repel hornworms and flies. You can also chop and scatter basil leaves to repel aphids, mosquitoes, and mites in the vegetable and flower beds.

Dill, mint, sage, and thyme. All four protect plants such as cabbage, cauliflower, broccoli, and Brussels sprouts from the dreaded cabbage moth.

Catnip. Plant catnip by eggplant to deter flea beetles and near cabbage to deter cabbage pests.

Onions and garlic. These pungent plants help protect your plants from Japanese beetles, carrot flies, and aphids. Plant onions and garlic near beans, beets, carrots, tomatoes, and lettuce.

Horseradish. The potato beetle hates horseradish, so if your area is plagued with these beetles, try planting some of this near your potatoes.

Anise and coriander. Plant this duo to discourage aphids.

Marigolds. Plant marigolds in rows with your vegetable garden. The odor repels many pests, such as tomato hornworms, nematodes, and whiteflies.

Radishes. Planted near cabbage, radishes keep maggots away.

Soap and water. Plain old soapy water is one of the best insecticides around. Take a bucket of warm water and add 1 tablespoon liquid soap. Spray the soapy water liberally on plants that are bothered by insect pests.

Keeping Pesky Animals Away

Four-legged pests can really munch down on your garden. Here are some ideas to send them packing.

Discourage Deer

Deer can eat more than you can grow, and if you don't quickly find a remedy to keep them away from your garden, you won't see a harvest. This can be tricky, but there are some ideas to try.

➤ Scatter or hang little bags of human hair around the perimeter of the garden. If you don't cut your own hair, ask your barber or beautician to save some hair clippings for you. To make little bags to hang, save old panty hose and simply fill them with the hair.

➤ String bars of strongly scented soap about 3 feet from the ground all around the garden. The smell of soap will encourage deer to move on. Replace the soap every two months or when you notice the deer are coming back.

➤ Spray trees and shrubs all around the perimeter of your garden with a mixture of 1 teaspoon liquid soap, 1 egg, and 1 quart water. When deer start to nibble, they'll be turned off by the taste.

➤ String small blinking Christmas tree lights around the perimeter of the garden, and keep them on from dusk to dawn. The blinking lights scare them away. They are not familiar with the lights so they move on.

Rabbit Remedies

Scatter mothballs around your garden to keep rabbits and other pests from eating your lunch. Replace as they dissolve.

Rabbits hate talcum powder, so sprinkle some on and around your plants.

Rabbit Repellent

For really persistent rabbits, try the following rabbit repellent formula. This will keep the rabbits away, and it also works to repel flea beetles. You'll need to apply more powder after each rain.

$1/2$ cup talcum powder

$1/4$ cup cayenne pepper

Mix together, then sprinkle the mixture wherever you don't want rabbits to feed. It won't hurt the rabbits, but it will encourage them to move on to more hospitable pastures!

Saving Seeds

The best way to keep vegetable or flower seeds dry and organized is to store them in little bottles (baby food bottles are perfect) or plastic margarine containers that have a tight-fitting lid. Simply place the extra seeds into the clean, dry bottle or container, and add a few tablespoons of flour or corn meal to each container to keep the seeds dry. Put the containers in a cool, dark place until you are ready to plant again. You can tape a picture from the seed packet on the outside of the container so you will know what seeds are inside the container. If the jar is clear, just place the folded seed package inside so you can see what the jar contains.

The big chill. If you have room, the best place to store seeds is in the refrigerator. The seeds will keep in the refrigerator, and most will still germinate several years after the expiration date.

Growing Plants Indoors

Seed starting. Don't waste money on special "grow lights" for indoor plants or seedlings. Ordinary white fluorescent lights are cheaper, last longer, and work just as well. Also, start seeds in egg cartons instead of wasting money on special seed-starting containers.

Free plants. Save the top of a pineapple for a free house plant. Remove the fruit and a few of the bottom leaves. Place the stem in an inch or two of water for a couple weeks. When you have roots, you can plant it in a pot or even outside (if you live in a warm climate). You can also save the large seed from avocados to make a house plant. Plant the seed in a small pot of dirt, and keep it moist until it sprouts.

Watering

Save water and save plants by knowing when to water them. Stick a pencil down in the dirt in the flower or plant pot (be careful to avoid damaging the roots). If the pencil comes out with dirt clinging to it; don't water. If it comes out dry; the plant needs a drink.

Veggie water. After cooking vegetables in water (boiling or steaming), cool the water to room temperature and use it to water your house plants. Your plants will slurp up the minerals in this free fertilizer! But don't add salt to the water because while the plants love the vegetable water, they hate salt. It can kill them.

Tightwad Tip

Small flowering house plants such as African violets, begonias, and bulbs (hyacinths, narcissus, or tulips) make lovely centerpieces and also cost less and last longer than fresh cut flowers.

Home-Brewed House Plant Polish

You can make your indoor plants look shiny and beautiful with this plant polish formula. Whenever your plants get dusty or you want to clean them up, mix up a batch.

>   4 cups warm water
>
>   1 tablespoon liquid soap
>
>   1 teaspoon wheat germ oil

Mix together the water, soap, and wheat germ oil. To use, first wash the dust off the plant with water. You can wash the plants in a sink, in a bathtub, or outside if the weather is nice. Wet a cloth with the house plant polish and gently wipe the leaves. Do not rinse off. If the plant has very small leaves, you can pour some of the mixture into a spray bottle and lightly spray the leaves. Use this solution on plants with smooth, shiny leaves such as philodendron or indoor ivy.

A Heap Of Savings with Composting

Instead of paying to have kitchen scraps, leaves, and grass trimmings hauled off, make a compost pile and you'll end up with a great soil enhancer that needn't cost you a penny. Compost is a dark, easily crumbled substance that develops from the partial decay of organic material. Making compost greatly reduces the volume of garden refuse, provides mulching materials for garden plants, and contributes nutrients and organic material to garden soils.

Piling It On

One of the easiest and cheapest way to compost is in a compost pile. Start the pile directly on the ground by layering a variety of plant materials and vegetable and fruit scraps (no meat scraps or diseased or insect-infested garden plants) until you've got a pile at least 3 feet high and 3 feet wide. Materials low in nitrogen, such as leaves, should be mixed with nitrogen-rich ones, such as grass clippings and (if you can get it) animal manure (either bagged or fresh). If the weather is dry, water the pile occasionally so that it stays just slightly moist. Turn the pile every two weeks so that the materials get mixed together and the pile is aerated. Air is necessary for good decomposition. In six to 12 months, the compost will be dark brown and crumbly and ready to use.

The ABC's of Container Gardening

If you think you can't reduce your grocery bill because you live in an apartment or condominium, think again. The answer to your problem is container gardening—and it's easier than you think. You can grow an abundant crop of fresh vegetables with flowerpots on a sunny patio. Here's what you need to know to get started.

In most parts of the country, you can grow vegetables anytime from the first of May until the first fall frost. If you live in a warm climate, you may be able to have a year-round harvest.

Pots and Soil

To get started, fill a couple of large pots with commercial potting soil. It's better to go ahead and spend the money on potting soil rather than getting soil from outside. Potting soil has a lighter texture that allows roots to develop more efficiently. Plus, you can be sure you're not importing any insects or soil-borne diseases into your pots. Use any type of large pots you have around the house; even plastic buckets work fine once you cut a few holes in the bottom for drainage. If you don't have any pots, stop by a local nursery and ask to buy some large, black, plastic "disposable" pots. Garden centers buy these pots in bulk and probably will sell you several for less than a dollar each. If you are buying other supplies, they may even give you a few used pots that they have sitting around.

Cheap plastic pots actually are better than expensive clay pots because they tend to keep the soil moist longer, which means you'll need to water less frequently.

Planting

You can plant most any type of vegetable in a container, but the best choices include tomatoes, squash, cucumbers, eggplant, and peppers. Herbs grow easily in containers, too. Smaller varieties, such as cherry tomatoes, Patio Hybrid, or Tiny Tim, are better choices than large slicing tomatoes. Look for small versions of each vegetable you plant.

Place pots in a sunny location. Most vegetables need about six hours of sun every day. Water regularly, but wait until the soil is dry on top before watering.

When you select vegetable plants that will stay relatively small, you can expect a good harvest. Avoid larger plants because their roots will not have enough room in the pots.

The Least You Need to Know

➤ If you plant your yard and landscape to be low-maintenance, you'll use less water and less fertilizer. You'll also save money and effort.

➤ You don't have to spend a fortune to landscape your property. Simple things such as choosing the right flowers and knowing where to shop can make a big difference.

➤ There are many natural pest-control measures you can take to avoid the cost and safety issues of using chemicals.

➤ Compost, easy to make and free, is the best soil additive for your garden.

➤ Gardening in containers lets you garden even when you have no garden.

Chapter 8

The Parking Zone: The Garage and Basement Solutions

> **In This Chapter**
>
> ➤ Getting your garage organized
>
> ➤ Easy and inexpensive ways to add storage space
>
> ➤ How to clean up greasy spots
>
> ➤ Keeping tools and hardware in tip-top shape
>
> ➤ Dry, clean, and bright basements
>
> ➤ Making the most of your basement space

We use our garages for storing all kinds of stuff, as a work area, maybe as a play area for the kids and—sometimes even a place to park the car!

Basements, other useful areas that are often dark, damp, and smelly, can be turned into more useable spaces with a few solutions.

Parking the Car

Parking your car in the garage will keep it looking new longer, and in the winter you won't have to deal with scraping ice off the windshield. What, no room? Read on!

Hit the target. Because space is always at a premium in the garage, it's nice to be able to pull the car inside just enough to get the garage door closed. That way you'll have space to store things along the back wall. To know exactly how far you can pull in, get yourself a thumbtack or small nail, a piece of string or fishing line, and a tennis ball. Position the car where you want to park it each night. Punch a couple of small holes in the tennis ball with the tack or nail, and push the string or fishing line through the holes and tie it fast. Hang the tennis ball from the garage ceiling with the tack or nail so it hits the car windshield at eye level when the car is pulled in far enough.

Front-end protection. If you pull your car all the way in the garage, protect the back wall and your car by hanging an old tire at bumper height on the back wall of your garage. This way you can pull the car in very close, and if you accidentally hit the tire, you won't scratch the car.

Avoid dents. To keep from making small dents and dings in your car doors, put a piece of carpet on the garage wall where your car door hits when you open it. If you have a small garage or squeeze both cars into a double garage, you'll appreciate this safety measure.

Cleaning Up Oil Spots

Your garage floors really get messy. Some of the spills and drips can be tough to remove. Here's some ideas to get rid of the spills and stains.

Oil on concrete floors can make a big mess. The quicker you work on the oil spots, the better your chances of completely removing them spots. Soak up fresh spots by any of these means: Here are a few solutions to try on fresh oil spills.

➤ Spread several thicknesses of newspapers over the spill. Saturate the newspaper with water, and press firmly against the floor. Let the newspapers dry thoroughly and then remove them.

➤ Sprinkle the area with sand, sawdust, or cat litter. All will absorb the oil. Leave the sand or litter on the oil spot for a day or two before you sweep it up.

➤ Pour baking soda on the oil spot to soak it up. Let it dry thoroughly, then sweep it up.

➤ Pour a little paint thinner on the oil area and cover it with baking soda. Let it set overnight, and then sweep up.

Watch Out!

While mineral spirits work great to get rid of oil stains on concrete floors, be aware that they're flammable. Ventilate the area well and don't light a match, have a space heater on, or burn anything while cleaning with mineral spirits.

Removing Oil Stains

When you've soaked up the oil, you can try either of these methods for removing any stains left behind:

➤ To remove oil stains on concrete, pour mineral spirits on the spot and leave it on for 30 minutes, then scrub with a stiff brush as you add more mineral spirits. Immediately after the scrubbing, soak up the diluted oil with newspapers. Allow the concrete to dry. Then wash with a solution of $1/4$ cup laundry detergent, 1 cup bleach, and 1 gallon cold water. Repeat until the stains are removed.

➤ Use a prewash laundry spray to remove oil and grease spots. Spray the prewash on the spot and let it stand for about 10 minutes. Sprinkle on powdered detergent, scrub with a broom or stiff brush, and hose off.

Drip Prevention

If you have a car that has a regular little oil leak, spread cat litter on the garage floor to catch the oil drips. You can sweep it up when it becomes saturated and put down fresh litter.

Garage Floor and Concrete Cleaner

This cleanerworks for oil, grease, and transmission fluid that drips from your car onto a concrete surface. It is a pretty heavy-duty formula that often works even on old stains that can be almost impossible to get up with anything else. Be sure to ventilate the area if you're working indoors.

Here's what you'll need:

Paint thinner

Cat litter

Broom

Pour paint thinner straight from the container to cover an area 6 to 12 inches larger than the spot. Saturate it well. Then spread a thick layer of cat litter over the entire treated area so that you cannot see the concrete surface underneath. Let the cat litter stand for about an hour to absorb the stain and then sweep it up. Older stains may require two applications. Oil is a fairly toxic waste, so place oil-soiled rags, newspapers, litter, sawdust, etc., into double plastic garbage bags and dispose of it properly. (Oil might even be considered a toxic waste in some jurisdictions.)

Sweep It Out

Before sweeping out a dirty or dusty garage, shred some old newspapers and dampen them with warm water. Spread the moist pieces of newspapers on the floor, and they will prevent dust from rising and resettling as you sweep. Alternatively, you can use fresh grass clippings in place of newspaper.

A Place for Everything

Handy twine. To keep twine untangled, hang a large kitchen funnel on the garage wall and put the ball of twine inside, feeding one end of it through the small end of the funnel. You can pull off just as much as you need easily and neatly, and you'll always know right where twine is when you need it.

Small hardware storage. Use baby food jars, coffee cans, or plastic margarine tubs to store screws, nails, bolts, and other small hardware items. To save space, you can even use screws to secure the jar lids under a convenient shelf. Fill the jars with nails and the like, and then screw the jars onto the lids. The jars are up and out of the way, and you can easily see what's inside.

Rope or garden hose organizer. To hang up a long length of rope, wire, or even your garden hose inside the garage so that there's no chance of its slipping off a hook or unraveling, all you need is a big nail and a loop of inner tube from a tire. Nail the inner tube to the wall, pull the free end of the loop through your coiled-up rope or hose, and hang it on the nail. Now you have double the thickness of the inner tube holding up the rope or garden hose.

Glass storage. Always store large pieces of glass (such as windowpanes) on their edges rather than laying them down flat. You'll be much less likely to break them this way.

Extra Storage Space

You'll want to make the most of your garage storage space, because no matter how big your garage is, there's probably not enough room for all the things you want to cram in there. Here are some ideas for getting the most from the space you've got.

Second-hand shelving. Always keep your eyes open for stores that are remodeling; their old shelving can come in mighty handy in your garage—and the price is usually right. When you see that a store that's getting ready to remodel, ask if it will be getting rid of any wire racks or shelving units.

The store manager may be quite happy to give them to you if you will haul them away.

Wall shelves. Even if your garage is small, you'll have room for shelves or cabinets on the back wall because the hood of your car doesn't go that high. You can make inexpensive shelves out of thick plywood, cut to size and properly braced with metal brackets.

Between the studs. Build shelves between the studs of unfinished walls in your garage for bonus storage space. Simply nail old boards between the studs.

Baskets. Staple plastic berry baskets on the wall above a workbench or the area where you keep your tools in the garage. Use these small plastic baskets to hold little packages of nails, seed packets, and other small, light objects.

Garage sale finds. An old chest of drawers or a ratty-looking bookshelf that you no longer want inside the house might be quite acceptable in the garage for extra storage. If you don't have anything on hand that will work, shop garage sales. Chances are you will be able to find something at a very reasonable price.

Old kitchen cabinets. When you remodel your kitchen, don't get rid of the old cabinets; put them to good use in the garage or laundry room.

Up and out of sight. Lay a board or two across the cross ties, and use the space between the ceiling and the roof for long-term storage. If you're going to lay boards in such a manner to create overhead storage, it's best to use fairly long, wide boards (2x6s or larger) and nail them in place to keep them from moving.

Tuck away seldom-used items such as Christmas decorations and beach chairs. You'll get them off the floor to make room for lots more good stuff.

Shoe bags. A hanging pocket-style shoe bag is great for storing everything from gardening gloves to paint brushes. If you get one with clear pockets, you can quickly see what's inside.

Cardboard tubes. Use old cardboard tubes from paper towels or toilet paper to store electrical cords. You can either put the cords inside the tube or wrap them around the outside.

Tool Time

Good household and garden tools are a big investments, but with proper use and care, they can last a lifetime. And who know they could even be passed on to the next generation if they haven't figured out how to program a computer to do the job.

Organization's the key. Just getting all your tools together and organized into one area in the garage is the first step in good tool maintenance, and the biggest part of your battle. If you can't find the tool, you can't take care of it, and you can't get the job done. By the time you spend an hour or so hunting down the tool, you'll probably be out of the mood to do the job (if you can even remember what the job was!).

Separate your tools and hardware into categories, and store them in ways that will help you find them quickly. For example, keep all your screwdrivers of different sizes and types together in one section, and keep your pliers in another. And keep nails separate from screws, and electrical parts separate from plumbing.

If you can start out organized, you'll find it easier to stay organized.

Buy Right

When buying a tool, a good rule of thumb is to buy a mid-priced one. Cheap tools usually don't work well or can break easily, and the most expensive tools tend to be designed for experts. Typical homeowners are usually somewhere in the middle, so that's where you should be.

Watch Out!

Never store your tools under basement pipes that may drip in humid weather. They'll rust before you know it.

Bet You Didn't Know

You can sharpen a dull pair of garden scissors by cutting through several thicknesses of aluminum foil.

Smart Solutions

Don't throw away those little plastic squares designed to keep bread bags closed. They're great for scraping off excess glue from woodworking projects and repairs. The twist ties that also close bread bags are handy, too. Save them to use for keeping keys organized and to keep washers together.

On the flip side, if you plan to use the tool a great deal, buy the best one you can afford and take good care of it.

Power tool tip. Buy your power tools the same way you would a kitchen appliance or car: from a reputable dealer that stands behind what he sells. Always consider where you will get parts and service for the tool when needed.

Dampness alert. Don't store your tools any place that's damp, even for part of the year. Dampness can speed rusting of metal and also can damage wooden handles. (See later in this chapter for ways to remove and prevent rust on tools.)

Tightening wooden handles. When the wooden handle of your hammer or ax head begins to loosen, take it off and soak it in a solution of glycerin and water. Reinsert the handle in the head while still wet, and the wood will swell to give it a tight fit.

Keep a couple magnets in your tool box or on the work bench. These will come in real handy when you want to pick up hardware that you've spread out or spilled.

Tool box solution. To make frequently used tools easy to carry around, and to keep them from rusting, store them in a closed container, such as a metal or plastic tool box. Keep a piece of chalk or a few charcoal briquettes inside the tool box to help absorb moisture. (You can also use moth balls to keep things dry, but then you have that awful smell to deal with!)

An old lunch box makes a perfect tool box for small, frequently used tools, and its compact size makes it easy to carry from one job to the next.

Tool protection. Seldom-used tools should be sprayed with a silicone lubricant and wrapped in aluminum foil. Before using, wipe them off with a rag.

Saw blade protection. Protect a straight saw blade by inserting the teeth end into a slit in a length of old garden hose.

Free or cheap tool loans. Planning to do a special project? If you plan to use a special tool only once or twice, it makes more sense to rent or borrow it than buy it.

If you're buying your supplies from a home center or nursery, see if the center will lend you the equipment you need for free or at a nominal cost. For example, if you're buying seed to plant a lawn, ask if you can borrow a seed spreader; if you're putting in a sprinkler system, see if they've got the tools for the installation.

Funnel substitute. You can make your own funnel by cutting the spout and neck off a plastic bottle. Different size bottles will make different size funnels. If you use the funnel for an especially messy job, just throw it away and make a new one next time instead of taking the time to clean it.

Acid neutralizer. Keep a solution of 1/2 cup baking soda and 1/2 cup water in a container in the garage or workshop to neutralize acid spills from leaky batteries and the like.

Portable caddie. Use a gallon plastic milk or bleach bottle to make a portable caddie for garden tools. Cut away the upper side opposite the handle and use it to store gardening gloves, hand tools, and seeds.

Garage and garden cart. Buy a child's used red wagon at a garage sale and use it to cart heavy items around the garage, yard, or garden.

Rust Relief

To prevent larger tools from rusting, try rubbing them with a light coat of car paste wax, oil, or petroleum jelly. The wax or jelly will prevent rust for a long time.

If you live in a humid climate, it's a good idea to store small tools such as garden trowels in a bucket of sand in the garden shed or garage. Just make sure the sand is dry, and push the working end of the tool into the sand and leave the handle out so you can easily pull it out when you need to use it.

Clean tools after each use with a stiff-bristle brush, and rub them with an oily rag before putting them away. Next time you need to use them, they will be clean and rust-free.

Smart Solutions

Always keep a utility knife on hand. Use it for projects that might ruin an ordinary knife blade, such as cutting vinyl flooring, shingles, insulation, or other rough materials. When it gets dull, either flip it to the other side or put in a new blade.

Smart Solutions

Paint the handles of your garden tools a bright color such as pink or orange. Then when you leave them in the yard, they'll be easy to find. When you lend tools to neighbors, the colored handles will remind them that these belong to you.

Tightwad Tip

Don't throw away an old mop or broom before you salvage the handle. You can use it to replace broken handles on other tools, use it as a walking stick, or make a garden stake out of it.

119

Rusted-on Screws, Nuts, or Bolts

Screws, nuts, or bolts rusted tightly in place can slow down any home project. Here are some ideas to help you get them loose without breaking a sweat.

➤ Spray on a lubricant such as WD-40. Let the oil soak in a while and do its work before you apply pressure again. If you don't have any, you can use a non-stick cooking spray such as Pam instead.

➤ Soak a rag in a cola drink, club soda, ammonia, or apple cider vinegar, then leave the wet rag on the nut or screw for about an hour or until the nut or screw can be loosened. You may find that it loosens a little and then you have to apply more of the liquid to get it going again.

➤ To loosen a screw that is stuck, insert your screwdriver in the screw head and tap the handle of the screwdriver with a hammer as you try to turn the screw with the screwdriver.

➤ You can also press a hot clothes iron, soldering iron, or curling iron against the bolt or screw for a few seconds. Many times the heat will loosen it.

Smart Solutions

Concrete floors can be really tough on your feet, especially if you stand a lot at a workbench. To make it easier on your feet, cover the concrete there with old carpeting or even cardboard. The extra softness will also help prevent items you're working with from breaking, should you drop them.

Removing Rust from Tools

Clean metal parts with a wire brush or steel wool. Or, rub with a soap-filled steel-wool pad dipped in turpentine, then rub with a crumpled piece of aluminum foil. Then apply a protective coating of petroleum jelly, car wax, or oil with a clean rag to keep the rust from coming back.

Put a tool that has rusted beyond repair to good use. Cover it with water and let it sit until the water turns brown, then pour the water around your plants to give them a mineral boost!

The Basement

A basement offers lots of extra space that you can turn into usable space with these hints.

Getting Maximum Light

To give you better daytime visibility in the basement, paint the walls, ceilings, and window wells the whitest paint you can find. White best reflects the light from overhead fixtures and from windows.

Keeping Dirt Down

If you use the basement as a work area, you tend to track sawdust and dirt up the stairs and into the house. To remedy the problem, place a rug at the bottom of the steps, or carpet the basement stairs. You don't have to buy new carpet—used carpet or even carpet scraps will serve the purpose.

High and Dry

Storage in the basement can be tricky, especially if your basement floods from time to time. Don't store anything in the basement that will be ruined by humidity. The family heirlooms and any photographs should be stored in a dry place, not the basement.

For other items you think are safe stored in the basement, you'll still want to get them up off the floor in case water comes in. Here's an easy solution: Take two concrete blocks and place two 2-by-4 boards on top of them. Then place your goodies on top of the boards. When the floor gets wet, the items on the boards will stay relatively dry—at least they won't be sitting in a puddle of water.

Make your own storage shelving for the basement out of leftover pieces of wood. Use the upper shelves for storage, and leave the bottom shelf empty in case your basement floods.

Watch Out!

Store flammable substances, such as turpentine and oil-based paint, in metal containers away from the heating system, the hot water heater, and other sources of heat.

Know What You've Got, Where

It's a good idea to label all the electrical and plumbing systems in your basement. Identify each fuse or circuit breaker, water shutoffs, gas and water meters, heating and cooling system controls, and drain access covers. If possible, write a description on an adhesive label and attach directly to each part. If you can't put on a label, draw a quick map of each system and label the parts on the map. Post the map on the back of the basement door.

Odor Control

To get rid of odor in the basement, use activated charcoal (from the hardware store). If activated charcoal doesn't remove all the odor, then you probably have mildew growing somewhere in the basement. When you find it, sponge on a mixture of half water and half bleach to kill the mildew.

Bet You Didn't Know

Your basement is a natural air conditioner for your home. In the summer, open the door to the basement and use a fan to draw the cool air into the upper floors. (If you have a serious moisture problem, deal with that first, to prevent circulating mold spores into the main living areas.)

Controlling Dampness

Do anything you can to dry out your basement if it is damp and musty. Open the doors and windows wide, and set up an electric fan on the floor for added air circulation. A few precautions now will help eliminate mildew, and you won't end up dealing with the problem over and over.

If left alone, dampness in a basement can peel paint, rot wood, and promote rust and mildew. Here's an easy way to determine if dampness is caused by water leaking in from outside or by excessive humidity.

Cut several 12-inch squares of aluminum foil. Tape them to various spots on the exterior walls and the floor; seal the edges tightly with the tape so that the foil cannot vent. If moisture collects between the foil and the surface of the walls after several days, you'll need to deal with the exterior walls. Here are some ideas:

➤ Clear clogged drains and roof gutters so they can effectively carry water away from the perimeter of your house.

➤ Treat walls with epoxy masonry sealer. Sealing the outside of the exterior basement walls against leaks is far more effective than sealing the inside of these walls, but it's also much more expensive because it requires excavating around the foundation. Try your luck with sealing the insides first, and save this method only as the last resort.

➤ Regrade around the house so that water will flow away from the foundation.

If moisture forms on the foil facing into the basement, you've got an inside humidity problem. Follow these suggestions:

➤ Increase natural ventilation by opening basement windows and doors (but only if the humidity outdoors is lower than inside).

➤ Install a window exhaust fan.

➤ Vent your clothes dryer to the outside.

➤ Wrap cold-water pipes with fiberglass insulation or foam plastic sleeves.

➤ Use a dehumidifier, especially during the summer months.

➤ Check all combustion appliances to make sure they are properly vented. High indoor humidity is sometimes linked to a backdrafting furnace or appliance.

Watch Out!

Before you decide to convert a basement into a home office or other work space, test the walls and floor as described previously with aluminum foil squares for dampness. If you find that moisture collects between the foil and the floor or wall, you have a dampness problem that must be solved before you start the conversion process.

Basement Flooding

If your basement floods frequently, do everything possible to collect and divert the water *outside* the foundation, *before* it gets into the house first. For instance, make sure that rain gutters are in place and operating properly, diverting water away from the house, and that the ground outside the foundation is properly graded away from the house. An existing French drain that's clogged can sometimes be unclogged by a Roto-rooter-type machine.

If you still have flooding, the best solution is to have a plumber install an interior drainage system of pipes connected to a sump pump. The sump pit should be 1 $1/2$ to 2 feet in diameter to collect enough water and prevent the pump from turning on and off too frequently.

The Least You Need To Know

➤ You can squeeze extra storage space out of your garage by being creative. A few well-placed shelves, hooks, and cabinets can keep clutter under control.

➤ Soak up greasy spots with cat litter, newspapers, or sawdust first, then wash away the spots.

➤ Time spent organizing tools means you'll quickly be able to get started on a project instead of spending time hunting them down first.

➤ Tools can last for years if you buy good ones to start with (not necessarily top-of-the-line) and take care of them.

➤ The basement is a natural space to use for storage, but you'll want to take precautions to make sure your valuables are protected from humidity.

Chapter 9

Savings on Wheels

In This Chapter

➤ How to save money when you buy a new or used car

➤ Getting better gas mileage

➤ Saving on auto repairs and insurance

➤ Car cleaning solutions

Cars cost a lot to buy, and when you add the costs of repairs, gasoline, loan interest, and insurance, they're also expensive to operate. But there's no need to pay any more than you have to. Whether you're buying new or used, doing your own repairs or paying a mechanic, there's money to be saved.

Buying New

Do a little R & R (research and reference) before you go car shopping. Go to the library, where you can find very informative price reference books. Ask for this year's *Consumer Reports Auto Buying Guide* and any other car-buying guides they've got. With a bit of research, you'll be able to find out the dealer's cost on the car, plus the additional cost for each option added. You can also get information on the performance and maintenance records of different models.

For a reasonable charge, *Consumer Reports* will mail or fax you a detailed price list for any model car that interests you.

When you know the dealer's cost, you'll be in a good position to negotiate down the asking price, sometimes considerably. If you negotiate hard, you should be able to make a deal anywhere from 3 percent to 10 percent over dealer's cost on most new cars.

Timing is Everything

A well-informed, patient buyer can get a fair price on a car at almost any time, but it is generally easier to negotiate and get the lowest price when business is slow or the dealer is anxious to liquidate inventory.

Best Time of Month

The best time to shop for a new car is at the end of the month, for several reasons. At the end of the month, the dealer is not as anxious about covering the overhead costs he's already spent for the month; he's more interested in cutting such costs for next month. On the first day of the new month, he must pay interest on the money he's borrowed for each vehicle on the lot, so he's eager to sell as many cars as he can by the 30th or 31st. There's another reason buying a car at the end of the month can work in your favor: A salesperson may be on a bonus plan and need only one more sale to make this bonus. If that sale is you, he may be willing to make less commission to meet his quota.

Bet You Didn't Know

With the exception of Saturns and a few Japanese cars, all dealers will sell cars below the sticker price. If you're not comfortable haggling with a car dealer, the best advice is to "hire" yourself a haggler. Ask a friend or relative that enjoys bargaining to go with you and help negotiate the deal. Haggling is a quick way to save several hundred dollars—or even a thousand dollars or more—on a new car.

Best Time of Day

Go to the dealer at night, an hour or two before closing. The salespeople are tired and ready to go home, but they can't leave as long as a customer is on the property. Another plus for shopping at night: If you have a car that you are trading in, it may not be inspected as thoroughly at night, which could mean a higher trade-in allowance.

Best Time of Year

The best time of the year to buy a car is in late September or October, when the new models come out and the dealers are eager to move out last year's cars. December is also a good month to buy a car, as sales are traditionally slow during the holiday season.

The Bigger, Often the Better

The best car prices can usually be found at big-volume dealers because they profit most from manufacturer incentives and may pass some of the savings on to you. If you have two dealerships close by, get a written estimate from the dealer and see if a competing dealership will beat the quoted price.

You can also search for competitive prices on the Internet. When you find what you're looking for, you can even set up financing and delivery from the comfort of your computer. Check out the Website Auto-by-Tel—it can save you money and reduce hassles considerably.

Beware of Add-Ons

After you have made the deal, many salespeople will start to add costs on to the bill. Typical add-ons are rust-proofing and fabric protection. Both of these add-ons are overpriced. Cars are guaranteed by the manufacturers for many years against rust-through. And you can get the same fabric protection with a $4 bottle of Scotchgard.

Some dealerships will also add on a "dealer preparation" charge. This is a last-minute unexpected add-on. Refuse to pay the dealer prep, and pass on the rust-proofing and fabric protection.

High Finance, High Cost

Financing a car will cost you many dollars over the life of the loan. To save the most money, shop for the lowest interest rate, make a large down payment, and finance the car for a short period of time. The payment on a 5.5-year loan may look attractive, but you'll end up paying much more when you add in the interest (see the following table).

> **Smart Solution**
>
> Check with your auto club, credit union, or place of employment to see if they have a car-buying program that gives you low pre-negotiated prices.

Home Equity Loan

If you own your house, you may want to consider a home equity loan instead of a regular car loan. The home equity loan generally will have a lower interest rate, plus you will be able to deduct the interest paid from your income taxes, just like you do on your mortgage.

Get Your Loan Ahead of Time

Have the financing lined up before visiting the dealer, because it generally takes two to four weeks to get a loan approval and the borrowed money. The car dealer will work out the financing for you, but you can bet that it won't be the lowest rate in town (unless they are offering a factory-authorized low interest rate). A lower interest rate can save you a good deal of money over the life of the loan. Call several local financial institutions to find the lowest rate. You might also want to check on the Internet. If you are a member of a credit union, don't forget to check its interest rates. It pays to check around!

A $13,000 Loan with an 8 Percent Interest Rate

Years	Monthly Payment	Total Cost	Interest Paid
3	$407	$14,665	$1,665
4	$317	$15,234	$2,234
5	$264	$15,815	$2,815
5.5	$244	$16,112	$3,112

A $13,000 Loan with a 9 Percent Interest Rate

Years	Monthly Payment	Total Cost	Interest Paid
3	$413	$14,882	$1,882
4	$324	$15,528	$2,528
5	$269	$16,132	$3,132
5.5	$250	$16,530	$3,530

Figuring the Annual Cost of a New Car

After you have picked out the car you want, do you know how much it's going to cost you? Not just the purchase price, but the total cost of owning and operating it? To figure this out, you have to calculate in depreciation, repairs and maintenance charges, the cost of gasoline, the interest on your car loan (if you've got one), and insurance costs. See the following table that compares the costs of owning two different cars.

Depreciation

The difference between the estimated resale value and the purchase price is depreciation. And when you drive a new car off the lot, it immediately starts depreciating.

To get a rough sense of how much a car depreciates each year, figure that after four years (the average length of time the owner keeps a car), driving 15,000 miles or less per year, a new car is worth 38 percent of its original price. (That's not 38 percent *less* than its original price, but 38 percent *of* its original price!) Divide total depreciation by four years to calculate your annual estimated depreciation.

Repairs and Maintenance

Estimated maintenance and repair costs should be fairly low because a new car warranty will cover most major repairs. But you'll still pay for oil changes, brakes, and routine maintenance that is not covered under the warranty.

Gasoline

You can calculate estimated gasoline expenses by dividing your estimated miles per year (15,000 in the example) by estimated miles per gallon. Then multiply by the current price per gallon of gasoline.

Loan Interest

Don't forget the cost of borrowing money to pay for the car, if you're not paying cash (see the previous section).

Watch Out!

Even cars that cost about the same amount of money can vary hundreds of dollars per year in insurance costs. If a car has a high theft or accident rate, you'll pay dearly in increased premiums. Before you buy a new car, talk to your insurance agent about how much the insurance will cost.

Yearly Cost Worksheet for a New Car

	Car A	Car B
Purchase price (including taxes)	$13,000	$18,000
– Estimated resale value (keep car 4 years, 60,000 miles)	$4,940	$6,840
= Depreciation (price minus resale value)	$8,060	$11,160
Annual depreciation (divide by 4 years)	$2,015	$2,790
Estimated insurance costs (Call your agent for a quote)	$975	$1,295
Estimated maintenance, repairs	$450	$650
Estimated gasoline (15,000 miles per year @ $1.20 per gallon)	$720	$857
Estimated annual loan interest (4 year loan @ 9 percent interest)	$632	$875
Total estimated annual cost	$4,792	$6,467

The Trade-In

If you don't think selling your old car yourself is worth the effort, consider this: The average difference between the retail and the wholesale selling price of used cars, according to the *NADA (National Auto Dealers Association) Used Car Guide*, is about $600 to $700.

To see what your difference could be, check the wholesale price in the guide and figure that you can expect the dealer to pay you slightly less than that. Not enough for you? Then wash the car and put it on the market. Place a sign in the car window and run a small classified ad in the weekend edition of your local paper. To figure your asking price, look up the retail price in the NADA guide and ask a bit more for it, especially if the car is in good shape.

Buying Used

A new car drops in value the minute it's driven off the lot, and it keeps dropping as it further depreciates (see the previous section). Knowing that—plus the annual increase in sticker prices—the option of buying a used car can be pretty attractive.

Best Buys

According to consumer car experts, the best buy in a used car is one that is three years old or less, is in good condition (both interior and body), and has been driven no more than 15,000 miles per year. The largest portion of depreciation will already have occurred on the car; any problems or defects will probably have worked themselves out and been repaired; and with reasonable care, the vehicle should still be reliable for at least another 50,000 miles.

To determine if the car is priced high or low, check in one of the used car guides in your the library, such as the NADA guide or *Kelly Blue Book*. These books list the national average sale price, which may or may not apply in your particular area. Compare prices in your local newspaper (classified ads) and perhaps also on the Internet to get a feel for prices where you live.

Know What You're Getting

When buying a used car, you should look it over carefully for signs of damage, excessive wear on the upholstery and carpets, missing or broken accessories, and repainting in certain areas. Ask to see the maintenance and repair records.

Test-drive the car on streets and highways. See how it handles during fast and slow speeds. Listen for unusual noises. Turn on all accessories (don't forget to turn on the heater and air conditioning in off months) to make sure they work.

Finally, if everything checks out and you are interested in the car, have your mechanic examine it. To do this, you'll have to have the permission of the seller. If he refuses an inspection, walk away because you've got to assume he has a good reason for *not* wanting you to find out more about the car!

The Low-Down on Leasing

Leasing a car instead of buying it can considerably reduce your down payment and the amount you pay monthly, but it will cost you more money in the long run. Leasing is more expensive because when you're done paying monthly lease payments on a closed-end lease, you are left with nothing. If you'd bought the car instead of leasing it, you'd own the car when the payments end.

Bet You Didn't Know

If you buy a used car, always check out the warranty situation. Still-valid factory or extended warrantees, or even service contracts, can be transferred to the new owner in some cases.

The value of the car after four years should far exceed the difference between what you paid for it and what you would have paid to lease the car. In the example below, even though the monthly lease payment is $73 less each month, you'll still save $2,569 buying the same car instead of leasing it.

Leasing a car may be your best bet, however, if you are using the car as a business expense and you need to drive a new car. Opt for a short lease (say, two years) and get a new leased car when your lease runs out.

Cost of Leasing vs. Purchasing a Car

	Purchase ($398 monthly payment)	Lease ($325 monthly payment)
Cost of car	$16,000	$0
+ Interest expense	$3,111	$0
+ Total lease payments	$0	$15,600
Monthly payments	$398	$325
− Estimated remaining value (after 4 years)	$6,080	$0
= Estimated net cost	$13,031	$15,600
Savings of purchasing vs. leasing	$2,569	

Better Gas Mileage

Gasoline will more than likely be your biggest operating expense. Only a few high-performance engines require premium gasoline (91 octane or higher) to avoid pinging. All other cars run on 87 octane, which is 10¢ to 30¢ cheaper per gallon. If you find that one brand knocks, before you spend the extra money on higher octane, try a different brand; you may find one that doesn't ping. Many people buy high-octane gasoline because they think it will make their car perform better and run faster. This is just not the case.

Consider these two additional ways to get discounts on gasoline:

➤ Pump your own gas. At some stations, the price difference is as much as 20¢ per gallon.

➤ Pay cash. You can save 4¢ to 5¢ per gallon by paying cash instead of charging it at certain gas stations.

Also, don't "top off" your gas tank after the pump automatically shuts off. Pay the $12.35 instead of trying to squeeze in $13! The gas in your tank will expand when it gets hot and can overflow. Plus, you risk spilling gasoline on the concrete and possibly all over yourself—a mess and a waste of money.

Tire Check

You can extend the life of your tires by rotating them every six months or 5,000 miles. When you buy new tires, ask if the shop will rotate them for free. Many tire centers offer this service, and you really should take them up on it.

To get maximum wear on your tires and the best gas mileage, keep the proper tire pressure. Even a slight variation can cause your tires to wear out prematurely and your gas mileage to decrease. Check your tire pressure once a month. You'll want to keep a tire gauge in your glove box. The gauges on air pumps at gas stations are notorious for being way off.

Smart Solution

To get the best gas mileage, empty any heavy stuff you've got stashed in your trunk and check your tire pressure often. A tune-up can significantly increase your gas mileage, too. Call local repair shops and gas stations for a price quote. Prices on tune-ups can vary more than 200 percent!

Tightwad Tip

Don't speed. The average car uses 17 percent less gasoline at 55 miles per hour than at 65 miles per hour, according to the United States Department of Energy.

Smart Solution

When your tires start to get worn, you can determine if you need new tires by using a penny. Simply insert the penny into the shallowest tread on the tire, with Lincoln's head in. If you can't hide the top of his head in the tread, it's time to buy a new tire.

Bet You Didn't Know

It's always a good idea to comparison-shop your auto insurance each year because rates can change. When your driving record or situation changes, a different company may offer a better rate than you get with your current policy. Companies have been known to raise rates through the roof when a driver gets a speeding ticket; others may be more lenient. When you add a driver (such as an inexperienced teenager), expect rates to vary quite a bit from one company to another.

Join The Club?

Before you sign up or renew your auto club membership, think about the services you will use and how much they cost. Most people join an auto club for the towing benefit. If that includes you, check with your auto insurance about towing coverage. In states that allow this type of coverage, the costs are minimal—usually about $10 to $20 per year. Before you sign up, find out who will tow your car and how long you can expect to wait. You may find the reliability and added convenience of your auto club well worth the added expense.

Ways to Save on Auto Repairs

Savings are out there, just for the looking:

➤ Buy auto supplies such as motor oil and other fluids at a discount auto parts store or a large discount store. You can pay almost double the discount price if you buy these items at the gas station or a convenience store.

➤ When you need to replace a part (such as a mirror, a glove compartment door, or fender) check out your local salvage yard before buying new. This is a good way to save money and recycle.

➤ Shop around for routine maintenance services such as oil changes, tune-ups, brakes, and tires. Often a local service station or repair shop will be priced much lower than the dealership. Look for discount coupons in local newspapers and in the coupon section of the *Yellow Pages*.

➤ Check with your local high school and see if it's got an auto mechanic shop class. This is a good way to get repair work (mechanical and body work) at a very low price. If you can spare the time, you can save dramatically.

Your Silent Partner: The Insurance Company

You can save about 15 percent to 20 percent off your total insurance bill by insuring all your cars with the same insurance company on the same policy. Some companies give discounts for insuring both your car and your house with them.

Any Discounts?

Always ask about insurance discounts. They might be offered for being a good student (most consider those with a B average eligible for the discount), taking a driver-training course, or driving fewer than a stipulated number of miles each year. Other discounts may be available for senior citizens and for women who are the only drivers in a household. Some policies give discounts for cars that have automatic seat belts, air bags, or anti-theft devices.

Buy Only What You Need

Increase the deductible on your auto policy and bank the savings. Increasing your deductible from $200 to $500 could reduce your collision premium by 15 percent to 35 percent. Take the premium savings and put them into a savings account. Then, if you have to make a claim, you won't have a hard time scraping up the money for the deductible.

Tightwad Tip

Letting your driver's license, car registration, or license tag expire can be very expensive. You'll end up paying the original fee plus an additional late fee. Some states have found that this is an easy way to raise revenues. Don't be surprised if the late fine is double or even triple the original amount due.

If you have an older car, consider dropping your collision and comprehensive coverage altogether. If your car is worth less than $2,500, you'll quickly pay more in premiums than you'd be able to collect.

The Clean Machine

Don't wash your car in the sun; direct sunlight can cause streaking. Move to a shade tree or other shady area if you must wash the car on a bright, sunny day.

Always wash the car with something soft so that you don't scratch the paint. A soft cloth (such as a diaper), an old dish cloth, or a chamois are all good choices.

Use cold or warm water (not hot) and a mild dishwashing detergent, or the home-brewed car wash solution below.

Car Wash Solution

$^1/_4$ cup liquid soap

$^1/_4$ cup baking soda

1 cold or warm (not hot) water

Pour the liquid soap and baking soda into a clean plastic gallon-size jug. Add warm water to fill.

When you want to use it, shake the container to mix ingredients. Pour 1 cup of the solution into a bucket and fill with warm water. Spray your car wet with the garden hose to loosen the dirt. Then dip a sponge or soft cloth into the solution and scrub gently in a circular motion. Rinse each section as you go along.

Stubborn Spots

Loosen hardened spots of dirt and grime by placing a wet rag on them for a few minutes instead of trying to scrape them off. It's hard to scrape off dirt without scraping the paint as well.

Tar. Remove tar and other stubborn stains by spraying on prewash laundry spray. Let it soak in for a few minutes, then use a soft cloth dipped in the prewash to gently scrub off the tar or stains.

Bugs. Wash bugs off the car by spraying a mixture of $^1/_2$ cup baking soda and 2 cups warm water on the area. Then take a soft cloth and loosen up the bugs. Apply more of the mixture if needed. Wait a few minutes, then gently scrub away the bugs.

Smart Solution

To get tree sap off your car, just hold a cube of ice on the sap until it gets hard, and then peel it off.

Leather Cleaner

$^1/_2$ cup rubbing alcohol

$^1/_2$ cup white vinegar

1 $^1/_2$ cups water

Mix together and store in a clean glass jar or plastic bottle. Moisten a cloth with the solution and wash leather seats and trim with a circular rubbing motion, then buff dry.

This works great for leather furniture, too.

Vinyl Cleaner

This cleaner will make the vinyl seats and dashboard look beautiful. It gets rid of dust and dirt and leaves a nice clean finish.

$1/4$ cup liquid soap

$1/2$ cup baking soda

2 cups warm water

Mix together and rub on vinyl seats and trim with a cloth moistened in the solution. Then rinse with clean water. If the vinyl is heavily soiled, start with a paste of baking soda and water. Rub it in and let it dry on the dirt for at least 1 hour. Then wash with the cleaner and rinse with clean water.

Smart Solution

Get in the habit of washing your car windows and the windshield every time you get gas. There's usually a squeegee there that you can use.

A Clear View

The car windows seem to get dirty every time you turn around. Here are some tips to help you get them clean.

Wash windows with a cloth dipped in white vinegar, then polish clean with a dry, lint-free cloth.

Add $1/4$ cup clear ammonia or white vinegar to 1 quart of water. Wash the windows with a clean sponge or soft cloth. Dry with paper towels, old newspapers, or a clean, lint-free cloth.

Windshield Washer Fluid

3 cups rubbing alcohol

1 tablespoon liquid soap

10 cups water

1 or 2 drops blue food coloring, if desired

Pour the alcohol and soap into a clean gallon-size plastic jug. Add water and food coloring, put the lid on, and shake to mix. Add as much as needed to your car's windshield washer reservoir. Always shake before pouring.

The alcohol speeds drying and prevents freezing in the winter. You can also use this formula to wash the windows.

Wiper Blades

Here are three good ways to clean the wiper blades:

➤ Wash the blades with a solution of $1/4$ cup ammonia and 1 quart cold water. Apply with a rag or paper towel saturated with the solution, and then dry.

➤ Clean away the dirt and grime with a solution of half white vinegar and half water.

➤ Wash with full-strength rubbing alcohol.

Corroded Battery Cables

To clean corroded battery cables, scrape off as much of the corrosion as you can with a stiff brush.

Then make a thin paste of baking soda and water. Rub it on the cables with a soft toothbrush or scrub sponge, then rinse off with water.

Prevent further corrosion by coating the cables with petroleum jelly after cleaning and drying.

Removing Sticky Stickers

To remove a bumper or window sticker, try one of these:

➤ Scrape the sticker away very gently with a single-edge razor blade, an expired credit card, or a putty knife.

➤ Put white vinegar on the sticker and allow it to soak in, then scrape it off with a plastic scrubber. Add more vinegar and let it soak to remove the sticky mess. Rub again and rinse.

➤ Spray a lubricant such as WD-40, or apply some vegetable oil to the sticker, leave it on for a while, then rub it off with a plastic scrubber.

Smart Solution

To keep your car smelling fresh, keep the ash tray filled with baking soda and place a used fabric softener sheet under the seat. The baking soda will absorb odors in the ash tray and encourage people not to use the tray.

➤ Heat the sticker with a hair dryer, then lift the corner with a single-edge razor blade, an expired credit card, or a putty knife. Apply more heat from the dryer, if needed. Dip a cloth into white vinegar and rub the remaining glue off the bumper or window.

Clean Up

After working on your car, your hands can be very messy. Here are some ways to get them clean:

➤ Wet your hands and rub with dry baking soda before washing as usual.

➤ Pour about 1 tablespoon of vegetable oil on your hands and wipe dry with a paper towel before washing with soap and water.

➤ Add a little sugar to hand soap when you wash your hands, rub in well, then rinse with clean water.

➤ Pour a little laundry presoak on your hands and work it into a lather. Wipe your hands dry with paper towels before washing with soap and water.

➤ Clean your fingernails with a damp nail brush that's been sprinkled with baking soda. Or, for really tough stains, soak your fingers in lemon juice for 15 minutes before using the baking soda. (To make clean-up easy, rub your fingernails over a bar of soap before you start work.)

➤ Rub salt on your hands before washing them to remove any gasoline or other strong odors.

The Least You Need to Know

➤ You can buy a car for about 3 percent to 10 percent over dealer cost if you come armed with information about the dealer's costs and are prepared to negotiate.

➤ To get the most money for your old car, sell it yourself instead of trading it in.

➤ You'll have lower monthly payments if you lease a car, but in the long run it's more cost-effective to buy a car.

➤ Save significantly on your insurance costs by buying all your insurance from the same company, buying no more insurance than you need, and comparison-shopping the costs every year.

➤ Homemade car-cleaning products are easy to make, inexpensive, and environmentally friendly.

Part 4
All in the Family

Between the kids, the pets, and the holidays, parties, and other special get-togethers, caring for your family takes lots of time and effort. If you agree, then you'll appreciate the time- and money-saving ideas for keeping everyone happy in the chapters here. And you'll enjoy the down-to-earth health and beauty solutions for yourself and those you love.

Weekend getaways and vacations can be a treat, and Chapter 15, "On the Go: Travel Tips," will help you plan, pack, and organize them so that they're fun and stress-free for everybody (including you!). Got a home office? Then look to Chapter 16, "The Home Office," for advice on how to keep it organized and running smoothly.

Chapter 10

Tips for Kids

In This Chapter

➤ Getting the most for your money when buying kids' clothes

➤ Easy-to-make breakfast, lunch, and snack-time foods

➤ Ways to make bath time more fun

➤ Creative toys and activities

➤ Teaching children to handle money

➤ Savings on school supplies

Children bring such joy to the household and numerous opportunities for solutions! Use the tips in this chapter to save time and money—and also have some fun!

Clothes on the Cheap

When buying clothes for small children, it's important to remember that until about the age of 8 years, kids could care less where you buy their clothing. But as they get older, they'll become more picky. Take advantage of the younger years to save money shopping at thrift stores, getting hand-me-downs from friends and relatives, and buying from discount stores.

Tightwad Tip

Recycle worn winter pajamas into summer sleepwear by cutting off legs to make shorts. You can also cut off long sleeves into shorter sleeves, or you can cut them off completely for sleeveless sleepwear.

Smart Solution

Store kids' clothes that they've outgrown in labeled boxes to keep them organized. This makes it easy to pass them down to younger siblings.

Tightwad Tip

Look for T-shirts, shorts, jackets, and other unisex items for girls and young women in the boy's and men's departments. These items will almost always be much cheaper there than in the girl's or junior's department.

Buy to Last

Buy clothes for children in durable fabrics that will stand up to a lot of wear, especially if you're counting on hand-me-downs. Avoid thin, flimsy fabrics and shirts with novelty items glued on that will come off in the washing machine. Choose clothes with an elastic waist or without a defined waistline so they'll grow with the child.

You can make clothes handed down from a brother more feminine for a girl by adding some lace around the collar or sleeves.

Try to buy play clothes in darker colors or prints that will not show stains as easily—most kids will end up getting spots on everything they own (especially the white shirts or pants).

A Stitch in Time...

Inspect clothing often for small tears and or seams that are starting to unravel. Take care of small problems quickly, and you'll find that you can extend the life of children's clothing.

Back-to-School Clothes

Just as with school supplies, many stores will have bargain prices on socks and underwear during the back-to-school season. Stock up on socks and underwear for the *entire family* during these terrific sales.

Older children's clothes. Starting at about age 11, children will want to have clothes like their peers. Self-esteem is very important for pre-teens and teenagers; they need to pick out their own clothes. At this age it is a good idea to give them a certain amount of money and let them pick out exactly what they want to wear. Try not to be critical of their choices (so long as they're appropriate). Let your children learn to shop and stay within a budget.

Special-Occasion Clothes

Make sure that each child has at least one outfit to be worn only for special occasions. Have the child change out of the outfit as soon as she gets home so the outfit stays looking nice.

Buy holiday outfits at after-Christmas sales for next year. Buy one size larger than you expect your child to be wearing next year. You'll save at least 50 percent, and you can take advantage of early-bird holiday picture sales (at portrait studios or at local discount stores) because you already have a holiday outfit for them to wear.

Frugal in the Kitchen

This is where you can save big-time when you stay away from prepared and prepackaged foods.

Treats

Instead of buying expensive novelty ice cream treats at the grocery store or from the ice cream truck, make your own. Buy a low-cost gallon of ice cream and some cones. Dip the ice cream into the cones and let them freeze hard. You can even dip them in chocolate or sprinkles for an extra-special treat. By making a bunch of them at one time, you'll have treats on hand without having to stop and dip ice cream for them. When the ice cream truck drives by and the kids start begging for a treat, simply pull one out of the freezer and save.

Fudge bars. Freeze chocolate milk in ice pop containers that you can buy at grocery and discount stores.

Ready-Made, Homemade Breakfasts

Don't spend big bucks on frozen breakfasts for kids. When you make pancakes, waffles, or French toast, make an extra batch and freeze them. Your homemade breakfast entrees will heat up just as fast as the prepackaged microwave breakfasts, and they'll probably have more flavor, too.

Lunch Box Bargains

A lunch box filled with prepackaged snacks and other expensive foods will quickly cost more than the price of a school lunch. But you can save 50 percent or more by packing your children's lunches with inexpensive items.

Here are several low-cost lunch items to choose from:

➤ Sandwiches: turkey, tuna, bologna, egg salad, peanut butter and jelly, leftover meat (such as pot roast and chicken)

➤ Leftovers, such as chili, spaghetti, goulash, and soup. These can be reheated in a microwave or packed in a thermos.

➤ Cookies (homemade or store-brand)

➤ Fresh fruit (in season)

➤ Vegetable sticks (cut yourself, of course)

➤ Crackers

➤ Popcorn

➤ Homemade brownies

➤ Homemade cupcakes (put frosting in the middle instead of on top)

Here's the wrong way to pack a school lunch:

	Cost
Roast beef sandwich	1.00
Pudding cup	0.25
Chips (prepackaged bag)	0.32
Animal crackers (individual box)	0.89
Juice box	0.37
Total cost	2.83

Cost over the average price of an elementary school lunch ($1.25) = 1.58

Here's the right way to pack a school lunch:

	Cost
Peanut butter and jelly sandwich	0.22
Popcorn (bagged at home)	0.10
Homemade brownie	0.08
Carrot sticks	0.05
Juice (made from concentrate and put into a recyclable container)	0.08
Total	0.53

Savings over the average price of elementary school lunch ($1.25) = 0.72

Lunch desserts and snacks. Prepackaged individual bags of crackers, chips, or cookies are very expensive per ounce. Buy potato chips, popcorn, cookies, and other lunch goodies in large bags or boxes, and repackage into just the right amount for your child. Keep the remainder tightly sealed so that it doesn't get stale.

Lunch-time drinks. Instead of buying expensive drink boxes for lunches, put your child's favorite drink into a plastic container with a lid. (Some margarine tubs are perfect for a drinking glass because they are tall and slim.) Buying the store and sip plastic containers made for this purpose is a good idea also. Freeze the drink (noncarbonated) to keep it cold until lunch-time.

Bet You Didn't Know

Plastic bags used for chips and cookies can be used several times. Have your child bring home their lunch box (or bag) with the plastic bags inside so you can decide whether to wash and use them again or toss them.

Fun in the Tub

Little kids love the bath, especially when they can play as they get clean.

Bath Toys

Bath-time sponges for kids in animal and other shapes are at least twice the price of regular sponges. Buy inexpensive foam sponges and cut your own shapes.

Colored water. For more low-cost bath-time fun, add a drop or two of food coloring to the water. You can make the tub a blue ocean, green lake, or pink paradise. Or, you can put a few drops of coloring into a plastic jar and add water. Give the jar to your kids and let them pour the mixture into the bath.

Bath foam. Inexpensive shaving cream is a great bath toy. Foam some into a plastic cup and give kids a little brush to paint the walls around the tub. Kids love it, and a single can will last a long time.

Plastic containers. Plastic measuring cups, spoons, and funnels can make bath-time fun and educational. Kids learn to pour and estimate amounts without making a big mess.

Bubble fun. Save plastic strawberry baskets and use them to entertain kids in the tub. Dip them in soapy water, then wave them through the air. They will make clouds of bubbles.

Let your little ones join in the fun of cleaning.

Tightwad Tip

Check out a book or video from the library on haircutting, and learn to cut kids' hair. The current short hairstyles for boys are especially easy to cut. Buy a few tools, and save quite a bit of money over the course of a year. Even if you do not feel confident doing a complete haircut, you can trim the bangs out of your kid's eyes to extend the time between haircuts.

Smart Solutions

Baking soda is a safe nontoxic cleaner that kids can use to wash the tub. Take advantage of this while they are young, because once they get older they will realize that this is work!

Shampoo. If your kids love the shampoos in novelty bottles, look for the type that you can refill with a less expensive product once the original is used up.

Toys for Tots

A good source for low-cost (or actually no-cost) toys is from friends and relatives. Mention to parents of older children that you're looking for toys, and you might get more freebies than junior has time to play with.

No Expensive Toys Required

Kids can entertain themselves for hours with things you probably have around the house. Try some of these low-cost activities that will encourage creativity.

Recycled Boxes and Papers

Food boxes. Save small boxes of empty food products such as cake mixes, corn bread mixes, and rice. Tape the top shut and let children play grocery store or kitchen with the food boxes.

Big boxes. Large cardboard boxes such as those that once housed a refrigerator or other large appliance can entertain kids for days as a playhouse or fort. Holes can be cut for doors and windows, and kids can decorate the inside and outside with water-based paints.

Junk mail. Collect colorful junk mail for children to play with. They can spend hours cutting out pictures and pasting them on paper. The stickers from magazine solicitations are especially fun to punch out and stick on paper.

Used paper. Used computer paper or other office paper with writing on one side is perfect for drawing and coloring. Bring a big stack home and let your little artists get to work.

Egg cartons and play money. Save a clean, empty egg carton (plastic or cardboard), fill it with play money, and let children play cash register or bank teller. They can even make their own play money out of cardboard. Save the cardboard from pantyhose or shirts; trace the outside of coins on the cardboard. Cut out the coins and draw pictures and put amounts on them.

Coupons. Give children old magazines and newspapers, and ask them to cut out all the coupons inside. Then you can quickly go through the pile and decide which ones you want to keep. Most children love to help their parents be thrifty. Show them when you save with some of the coupons, and you'll have an eager coupon-clipper.

Dress Up

Keep a box of old clothes for children to play dress up. You can use old items from your closet and add a few things from garage sales or thrift stores. A few dresses, old men's shirts, high-heeled shoes, cheap jewelry, ties, pocketbooks, and other miscellaneous items can add up to a box full of entertainment.

Pipe Cleaners

These are fun low-cost entertainment. Kids can shape pipe cleaners into almost anything, such as eyeglasses, crowns, rings, antlers, or candy canes. They're also great for keeping kids occupied during car trips.

Finger Paints

  2 cups cold water

  $1/4$ cup cornstarch

  food coloring

  liquid detergent (optional)

Mix cold water and cornstarch together, then boil the solution until thick. Let it cool slightly before pouring into small containers (baby food jars work great). Add a couple of drops of food color to each container. To make clean-up easy, add a drop of liquid dishwashing detergent to each container. Let the paints cool to room temperature before using.

Tightwad Tip

Buy pre-owned toys from second-hand stores, thrift shops, garage sales, or flea markets. Many times you can find used toys that look just like new with just a little cleaning.

Smart Solution

When you take your children to the library, take all the library cards out of the books and put them in a plastic bag. Hang the plastic bag near your calendar. Make a note on the calendar when the books are due so you can make sure they are returned without a fine.

Tightwad Tip

Shop for low-cost craft supplies such as glue, glitter, stickers, and colored paper on sale. Keep a box of craft items for a rainy day project.

Homemade Play Dough Recipe

Mix in a medium pot:

> 1 cup flour
>
> $1/2$ cup salt
>
> 2 tablespoons cream of tartar

Add:

> 1 cup water
>
> 1 tablespoon cooking oil

Mix ingredients as above and cook over medium heat for about three to five minutes, until the mixture becomes the consistency of dough. Let it cool, and add a few drops of food coloring if desired. Store in an airtight container or plastic bag.

Rainbow Chunk Crayons

Don't throw away broken pieces of crayons; recycle the stubs by melting them and making big chunk crayons. They even make nice stocking-stuffer gifts or party favors for children.

Supplies needed are old crayon pieces; empty clean soup or vegetable cans (pinch one side to form a pouring spout); a saucepan; water; and paper muffin liners and a muffin tin. Note: Adult supervision required for this project.

Peel wrappers from crayons. Sort crayons by colors. (Mix all together, and you'll probably wind up with a lot of brown crayons!). Fill the empty soup or vegetable can about half full of broken crayon pieces. Put about 2 inches of water in the saucepan, and heat the water over medium heat. Stand the can of crayons in the warm water, and continue simmering to allow the crayons to melt. Be careful that the melting crayons don't start to boil.

When they've melted to a liquid wax, pour about $1/2$ inch of wax into each muffin liner. If you melt several colors in separate cans, you can swirl the colors to make a pretty design. Cool the new crayons by placing them into the refrigerator or freezer.

You can add several different colored layers to the new crayons; just let each layer cool before pouring another color on top. Peel away the paper liners when crayons are completely cool and hard.

Bead Necklaces

Make colorful beads from cut macaroni. In a zip-lock plastic bag, combine 2 tablespoons rubbing alcohol, a few drops of food coloring, and a handful of macaroni (select a shape that's easy to string). Drain the macaroni and lay it out on several thicknesses of newspapers to dry thoroughly. Pour the beads into small paper cups and let children make their own beautiful necklaces and bracelets. To make stringing easier, wrap one end of a string with a scotch tape to keep it stiff.

Big, BIG Bubbles

You and your kids can create really wonderful, huge bubbles by mixing up your own bubble recipe. In a half-gallon jug, mix together 1 cup liquid soap (the brand Dawn works particularly well), and fill the rest with water. These bubbles are really for outdoor play—so once outside, pour about 2 inches of the soap mixture in a cake pan, dip in your wand (see below), and have fun!

Experiment with creative bubble wands. Strawberry baskets make amazing bubble clusters. The plastic holders for soft drink six-packs make big bubbles, and for really huge bubbles take a wire coat hanger and bend it into a circle.

Cleaning Stuffed Toys

To clean stuffed toys try one of these methods:

➤ Read the label. If it is washable, tie the toy in a mesh bag or pillowcase and wash in warm water on a gentle cycle. Add a few towels to the load for balance. Dry the toy in the dryer unless it has foam rubber inside; then air dry.

➤ Rub in dry cornstarch, let stand for a few minutes before brushing off.

➤ If the toy is more dusty that dirty, toss it in the dryer for a few minutes. Set the dryer on the lowest setting, usually called "air fluff" or "no heat."

➤ Baking soda works great to get rid of dirt and odor. Rub dry baking soda into the toy and brush off. Or, take a plastic bag large enough for the toy to fit inside, and add $1/2$ cup baking soda. Put the toy inside the bag, close the top, and shake vigorously. Remove the toy from the bag and shake off as much baking soda as possible before brushing the rest off with a soft brush.

Bet You Didn't Know

Clean and deodorize kids' toy chests and toys by wiping them clean with a damp sponge sprinkled with baking soda. Clean dolls and other plastic toys with a paste made by mixing dishwasher detergent and baking soda with a few drops of water. This dynamic combination will remove most dirt and stains. It even removes ballpoint-pen marks. Use an old toothbrush or cotton swab to reach in the small cracks and crevices.

Removing Chewing Gum from Hair

With kids, it's bound to happen. Here's what to do:

➤ Rub lotion or cream into the hair. Work it into the gum and use a paper towel to pull out the gum.

➤ Take a spoonful of peanut butter or vegetable oil and massage the gum and the peanut butter or oil between your fingers until the gum loosens. Remove with a paper towel.

➤ Apply liquid laundry detergent or a prewash spray generously to the gum and work it in with your fingers. Comb the gum out or use a paper towel to remove.

➤ Take an ice cube and hold it on to the gum. The ice will harden the gum and you should be able to peel it off.

Smart Solution

Little children and playful cats or dogs love to watch a roll of toilet tissue spin off the roll. To prevent roll-off, before inserting the new roll of tissue on the holder, squeeze the roll together so it is no longer round. This will also keep everyone in the house from pulling off and using more paper than is needed.

Unwanted Art

When you come home to find that little Junior has tested out his artistic ability on your walls, you can give him some paper to draw on and use these tips to remove his masterpiece.

➤ On painted walls (especially white walls), regular white toothpaste usually works great. Rub a dab of toothpaste on the crayon marks and wash away with warm water.

➤ Baking soda is also effective for cleaning crayons off painted walls. Either make a paste or sprinkle baking soda on a wet cloth dipped in hot water.

➤ For large drawings on painted surfaces, and for any drawings on wallpaper that could tear with washing, try removing the crayon marks with a hair dryer. Set the dryer on low to warm the marks for a few seconds, then wipe the area clean with a damp cloth.

Doctor Mom, Doctor Dad

Cuts and scrapes. Instead of applying a salve or antiseptic directly to a boo-boo, try putting the medicine on the bandage before putting it on the skin. Young children usually find it less traumatic.

Clean a cut or scrape with a brown or red washcloth instead of a white or light-colored one. The blood won't show and then maybe, just maybe, your child won't be as hysterical.

Fever. Lower a feverish baby's temperature by putting him or her into a bath of lukewarm water with $1/2$ cup of baking soda mixed in.

Medicine. Freeze juice or any type of drink your child likes in an ice cube tray. Before giving her a bitter-tasting medicine, give her a flavored ice cube to suck on. The ice cube will desensitize the taste buds a little and the medicine will go down easier.

Splinters. If you can't see the splinter in a finger, touch the spot with iodine. The iodine will make the splinter darken, making it easier to see so you can remove it.

Stuffy nose. You can treat a baby or young child's stuffy nose with a mixture of $1/4$ teaspoon baking soda and $1/2$ teaspoon salt added to 1 cup boiled water. Let the mixture cool down to room temperature before putting it into a clean bottle with an eye dropper (if you don't have one you can recycle, you can buy one at the drugstore). Apply only a drop or two at one time into the nose, and if the problem doesn't get better in a few days, consult your doctor.

Ice Packs

When kids are around, you're gonna have lots of bumps and bruises to tend to. You can make your own ice packs ahead of time and keep them ready in the refrigerator to soothe aches and pains. Here's how:

Small Ice Pack

> 1 cup rubbing alcohol
>
> 2 cups water
>
> 1 quart-sized, self-sealing plastic freezer bag

Large Ice Pack

> 2 cups rubbing alcohol
>
> 4 cups water
>
> 1 gallon-sized, self-sealing plastic freezer bag

Mix together the alcohol and the water, and pour into the bag. Zip the bag shut and place it in the freezer. Leave the ice pack in the freezer until you need it. You can re-use these bags many times. After using, simply place the bag back into the freezer for next time. The alcohol and water mixture will not freeze solid but will stay slushy and can be shaped around difficult places such as knees or elbows.

That's My Baby

The cost of feeding, clothing, and diapering a little one can be astounding. Here are some ways to save.

Homemade baby food. Puree home-cooked foods in a food processor or blender, and freeze individual portions in an ice cube tray. Transfer the baby food cubes into freezer bags.

Baby formula. If you're bottle feeding, remember that powdered formulas are much cheaper than ready-mixed formulas.

Baby shoes. Don't spend money on shoes for infants. Most pediatricians agree that babies really need bare feet to get a good balance on the floor while they are learning to walk. Keep socks on their feet for warmth. Once they have mastered the art of walking, it's time to buy a pair of shoes.

Diaper rash. Fight diaper rash by adding $1/4$ cup baking soda to 3 cups of warm water for cleaning baby's bottom. (But don't use baking soda as a dry powder on the bottom.) The baking soda in the water soothes and helps diaper rash heal by neutralizing the acid from urine.

Tightwad Tip

Call the companies that make baby products and ask if they have any information that they send out to new mothers. Most will have something to send you. The goodies will range from information and a few coupons, to free samples.

Alternatively, add $1/2$ cup baking soda to baby's bath water. You can use less than $1/2$ cup if you're bathing her in just a small amount of water, such as that in a sink or small plastic baby tub.

Diaper Presoak Solution

If you use cloth diapers, you'll want to keep a batch of this solution on hand. This presoak solution is also great for heavily soiled laundry for the entire family.

> 1 cup baking soda
>
> $1/2$ cup ammonia
>
> 1 gallon warm water

Combine the ingredients in a clean gallon-size plastic jug and shake to mix thoroughly. Label the jug and store away where children can't get to it.

To use, pour as much of the solution as you need into a pail or the sink, and soak the dirty items for several hours before washing. You can also put the diapers or clothing straight into the washing machine, pour the presoak solution over the clothes, and let them soak overnight. In the morning, fill the machine with cold water, agitate and rinse, and then wash with a full load of wash as usual.

Homemade Baby Wipes

  1 roll of paper towels cut in half so you have two small rolls

  1 to 1 ¹/₂ cups water

  1 tablespoon baby shampoo

  1 tablespoon oil (baby or canola)

Mix together the water, baby shampoo, and oil, and soak one of the small rolls of paper towels in it. Place the towel roll in an empty plastic baby wipes container or another plastic container with a lid. When the towels are soaked through, remove the cardboard tube and pull wipes as you need them from the center. You may need to add more liquid if the paper towels are not soaked all the way through. Save the other small roll of paper towels for next time.

Money-Smart Kids

It's never too soon to start teaching your child the value of a dollar—it will benefit both of you!

Money earned. Give your children a list of chores to complete before you give them their allowance. If they don't finish the list or don't do the chores properly, deduct from their allowance. This will help them learn the concept of being responsible and earning money.

Recycle for cash. If you live in a state that has the Bottle Bill (mandating glass bottle and aluminum can recycling), put your children in charge of saving aluminum cans and glass bottles for deposits. Let them make the returns and keep the money.

Tightwad Tip

Take your kids to garage sales and teach them how to bargain for what they want to buy. Kids can be taught how to be a smart shopper very early, and it's a skill they'll use for the rest of their life (at least you can hope so!).

Entrepreneurship

Encourage children to start a small business to make money. This will require some work from you because you'll have to be their "silent" business partner. But the rewards should be worth it. They will learn responsibility and work ethics and will earn some extra money.

Kids can mow grass, baby-sit, walk and feed pets, clean houses, iron, trim trees and bushes, clean out gutters, clean attics and garages, wash windows, wash cars—and just about any other projects that adults would rather pay a youngster to do. Have your kids get the word out in the neighborhood that they're hard-working and willing to tackle most any job. They can print up flyers and place them on the doors of neighbors. As a parent, you will need to supervise and make sure that your child is safe and is being paid a reasonable amount for the work performed. As children get older and wiser about working, you won't have to be as involved.

Save It

Once children start making money, encourage them to set up a savings account. Teach them about both short-term and long-term saving. Let them save up for a large toy or game purchase, and insist that some amount go into a college fund or other savings account.

Save on School Supplies

For about a month before school starts, discount, drug, and grocery stores will have back-to-school sales. The stores will typically offer one or two items at cost or even below cost to get you in the door. They hope you will pick up the "door buster" sale item and buy all the rest of the supplies you need (at regular price, of course). Before school starts, stock up on the bargains, then wait to buy any other things you need. (And keep checking the ads because other stores might have them on sale later.)

Smart Solution

Look for good buys on office supplies that you use around the house. Many times index cards, envelopes, and writing paper go on sale during the back-to-school blitz. Stock up!

Do They Really Need It?

At the start of school, or sometimes in the mail before school begins, teachers often give students a list of required supplies. Wait to buy any unusual supplies until your child's teacher personally requests that the students bring them in. If a teacher is planning a special project that requires additional supplies, he or she will let students know when to bring them in. If you buy all the school supplies on the "required" list, you could spend a lot more than you really need to, because chances are good that some of the supplies will not be needed after all.

Book covers. Rather than buy book covers, look around the house for something you can use instead. Paper grocery bags, newspaper comics, leftover wallpaper, or even old posters make fine book covers and cost nothing.

The Least You Need to Know

➤ For everyday wear, choose dark-colored durable kids' clothes; buy one special-occasion outfit a season.

➤ Making your own prepared-ahead foods, especially treats, lunch foods, and breakfasts, can save you big-time over the prepackaged stuff at the supermarket.

➤ Toys and entertainment for kids need not be expensive; sometimes simple things you have around the house are the best.

➤ Teaching children when they're still young to handle money and make smart consumer choices will benefit you both.

➤ Prepare for back-to-school in advance and take advantage of the season's super sales.

Chapter 11

Pampered Pets: Cats and Dogs

In This Chapter

➤ Tips for feeding your pet

➤ Easy make-at-home pet supplies and toys

➤ Tips for grooming and bathing pets and eliminating fleas

➤ Getting cats and dogs to break bad habits

We love our pets just like we do other members of the family. Here are some smart solutions to make both you and your pet happy. You'll enjoy these effective and natural homemade products and clever ways to care for your pets. Many tips and hints can be used for both cats and dogs, so when not specified, assume you can use for either pet.

Big or Small?

Although many times our pets seem to "find" us, when choosing a pet, you'll want to consider the pet's personality, size, and grooming requirements. A long-haired pet looks adorable, but do you have the extra time and patience to deal with grooming the long hair? A smaller pet may make more sense if you plan to keep it inside for companionship. On the flip side, you'll want to get a big dog (with a big bark) if it's personal security and protection you're seeking.

Adopt a Pet

Animal shelters almost always have cats and dogs just waiting for new homes. If you're thinking of getting a new pet, you might want to visit your local shelter first to see what it's got. There's no obligation to leave with an animal. If you are searching for a particular breed, ask the shelter if someone there can call you when one is available for adoption.

Most shelters charge a small adoption fee (usually about $25 to $30), the cost of adopting a pet is minimal—you'll still save money (and you'll make an abandoned animal happy). The same animal may have cost several hundred dollars when purchased from a pet store or a breeder. Many shelters initially offer reduced fees on basic veterinary care, and often shots and neutering or spaying is included in the adoption fee.

Feeding Fido and Fluffy

Our four-legged friends depend on us for every meal. Just like us, they like a little variety. Here are some hints to make meals more interesting.

Dry Food

If saving money is your focus, you'll get more bulk for your buck buying dry food. When you buy wet food, you're paying extra money for water and more packaging.

Juice it up; spice it up. Dry food is easier and less expensive than canned food, but that doesn't mean the dry food has to be boring. Every once in a while, "juice up" the dry food. Add some leftover gravy or even water used to cook vegetables to the dry food. Your dog or cat will enjoy the extra flavor.

When you first open a large bag of dry dog or cat food, put a stick of beef jerky inside the bag. The smell from the beef jerky will make the dry food seem more enticing to your pet.

Buy small. Resist the temptation to stock up on dry pet food. Even with proper storage, the vitamins and minerals in the food deteriorate after a few months, and there is a good chance the food will become moldy. Buy only the amount your pet will eat within a couple of weeks, even when it is on sale.

Pricey Isn't Always Better

Don't assume that a fancy name and a big price mean better food for your pet. Feed your pet generic or store-brand food. You'll find that your pet is just as healthy and satisfied with a low-cost brand, as long as it provides the proper nutrients. The savings can add up to 25 percent to 50 percent or more.

Check pet food prices at a local pet discount store instead of automatically picking up pet food at the grocery store. You may be able to save 15 percent to 25 percent on pet food, and even more on pet supplies.

Don't Overfeed

Save money and preserve your pet's health by not overfeeding her. If you can't feel the ribs easily, ask the vet of you should reduce the amount of food intake, and reduce her food a little bit at each meal if so advised. Ask your veterinarian approximately how much your pet should weigh.

Meaty Dog Biscuits

You can make your own treats for your dog. They will love these tasty dog biscuits.

> 1 pound liver, organs, or other meat (enough to make 2 cups cooked meat)
>
> 2 cups bran
>
> 2 cups old-fashioned oatmeal
>
> 1/4 cup cooking oil

Preheat oven to 250° F.

Cover meat with cold water and bring to a boil. Lower heat and simmer for 30 minutes. Remove the meat from the water (reserving the water) and let cool.

When the meat is cool, chop it into small pieces and grind it fine. You can use a blender, meat grinder, or food processor to speed up the grinding process.

Mix the meat, bran, oatmeal, and oil, adding the cooking water from the meat as necessary to make a thick dough. Be careful not to add any more liquid than needed to make a dough that is coarse and just wet enough to work with. You can always add a little more water, but it's hard to take some away when you find you've added too much.

Watch Out!

To prevent a stomach ache or bloating, avoid feeding a dog immediately before or after strenuous exercising. Wait at least 30 minutes. Also, 2 smaller feedings per day instead of one large feeding will help.

Bet You Didn't Know

Once a week, add a scrambled egg to your cat or dog's menu. Most love eggs, and it makes their coat shiny. While most pets love this added treat once in a while, some dogs will get spoiled by it and refuse to eat their regular food unless you add something extra to it.

Smart Solution

To keep your pet's bowl from sliding around on the floor, put the dish on a piece of foam rubber. Or, you can glue rubber canning rings or some rubber pads on the bottom.

159

Shape the dough into flattened balls or little bone shapes, and arrange on a greased baking sheet. Bake for three hours. Then turn the oven off, but leave the biscuits inside the oven while it cools down. This will make the treats nice and crunchy.

Let the biscuits air-dry for 24 hours. Store them in a plastic bag or a covered container.

Save on Accessories and Toys

Some of the most used pet accessories and toys are homemade gizmos instead of store-bought items. Here are some ideas to get you started.

Collars

No need to buy dog or cat collars. Instead, go to garage sales, thrift stores, and flea markets; they always have low-priced belts. Buy a skinny leather belt, cut it to the correct size, and punch holes in it with an ice pick. It works just like a dog or car collar for a fraction of the cost. Or look for pet collars at garage or yard sales.

Playful Pups

Most dogs have lots of energy and spend many hours running and playing. Here are some ideas to make their playtime more fun.

➤ Make it a habit when you go outside to take your dog with you. He will love the attention and the exercise. If you are working out in the yard, let your dog stay with you and play. If you don't have a fenced yard put him on a leash or chain near you while you are working outside.

➤ Puppies and even older dogs enjoy having a stuffed animal to drag around the house and sleep with. When your child gets ready to throw away an old stuffed animal, give it to your dog and see if they "bond." Remove any plastic eyes or other parts that your dog could chew and swallow before letting him play with it.

➤ Save plastic margarine tub lids and let your small dog fetch them instead of using a Frisbee. The lids are much lighter and easier for a little dog to handle.

➤ When tennis balls lose their bounce and are no longer usable on the court, give them to your dog to play with.

➤ A plastic soda bottle on a rope can provide hours of fun for a playful dog. You can use a 1-liter bottle for a smaller dog or a 2-liter bottle for a larger one. Put a little sand inside if you want to make it heavier.

Toys for Cats

Cats are just as happy playing with something you've made as they are with a store-bought toy. Here are some ideas for quick and easy things to amuse them:

➤ Make an inexpensive cat scratching post by stapling a carpet remnant or cork board (available at home improvement centers) onto a log. You can then nail the log to a wooden base. Your cat will enjoy playing with this for hours—and hopefully it'll discourage her from clawing the furniture.

➤ Use old socks to make an inexpensive cat toy. To make the toy, tie off the toe end and pour a little catnip into the sock. Tie the other end closed.

➤ Place a coin, button, paper clip, or anything else that will rattle in an empty film canister or prescription bottle to make a fun toy for your cat.

➤ Hang a small plastic toy on a string from a door knob, and your cat will have many hours of enjoyment.

Bet You Didn't Know

If you have a cat that goes crazy for catnip, you can grow your own. One packet of seeds should give you enough catnip for the year. And it's very easy to grow. You can expect to get three or more cuttings from each plant. Give a bit of the fresh stuff to your cat, and dry the rest for other times.

➤ Cats love to bat around small objects. Give your cat an empty thread spool or a crumpled-up piece of aluminum foil to play with.

Grooming Your Pet

A cat will usually keep himself clean, so give him a bath only if he has grease or grime on his coat that he can't clean by himself. A dog, however, is another matter.

Doggie Baths

Always brush your dog before giving him a bath. You'll remove quite a bit of dirt with the brushing. Next, place a cotton ball in each ear. The cotton balls will keep his ears dry, which will make him happy (well, as happy as a dog getting a bath can be!). Put a towel on the bottom of the tub so he'll feel more secure and won't slip around. First make a ring of lather around the neck of your pet to keep any fleas from running up on his head while you are washing the body. To keep Fido more calm, work from the tail and do the head last. Most dogs hate to get their face wet, so do it last.

Down the drain. If you give the dog a bath in the sink or tub, be sure to place something over the drain to collect the hair. A nylon kitchen scrubber or a small strainer will do the job. The hair will collect on the scrubber or in the strainer, which will prevent it from blocking the drain.

Pet shampoo. You can use any inexpensive shampoo or liquid soap to bathe your dog (and cat, for that matter, if you wash her). Shop for inexpensive "people" shampoo to use on your pets. If you buy an inexpensive shampoo and conditioner in one, it will

161

Smart Solution

To clean and deodorize your pet's bed between laundering, sprinkle baking soda on the dry bedding and let it sit for 30 minutes. Then shake out the cushions or vacuum up the soda.

Smart Solution

Skunk odor will eventually wear off, but it takes a while. You can get rid of the smell if you act fast. As quickly as possible, apply either tomato juice, half water and half white vinegar, or stale wine (red or white) to the pet. All three solutions contain 5 percent acid. Then follow with a warm soapy bath and rinse with clean water. Usually one application will get rid of the odor, but repeat if necessary.

help to eliminate tangles in long-haired animals and make the coat soft; this is especially helpful with long haired pets. If your pet has fleas, use dandruff shampoo to bathe her. Look for an inexpensive brand or even a store brand of dandruff shampoo.

For freshness. Add 2 tablespoons table salt to the wash water when bathing your pet. The salt will help kill fleas and add freshness. You can also add a few tablespoons of baking soda into the rinse water. This will keep your cat or dog smelling fresh and help make his coat glossy.

Matted hair. To remove mat in your dog's hair, first shampoo, then use a conditioner. Work the conditioner into the matted area while it is wet. Try to work a comb with wide teeth through the area. When the hair is dry, rub talcum powder into the mats and gently use a comb to work through them.

Dry shampoo. Between regular baths, a dry shampoo can go a long way with a dog (or a cat). Cornstarch or baking soda works best because both will absorb oils. Baking soda is also an excellent deodorant. Sprinkle the cornstarch or baking soda on the pet, and rub it in with your hands. Then use a brush to work it in further, and brush out the excess.

Keep in mind that pets should not be bathed more than once a month. Bathing them more often will cause dry skin.

Fleas

Both cats and dogs (and as a result, people!) can suffer from fleas. Here are some things you can do to get rid of these pests.

A flea comb. Buy a flea comb, and comb your cat or dog three times a day for about two weeks, or until no fleas appear. Then comb the animal once a day to keep the fleas away. Most animals love to be combed.

Brewer's yeast. For cats, add $1/2$ teaspoon granular brewer's yeast or a crushed brewer's yeast tablet to the food once a day for two weeks. If after two weeks you don't notice any improvement, increase the amount until you do. From then on, add $1/2$ teaspoon to the food every day. The yeast will also give your pet a nice shiny coat of hair. Brewer's yeast will not work for all pets, but it is certainly worth a try.

If your cat is reluctant to eat the food with the yeast in it, rub the granular yeast on the cat's coat, and he will lick it off. When he has licked it off a few times, he probably won't mind the taste of it in his food.

For dogs, start out with 1 teaspoon of brewer's yeast. Continue to give him $1/2$ teaspoon every other day once he stops scratching.

Pine and cedar chips. Stuff a pillow with cedar chips or cedar sawdust, and use as a bed for your dog or cat. If you have an outside dog, put pine needles or cedar shavings inside his doghouse.

Salt. Salt also works to repel fleas. Wash the dog house out with salt water periodically.

Garlic. To get rid of fleas, crush a clove of garlic into your pet's food. This will keep fleas away and make her coat shiny. Half a clove should be enough for cats, and $1/2$ to 2 cloves is recommended for dogs, depending on their size. If your pet won't eat the food with garlic in it, bury the garlic in a piece of meat or other treat and hand-feed it to your pet.

The great thing about using garlic is that it works on several different problems in addition to fleas, such as constipation, coughing spells, indigestion, and worms.

Vinegar. Add a few drops of vinegar to your pet's water bowl every day. The vinegar not only helps eliminate fleas, but it also helps to get rid of ticks.

Lemons. Boil two unpeeled lemons cut into small pieces for one hour in 1 quart water. Let sit overnight, then strain. Sponge or spray the pet with the liquid.

Light-Bright Flea Trap

When you pet has fleas, so can your carpet and your upholstered furniture. Unfortunately, the fleas can jump off into your carpet and then can jump onto you or back onto your pet, even after Fido has been de-fleaed. But you can get rid of the fleas jumping about without using a chemical product. All you need is a light and soapy water.

Place a small pan of soapy water on the floor where you have seen fleas. Sit a lamp with a 25-watt bulb about a foot over the pan. You'll want to remove the shade so you get the most light. Turn off all the other lights near the flea trap. The fleas will jump toward the heat of the light and will fall into the water and die. In the morning, wash out the pan. You'll want to repeat the process every night for several weeks, or until you don't catch any fleas for a couple nights in a row.

Hairy Scary

If you seem to have an abundance of hair from your pet, your first line of defense is to brush him once or twice daily. If regular brushing does not solve the problem, massage the coat with a little olive oil once a week.

Dealing with hair balls and pet hair on your furniture can make you crazy. Here are some hints to get rid of it.

Cat Hairball Solutions

Regular grooming will help keep your cat free of hairballs. Brush your cat for a few minutes every day. Use a hairbrush with round tipped plastic or rubber bristles on your cat instead of buying a special brush designed for animals. The people hairbrush will work better and cost less. If your cat has long hair, comb out any matted areas after you brush him.

Oil it. When you find a hairball that you can't comb through, take some baby oil or vegetable oil and rub it into the hairball with your fingers. The oil will loosen up the ball so that you can comb it. Only as a last resort should you try to cut out a hairball. If you must cut one out, be very careful not to clip your pet's skin in the process.

Adding a little oil to your kitty's diet will help eliminate hairballs. You can add 1 teaspoon vegetable oil to the cat's food daily. Any time you have tuna or a can of sardines, be sure to let your furry pet enjoy this treat. Not only does it taste great to him, but it will also help keep the hairballs from forming.

Carpet and Furniture Pet Hair

To remove pet hairs on upholstery and carpets, try one of these solutions:

➤ Put on a rubber glove and rub it over the carpet or upholstery. You'll be amazed at how much hair you'll pick up.

➤ Scrape the hairs off with a lightly dampened sponge, a small terry cloth towel, a chamois, or even a squeegee.

➤ Wrap a length of tape (masking tape, duct tape, or adhesive tape) over your hand, sticky side out, and brush over the area. The animal hair will stick to the tape. When the tape is completely covered with hair, get a new piece.

➤ Rub the surface with a fabric softener sheet that has been used once. A used sheet works the best because while it still has some fabric softener in it, it's not overpowering.

The Portable Pet

Moving a cat or dog, or taking him to the vet, can be a challenge. Instead of buying a pet carrier, you can make one out of two large laundry baskets. Fasten them together with rope in the back, and use some more rope to tie the front shut after you have Fluffy safely inside.

If your kitty is small enough, you can use an old wicker picnic basket. Just be sure to secure the lid before heading out.

Home Sweet Home for Fido

Make an inexpensive entrance flap for a dog-house out of a piece of carpeting. Cut the carpet to size, make one or two slits in the middle, and nail it into place. In the winter, this flap will keep Fido much warmer.

Dog anchor. Make a portable dog anchor by tying his leash around an old tire. To keep it in place, put a few rocks or bricks inside the tire.

Bedding. To clean and deodorize pet bedding between launderings, first make sure it is dry, then sprinkle liberally with baking soda and let it sit for 30 minutes. Shake out or vacuum up the baking soda. If the bedding has a strong odor, leave the baking soda on longer before shaking it out.

Smart Solution

An old foam ice chest makes a good house for a small dog or a cat. Glue the lid on, turn it upside down, and cut a door with a serrated knife. Rags or old towels make it comfy, and the animal is out of the bad weather. Place a heavy board or rock on top to keep the house from blowing away.

Kitty's Litter Box

Instead of buying the more expensive kind of cat litter that comes with a built-in deodorizer, get an inexpensive brand and add baking soda or borax to the bottom of the litter tray to absorb more odors. You can mix $1/2$ cup borax or 1 cup baking soda to every 5 pounds of litter.

Cat Litter Box Deodorizer

> 1 cup baking soda
>
> 2 teaspoons dried mint

Mix the baking soda and dried mint together. Stir the mixture into your litter box when you clean it out. This combination of baking soda and mint will keep the litter box smelling fresh.

Spoon scoop. Instead of buying a special scoop to clean out a litter box, use a large slotted metal spoon (reserved just for this purpose) as a scoop.

Keep it neat. Keep the litter box on top of a carpet scrap or piece of Astroturf so the litter doesn't get all over the place. If your cat is especially messy, use a large piece to cover the area where the litter usually ends up.

Keep it clean. There is nothing a cat hates more than a dirty litter box. Many cats will refuse to use one. To save yourself a big mess, replace litter at least once every two weeks, or more often if your cat demands it. If you use cat litter that clumps, remove the clumps daily and add more litter as needed—there's no need to replace the litter.

165

Place a layer of newspapers on the bottom of the litter box before you add new litter. The newspapers will keep the litter box cleaner and make it easier to change the litter.

Watch Out!

Don't use old newspapers instead of cat litter, and don't let your cat sleep regularly on newspapers. The newspaper ink may contain toxic substances, and these can get on your cat's paws and hair. Then, when he cleans himself, he'll end up ingesting the toxic substances.

Bet You Didn't Know

You should talk to your dog or cat in a high voice. They associate lower voices with scolding.

When you replace the litter, wash the box with hot soapy water. Then wash it again with 1 quart of water and $1/2$ cup white vinegar. Let the vinegar and water solution soak for 10 minutes before rinsing thoroughly.

Rx for Pets

Minor problems are often easy to deal with, but always use common sense when it comes to the health of your pet. If you have any doubt or if the condition worsens, call your veterinarian.

Vitamin E for cuts. Clean a scratch or small cut on a cat or dog with lukewarm water, then apply vitamin E oil or use a vitamin E capsule. Repeat twice a day. No need to worry if the animal licks off the vitamin E— just apply some more to help heal the wound.

Skin injuries. Minor skin injuries such as scratches or insect bites can be treated with olive oil. First, wash the area gently, then dab the olive oil on the skin. This relieves pain and promotes the healing process.

Dry skin. If your dog or cat has dry skin, you probably can clear it up by adding 1 tablespoon olive oil to his food every day. In about one week, you should be able to see a difference. Continue to add the oil to his food to keep the dry skin from returning.

Gas relief for dogs. To relieve gas, rub your dog's stomach with apple cider vinegar. This should relieve gas within 30 minutes.

Itching. Dab apple cider vinegar over your cat or dog's coat to relieve itching. If vinegar doesn't do the trick, oatmeal can also be used to alleviate itching. Oatmeal is messier than vinegar but can provide effective relief. Mix 2 tablespoons oatmeal with 2 gallons of warm water. Rub the solution over the pet's entire body. This will provide itch relief for two to four days. This solution will work best if you blend the oatmeal until it is very fine. Regular or quick-cooking oatmeal will work just as well.

Ear mites. When your pet gets ear mites, you need to see the vet. To make him more comfortable while waiting to see the vet, put a few drops of vegetable oil into the cat or dog's ear and gently rub in. Then clean out the dirt with a cotton ball.

Dry, cracked paws. If the pads of your dog or cat's feet become dry or cracked, dab a little petroleum jelly or lotion on them. Rub off the excess so it won't get tracked into your carpet or on your furniture. It's also possible to prevent cracking by dabbing petroleum jelly onto paws in the winter before your pets go outside; the cracking can be caused by salt on driveways and walkways.

Nail cut too short. If you accidentally trim your pet's nail too short, all you need to do is press the bleeding nail into a bar of soap. It will stop the bleeding almost immediately. Or, use alum powder mixed with water to form a paste. Apply the paste to the nail, or put a little of the paste on a tissue and hold the tissue around the nail for a few minutes. Always be careful when cutting your pet's nails. When cut too short they bleed and cause quite a bit of pain.

You can buy alum at your local drugstore or pick it up in the spice section of the grocery store.

Worms. When your pet has worms, see the vet. To keep the worms away, give a small animal such as a cat, puppy, or small dog one clove of garlic daily. Give a larger animal two to three cloves daily. Mince or crush the garlic, and mix it well into your pet's food.

Nasty Little Habits

For the most part, animals are a joy to our lives, but their naughty little habits such as chewing on the furniture or spraying inside the house can make them less of a joy. Here's how to deal with them.

Smelly Carpets

The problem with pet odors in the carpet is that even though you may have removed the "accident" from the carpet, it probably soaked into the carpet padding as well.

To get rid of the smell, make up a solution of half warm water and half vinegar. Pour enough of the solution into the carpet to let it soak into the padding also. Then leave it there for 20 to 30 minutes before cleaning it up. Wash the area with cool tap water to remove the vinegar. You may have to rinse the area several times with lots of water. Be sure to let the area dry thoroughly. A hair dryer or fan directed at the spot will help dry it out. When the carpet is completely dry, sprinkle some baking soda on it before vacuuming.

Dogs Chewing on Furniture

Here are three things you can do to break your dog's habit:

➤ Put a little dab of oil of cloves on the wood that's chewed. The smell and bitter taste will stop him from chewing.

➤ Make a solution of $1/4$ cup clove oil, 1 tablespoon paprika, and 1 teaspoon black pepper. Sponge the solution on the furniture and any other areas being chewed. Apply more as needed.

➤ Make a paste of alum powder and water, and apply to the area being chewed.

167

Cat Spraying

Cats hate water, so one way to get your kitty to stop spraying indoors is to get him to associate water with spraying. Keep a squirt gun or spray bottle full of plain water handy, and give him a little dowsing every time you catch him spraying. (You might want to buy a few water guns or bottles so that you can keep them in several places throughout your house for quick action!)

You can also wash the sprayed area with white vinegar to remove the odor and discourage him from spraying the area again.

Cats Jumping on Furniture

To discourage a cat from jumping on furniture or other places, try one of these solutions:

➤ Cover the area temporarily with aluminum foil or plastic bags until the pet gets out of the habit. The noise will drive him crazy.

➤ Tie a few small, inflated balloons to the furniture he jumps on. When he jumps on the furniture the balloons will at least move, and one or more of them might burst, which will scare him. Cats hate loud noises.

➤ Touch the cat's lips very lightly with a cotton ball moistened with rubbing alcohol or vinegar each time it goes where it shouldn't, then leave the cotton ball at the area. Soon he will associate the bad smell with that area, and he will stay away.

➤ To discourage a cat from jumping on the kitchen counter, leave several aluminum baking pans near the edge so they'll clatter when the cat lands.

➤ Stick some two-sided tape on the kitchen counter. Your cat won't like the feel of his feet sticking to the tape.

➤ Take a spray bottle or squirt gun full of water, and spray the cat whenever he goes somewhere he shouldn't. Most cats hate water and will learn quickly what places are off-limits. (This is my favorite solution.)

Dogs on Furniture

To keep dogs off furniture, try any of the above solutions for cats, or fill a metal can that has a lid (a coffee can works great) with some coins, nails, or anything else that will rattle. Place the can on the sofa—when the dog jumps up, the can will make an awful noise. He will associate the noise with the sofa and think twice before jumping up on it next time.

The Least You Need to Know

➤ Dry food is just as healthy for your cat or dog as canned and costs much less. Price is not an indication of quality, so don't get your pet used to the most expensive brand if you want to save money.

➤ You can make toys for your pets out of simple things you have around the house.

➤ Grooming your pet at home saves you money you would otherwise pay a professional groomer. Most animals are easy to bathe and brush, and they feel more comfortable with you doing it rather than a stranger.

➤ You probably have all the things you need to solve your flea problem in your kitchen pantry: salt, vinegar, lemon, and garlic. Brewer's yeast, which you can get at a health food store, is also effective.

Chapter 12

Beautiful All Over

In This Chapter

➤ Low-cost, all-natural alternative products

➤ Simple ways to use soaps, scrubs, and skin care treatments

➤ Giving your hair the care it deserves

➤ Homemade solutions for clean teeth and fresh breath

➤ Getting the most from your fragrance

We all want to look and feel good; this chapter introduces you to some wonderful toiletries and beauty aids you can make at home that will make you feel truly pampered.

Low-Cost—and Just as Good

You can spend a small fortune on beauty products that may not work any better than much less expensive alternatives. A good example is makeup remover—why pay the numbers for a fancy brand of remover when baby oil or even plain mineral oil works just as well? Baby oil and mineral oil won't irritate the eyes, and they also act as a natural moisturizer.

Substitute and Save Money

Next time you're looking for a low-cost beauty product, try out some of these low-cost substitutes. They'll save you money and do the job just as well as their related products.

Commercial Product	Low-Cost Substitute
Makeup remover	Baby oil, mineral oil
Perfume	Cologne
Bath oil	Baby oil, vegetable oil
Deodorant	Baking soda
Cold cream	Vegetable shortening
Dusting powder	Baby powder, cornstarch
Toothpaste	Baking soda
Denture cleanser	Vinegar

Read the Label

A high price doesn't necessarily mean a better product; sometimes it simply means a fancier package or a bigger name because of more extensive advertising campaigns. When buying beauty aids and toiletries, read the label and ingredients. You'll be surprised at how similar some products really are—and you may be just as pleased with a low-cost or generic brand.

National Brand vs Generic Brand Savings *

This table compares the cost of generic and brand-name toiletries and beauty aids. Notice that the percent saved by buying generic products turns out to be an impressive amount.

	Generic Brand	National Brand	Savings	Percent Savings
Baby oil	$0.99	$2.79	$1.80	182%
Mouthwash	$1.48	$3.29	$1.81	122%
Petroleum jelly	$1.29	$3.89	$2.60	202%
Deodorant	$0.99	$1.89	$0.90	91%

* Discount store brand name prices compared to same size generic name prices.

Where to Shop

Where you shop for health and beauty aids also can make a big cost difference. Picking these items up at the grocery store may be convenient, but you may pay extra for that convenience. Instead, find a discount drug store in your area that offers deep discounts on health and beauty aids—it may be worth an extra trip once or twice a month to stock up.

Discount Store Prices vs Grocery Store Prices*

As this chart shows, prices often vary widely between discount drug stores and grocery stores. Be sure to shop around for health and beauty items to get the best price.

	Discount Store	Grocery Store	Savings	Percent Savings
Shampoo	$0.89	$1.99	$1.10	124%
Toothpaste	$1.75	$2.79	$1.04	59%
Shaving cream	$0.79	$1.39	$0.60	76%
Mouthwash	$3.29	$4.99	$1.70	52%

*Same brand names and sizes were compared.

Lipstick for Less

You can pay $20 or more for a tube of lipstick at department store counters. Have you ever wondered what makes these tubes cost so much more than other brands available at the drugstore? According to *Consumer Reports* magazine, all lipsticks are pretty much the same. They've all got basic ingredients (wax, oil, dye, and perfume), whether you spend $2 or $20.

The high priced lipsticks generally offer you a better case, more fragrance, and a "classier" image—but the performance is about the same as the lower-priced brands.

Avoiding Makeup Mistakes

When buying makeup, be sure to use a tester or try out a sample first, if at all possible. Remember, what looks great on the color chart might not look so good on you—and what looks fine on you in the store might look horrible when you're in natural sunlight. If you're not careful, you could end up with a whole drawer of makeup mistakes.

Always save your receipt when you try a new type or color of makeup. If you're not satisfied with the makeup, don't just toss it in a drawer; return it to the store where you purchased it. Most stores will either give you a cash refund or a store credit. If the store won't refund your money, call or write to the manufacturer. Explain the problem and ask for a refund. Most companies will bend over backward to accommodate you, to keep you as a customer.

How Long Will Cosmetics Last?

Ever wonder about the shelf life of your cosmetics? This chart should give you some guidelines.

Shelf Life of Cosmetics

Product	Opened	Unopened
Mascara	2 to 3 months	2 to 3 years
Eyeliner	3 months	2 to 3 years
Eye shadow	3 months	2 to 3 years
Eye pencil	1 year	3 to 4 years
Liquid foundation	6 months	2 to 3 years
Face powder	1 year	3 to 4 years
Powder blush	1 year	3 to 4 years
Cream or gel blush	6 months	2 to 3 years
Lipstick	6 months	2 to 3 years
Lip gloss	6 months	2 to 3 years
Perfume	1 year	3 to 4 years
Cologne	1 to 2 years	2 to 3 years

Cosmetics should be replaced after the time has elapsed. Over time and use they can collect dirt and germs. Perfume and cologne can be used but will start to lose some of their fragrance.

Bath Time

Some of the best bath-time luxuries are easy and fun to make at home. Try these recipes for bath oils or bubble bath.

Bath Oils

To make your own wonderful bath oil, pick up a large bottle of baby oil and add a few drops of your favorite perfume; then shake to mix. You can even add a few drops of food coloring to make it look pretty. Pour the mixture into a fancy bottle, and tie a ribbon around the neck. Then add about a tablespoon to your bath water for a luxurious bath.

Bubble Bath Oil

Try this recipe for homemade bubble bath:

2 cups vegetable oil

3 tablespoons liquid shampoo

2 to 3 drops perfume

Mix all ingredients together with a whisk, or put it in the blender for a few seconds; then pour the solution into a plastic bottle. Add one or two tablespoons to your bath water to make your skin soft. Shake well before using.

Sensitive skin bath treatment. Add 1 cup baking soda and $1/2$ cup baby oil to the bath water. You can pamper yourself with this formula even if you have been prone to skin rashes from bubble baths or oil—it's very gentle, and it will leave even the driest skin feeling silky smooth.

Soothing bath. For a refreshing bath that's very soothing to sore or tired muscles, add $1/2$ cup baking soda to your bath water. For just a few pennies, you've got yourself a relaxing bath additive.

Quick sponge bath. When you're rushed for time and want to feel fresh without taking a bath or shower, rinse a sponge or wash cloth in a sink filled with water and 2 tablespoons of baking soda. Give yourself a quick sponge bath—the baking soda will leave you clean and fresh-smelling.

Smart Solution

Plain old baking soda can be used as a deodorant. Simply pat or sprinkle a touch of baking soda under your arms after taking a bath or shower. Because baking soda does not contain harsh chemicals, it can be used comfortably right after shaving.

Soapy Ideas

As a general rule, it's "waste not, want not" with bar and soft hand soaps.

Sponge up the soap. To keep your soap bars from melting into a soggy mess, place a sponge under them and then use the sponge to wash yourself. This will help keep the area neat, and you will actually use most of the melted soap instead of washing the soapy mess down the drain.

Soap on a rope. Rather than throwing away the end pieces of soap, cut a leg off an old pair of pantyhose and place the small pieces inside it. Tie the open end of the pantyhose loosely so you can open it to add more soap pieces as you get them. Then hang the "soap on a rope" over the faucet or showerhead so it'll be handy.

Smart Solution

If you notice that your soap bar seems to have lost its suds, prick it with a straight pin or a fork—you should be able to get much more lather out of it because you are getting into the new part of the soap that still has fragrance and lather.

Soft soap. When the bar of soap gets too small to handle, don't throw it away. You can make it into inexpensive soft soap for filling hand soap dispensers, either by melting the pieces in hot water or by whizzing them through a blender or food processor.

Longer-lasting bars. Open bars of soap as soon as you buy them—they will harden in the open air and will last longer when you start using them. Place the open bars in drawers to make your clothes smell fresh.

Better hand soap. Instead of buying expensive liquid soaps for hand washing, fill your pump dispensers with the least expensive shampoo you can find. The shampoo works great and is very gentle to your hands.

Baby Face

Taking care of your face is a balancing act. You want to find something that cleans thoroughly *and* leaves your skin soft and smooth. These cleansing and moisturizing solutions are sure to please.

Facial Scrubs

For good skin circulation, use an exfoliating scrub once a week. (More frequent use can cause the skin to thicken.) Try these quick and easy homemade scrubs; they work just as well as the expensive ones you can buy.

Tightwad Tip

To get every last bit of skin lotion out of the bottle, put the container in the microwave for about 15 to 20 seconds until it's warm (not hot)—or toss the bottle in your bath water to warm it up. The warm lotion will pour right out.

Cleansing grains. Mix a teaspoon of sugar with your soap lather, and use it once a week to help remove any dead skin cells. Your skin will feel clear and very soft afterward.

Exfoliating scrub. Mix 1 teaspoon olive oil and 1 teaspoon baking soda together in your palm until it's a fairly thick paste. Massage it gently into your skin, and rinse with cool water before patting dry.

Gentle cleanser. Mix a little baking soda with your regular facial cleanser to give it a little extra scrubbing power. The baking soda boosts the cleaning power of your cleanser, but is very gentle on the skin.

Homemade Facial Mask

Use a facial mask twice a week to tighten pores, smooth your complexion, and rev up circulation. Afterward, splash on cool water to close pores, and then apply some moisturizer. This homemade facial mask cleans and revitalizes your skin for just a few pennies.

> 1 tablespoon instant dry milk
> $^1/_2$ cucumber, peeled
> 1 teaspoon plain yogurt

Puree the ingredients until smooth in a blender. Apply the mixture to your face, avoiding the eye area. Let it dry for about 20 minutes. Rinse off with cool water, and pat skin dry.

To save time, you can make several batches at once. Freeze the extra mixture in an ice cube tray; then pop out a cube and thaw out as needed.

Tightwad Tip

Refill trial-size bottles of lotion, shampoo, and other toiletries for traveling. When you return from your vacation, save the bottles and refill them.

Gentle Steam Cleaning

Steaming your face helps rid the skin of impurities. First wash your face with soap and water. Then hold a towel over your head to form a tent, and stand over a sink of steaming hot water for about five minutes. Keep your face at least 12 inches from the water, because intense heat can break capillaries. Next, splash lukewarm water on your face and apply a toner.

Face Cleaner and Moisturizer

This is a very nice, natural face cleaner and moisturizer. When your face is a little dry, this moisturizer will make it very soft.

> juice from 1 lemon
> $^1/_2$ cup mayonnaise
> 1 tablespoon melted butter

Mix all together, and place this cream in a glass jar; store in the refrigerator what you are not using immediately. Use a small amount, enough to cover your face, to clean your face and remove any makeup; then rinse your face with cold water. One batch will last for 2 weeks in the refrigerator.

Oatmeal Honey Scrubbing Cream

This natural scrubbing cream is perfect if you have oily skin or blemishes. It really cleans the skin and makes it feel tight. This is also good for teenagers.

$^1/_2$ cup uncooked oatmeal

1 tablespoon honey

1 tablespoon cider vinegar

1 teaspoon ground almonds

Combine all ingredients in a glass or enamel bowl. To use, first wash your face with very warm water to open your pores. Then apply the mixture to your face and let it dry completely. When dry, use a wet washcloth to work the mixture into your skin with brisk but gentle circles. Rinse with warm water and pat dry.

Oily Skin Conditioner

This solution will clean, take the shine off your face, and tighten the skin. When used often (once or twice a day) your skin will not be as oily.

$^3/_4$ cup witch hazel

$^1/_4$ cup rubbing alcohol

Mix the ingredients together, and store in a tightly capped, clean glass bottle. To use, moisten a cotton ball and clean your face with this solution after washing and before applying a moisturizer. This formula will take the shine off oily skin, tighten the pores, and make your skin feel tingly.

Blemish Control

To dry up a blemish or pimple, dab the area with lemon juice several times a day. This juice works just as well as any of the expensive products available, for a fraction of the cost. You might also want to make a paste of baking soda and peroxide and then apply to blemishes before going to bed. Plain white toothpaste applied to blemishes or pimples will also help make them go away.

If you or your teenager tends to have acne, you may want to try using salt without iodine in your cooking and on the table at home. Iodine is essential in the diet, but you will get plenty from other sources. This simple tip could save you tons of money on dermatologists' bills.

Smart Solution

When you wash face cloths, always add fabric softener. This will make them less abrasive to your skin.

Watch Out!

Wearing makeup overnight is not a good practice—makeup can clog pores and cause blemishes. Make it a habit to thoroughly wash your face before going to bed.

Moisturizers

Always apply moisturizer when the skin is slightly damp; the best time is right after you have washed your face. Rinse with cool water and pat until almost dry; then dot or dab on the moisturizer and gently blend it in.

Night cream. For normal to dry skin, use a lotion or cream at night. While you sleep, your skin is more receptive than it is during the day to the ingredients found in night creams. If you have oily skin, avoid using heavy night creams because they can clog the pores.

Eye cream. Apply eye cream sparingly and gently. The skin around and under the eyes is thin and delicate, so dot the lotion or cream there, never rub it in.

Smooth and Silky Face Softener

To add moisture and softness to your face make a batch of this face softener. It is so relaxing to use and your face will be very soft when you finish using it.

   $1/4$ teaspoon apple cider vinegar

   1 tablespoon honey

Beat the vinegar and honey together, and spread liberally over the face. Leave on for 15 minutes, then rinse off with warm water. Pat face dry.

Soft All Over

Your face needn't be the only place for soft skin.

Rough Elbow Paste

Elbows can be one of the roughest parts on your body. To keep these areas smooth, make a thick paste of baking soda and water, and rub it on your elbows. Then use a wash cloth to rub away the dry, flaky skin. Apply some petroleum jelly on the dry area, and let it soak in. Apply more petroleum jelly as it becomes absorbed.

Smart Solution

For healthy skin from within, drink at least eight glasses of water a day and get plenty of rest at night.

Bet You Didn't Know

Apply a light coat of moisturizer to the skin before putting on your makeup. Believe it or not, moisturizer helps make makeup last and keeps colors truer while protecting the skin.

Elbow Rub Softener

Rough elbows can be tough to soften. This formula will make them softer and when used daily you can probably eliminate the dry, cracked elbows.

1 teaspoon lemon juice

1 teaspoon vegetable oil

1 teaspoon honey

Beat all ingredients well until thoroughly blended. Rub mixture onto elbows, and massage for a few minutes. A stubborn case of dry elbow skin can be helped considerably by frequent applications. If used often, this formula will make the previously hard, dry skin soft and healthy-looking.

Bet You Didn't Know

If you use petroleum jelly as a body moisturizer, then you know that it is very effective—but it can be difficult to apply smoothly. To make the petroleum jelly go on more easily, microwave it briefly. Place a small amount of petroleum jelly in a glass cup, and microwave for 30 seconds or until it melts. Be sure to watch it closely, and let it cool before rubbing it on your skin. Not only will the melted petroleum jelly go on smoothly, but it will feel and act like an expensive oil.

Treat for the Feet

Give rough feet an overnight treat. Rub off dead skin cells with a pumice stone, apply petroleum jelly in a thin layer, and put on a pair of cotton socks. In the morning, wipe off any excess petroleum jelly. You'll be amazed at how much softer your feet are.

Hair Care

Want to save some cash on hair care? Check with local beauty (cosmetology) schools and see when class is in session. At many schools you can get your hair cut for *free* during the class. Either the instructor will cut it as a demonstration to the class, or a student will cut it with close supervision by the instructor.

Ask about other services such as coloring or permanents as well. Even if they don't offer class demonstration cutting, the beauty schools generally will cut your hair and perform other services for about 50 to 60 percent less than regular beauty salons. Many schools don't require appointments, either; they accept walk-ins.

Tightwad Tip

For the best results when coloring your hair, pick a hair color close to your natural color (a shade or two lighter or darker). With a close shade, you won't have to touch up the color as often.

Shampoo How To's

Always rinse your hair with warm water before you apply shampoo. The rinse will help loosen dirt and wash some of it away before you start to shampoo.

More isn't really better in this case—don't think that lots of lather means you'll get your hair cleaner. The lather comes from the shampoo's sudsing agents, which do nothing for cleaning. If your hair is especially dirty, shampoo and rinse twice.

Massage shampoo and conditioner into the scalp with your fingertips, not your fingernails. Wash your hair in warm (not hot) water, and finish off with a cool rinse. The cool water will flatten the cuticle of the hair shafts and make your hair look shinier; it will also close scalp pores.

Removing Shampoo Buildup

Over time, shampoos and hair sprays can leave chemicals in your hair that don't come out with normal shampooing. Try these ideas to really clean your hair and give it a healthy bounce:

➤ Mix 1 teaspoon baking soda in your hand with your regular shampoo. Lather and rinse as usual.

➤ After washing with your regular shampoo, rinse with equal parts lemon juice and water. Follow the lemon juice rinse with a cool water rinse. If you prefer, you can use half cider or white vinegar and water instead of the lemon-and-water mixture.

Dry Shampooing

Every once in a while you may need the quick fix of a dry shampoo. Dust your hair with dry oatmeal, cornmeal, cornstarch, or baby powder. Any of these will absorb some of the oil and

Smart Solution

To clean combs and brushes, place them in a sink of very hot water and $1/4$ cup baking soda. The baking soda and hot water will fizz away the dirt and grime.

Tightwad Tip

When you think your shampoo bottle is empty, fill it $1/3$ full with water. You'll be amazed at how many more shampoos you'll get out of it!

Smart Solution

If you find that your dandruff shampoo does a great job of eliminating dandruff but leaves your hair dry, try using it every other time. For the alternate times, use a shampoo suited for dry hair. (For dandruff remedies, see Chapter 13, "Home Remedies.")

grime in your hair. Then brush thoroughly to remove the "dry shampoo." The dirt will seem to disappear, and your hair will have more volume.

Extra Body Treatment For Hair

When your hair needs some heavy duty help try this treatment. It will bring back the bounce and shine. Use it once a month or more often if needed.

> 2 tablespoons molasses or honey
>
> 2 tablespoons unflavored gelatin
>
> 1 tablespoon milk
>
> 1 tablespoon beer (stale beer is fine)

Combine ingredients in a small bowl and then comb or brush the mixture into your hair. Cover your hair with a plastic shower cap, and wrap a towel around your head. Leave the conditioner on for 30 minutes. Rinse with warm water, then shampoo. Your hair will have incredible body and extra fullness.

Deep Conditioning

Any time you want to add some extra bounce to your hair you can use this conditioner. When used once a week, you'll find your hair looks great all week long.

> 1 egg white
>
> 1 tablespoon olive oil
>
> 1 tablespoon mayonnaise

Mix all together and comb the mixture through your hair. Wrap your head in a towel, and leave the conditioner on for 20 to 30 minutes. Rinse well.

Control for Frizzy Hair

Permed or naturally curly hair will not be as frizzy if you rinse with a mixture of vinegar and water after shampooing and conditioning. Combine 1 cup vinegar and 1 cup water. Pour on your hair and wait two minutes before rinsing with clean water.

Nail It!

Before applying nail polish, rub your fingernails with cotton balls dipped in vinegar. This not only cleans them thoroughly, but it also removes any oils on them so that your nail polish stays on longer.

Don't throw away nail polish that is too thick to use. Place the old bottle in a pan of hot water for a few minutes to thin it out and restore its smooth consistency.

Cleaning nails. Put a dab of baking soda on a small nail brush, and scrub gently on the top of the nails and under them. The baking soda helps dissolve dirt.

Cuticles. Keep cuticles smooth by slightly moistening baking soda and rubbing it in around the nails. Rinse off and dab hands dry.

Once a week give your cuticles a moisture bath. Warm about an inch of olive oil in a small glass bowl in the microwave for 15 to 20 seconds, or until warm but not hot. Soak your nails for 15 to 20 minutes to soften the cuticles. Keep cuticles pushed back with a wooden stick; never cut them.

Filing. File nails in one direction, from the sides toward the center. File from underneath the nail rather than on top of the nail; this helps keep nails from splitting.

Buffing. Buff nails before polishing them; this gives you a smooth base on which to apply the polish so that your polish stays on longer.

Bet You Didn't Know

You don't have to spend extra money on special quick-drying nail polish or sprays to make nails dry quickly. Instead simply dip your painted nails into ice cold water (being careful not to touch the sides of the sink or bowl) to dry them quickly.

Clean Teeth and Fresh Breath

There are several good home-brewed solutions that can help here.

Homemade Toothpaste

This natural toothpaste works great and even tastes great. Try it and you may not go back to the stuff in the store.

> 3 tablespoons baking soda
>
> 1 tablespoon popcorn salt (because of its finer grain)
>
> 1 1/2 tablespoons glycerin (from the drug store)
>
> 10 drops peppermint extract
>
> 1 or 2 drops water
>
> Note: You can omit the popcorn salt if you cannot find it in your local store. The salt adds a little extra scrubbing action.

Mix the ingredients together and use as you would store-bought toothpaste. Baking soda has been used for toothpaste for many years; it is less abrasive than most toothpastes, yet it is still strong enough to clean teeth effectively.

Teeth Whitener and Stain Remover

This solution will remove many stains from your teeth. When used once a week, your teeth will stay white.

Tightwad Tip

To get every last bit of toothpaste out of the tube, slip a barrette, a binder clip, or an old fashioned clothespin on the tube. They all work just as well as the plastic keys that you can buy.

$1/4$ teaspoon toothpaste

$1/4$ teaspoon baking soda

$1/4$ teaspoon hydrogen peroxide

Mix all together. Brush with this formula once a week to remove stains on your teeth. Do not swallow this solution and do not use it on children.

Fresh Breath

Add $1/2$ teaspoon baking soda to a cup of cold water, and rinse your mouth as your would with any mouthwash. The baking soda solution will remove strong odors (such as garlic and onion) and leave your mouth feeling fresh.

Homemade Mouthwash

Try this mouthwash instead of a commercial mouthwash. It works very well and you can make a batch quickly.

1 teaspoon salt

1 teaspoon baking soda

1 quart water

Mix all together and gargle twice a day (morning and night) or as needed.

Tightwad Tip

When the tube of toothpaste is almost empty, place the closed tube under warm water for a few minutes to get every last drop out. When you think there's no more left, cut open the tube, and you'll find there's enough for several more brushings.

Denture Soak

To clean dentures try this homemade solution. It will soak clean your dentures without scrubbing.

    1 cup water

    1 tablespoon powdered laundry detergent

    1 tablespoon baking soda

Mix ingredients together. To clean dentures, soak them in a cup for at least 30 minutes. Rinse well with water before using.

Sweet Smell of Perfume

To make your cologne or perfume fragrance last longer, dab a little petroleum jelly on your wrists and mix your perfume or cologne with it. The petroleum jelly will make the fragrance last about twice as long, so you will be able to put perfume on less often and still enjoy the fragrance all day.

Make your own perfumed moisturizer by adding a few drops of your favorite perfume to a small bottle of baby oil or unscented lotion. You'll enjoy your favorite scent every time you use the oil or lotion.

Test first. Before you buy a perfume, always test it on yourself. A scent can smell different on you than it does in the bottle, on a piece of blotting paper, or on someone else.

Heat intensifies scents. Wear lighter forms of fragrance in the summer (such as eau de toilette or cologne) and a more intense form (perfume) in colder weather.

Avoid mixing. Don't let your fragrances fight each other. When wearing cologne or perfume, stick to unscented soaps, deodorants, hand lotions, and hair sprays. Always wait at least six hours before switching scents.

Tightwad Tip

You can find good perfume and cologne bargains after Christmas. Stores want to get rid of their special packages wrapped for the holidays and often discount them substantially. Stock up on as much as you will use within a year (after which time they start to lose their potency) to save big.

The Least You Need to Know

➤ A fancy package and a high price do not necessarily mean that you're getting a superior beauty product. Cheaper ones are often just as good.

➤ You can make some wonderful bath oil and dry skin treatments inexpensively at home.

➤ You'll need to go no farther than your kitchen to find the ingredients to keep your face and skin clean and silky, and to deep condition your hair and give it body.

➤ Natural ingredients such as baking soda and salt work great to clean your teeth and freshen breath.

Home Remedies

Home remedies were around many years before you could run to the drugstore and pick up a bottle or jar of something to ease the pain. Indeed, many of today's over-the-counter and prescription drugs were originally created from home or herbal remedies.

Take for instance, parsley. It's been used as a breath freshener since ancient times. Parsley is rich in chlorophyll, an active ingredient in commercial breath fresheners now, including Clorets and Certs. Honey, which was recommended as a wound treatment in the Bible, has been shown in hospital studies to help prevent wound infections. Some surgeons cover surgical incisions to this day with a layer of honey.

This chapter covers these and other home remedies that will help ease, soothe, and heal.

Home Remedies A to Z

While home remedies are not a substitute for prescription medication and sound advice from doctors, many can clear up simple problems and ease pain. So before you dash out to the drugstore, consider trying some of these first.

Always consult a doctor if your condition worsens or does not improve within a reasonable time.

Arthritis. Many people claim that arthritis and other types of pain in joints is eased when they drink a vinegar and honey "cocktail." Mix 2 teaspoons of cider vinegar and 2 teaspoons of honey into $1/2$ cup of warm water. Drink the mixture three times a day.

You can also ease arthritic pain with an Epsom salts soak. Mix 2 cups of Epsom salts in a gallon of warm water. Wet a towel with the solution and hold it against the painful joints for about 15 to 25 minutes. Then remove the towel and massage in castor oil.

Watch Out!

Always consult a doctor if pain persists or gets worse. These home remedies are a quick fix for only occasional discomfort.

Athlete's foot. Soak socks or stockings in vinegar water. Combine 1 part vinegar and 4 parts water; soak the socks for 30 minutes before washing as usual. Relieve the itching of athlete's foot by rinsing the feet several times a day with undiluted apple cider vinegar.

Backaches. For a sore back, add 2 cups of apple cider vinegar to your bath water. Soak for 20 minutes. Add $1/2$ cup of baking soda or 1 cup Epsom salts for added relief.

Bad breath. Gargle with a solution of half vinegar and half water. If desired, use mint-infused vinegar for a refreshing mouthwash. You can also chew on some parsley.

Bee or jellyfish sting. To soothe a bee or jellyfish sting, mix a solution of three parts vinegar (white or apple cider) to one part water, and apply to the sting. This will soothe the skin irritation and relieve itching.

For bee stings you can also try any of the following:

➤ Make a paste of baking soda and water and apply it directly to the stung area for 10 to 20 minutes to relieve the pain.

➤ Carefully dab a cotton ball with household ammonia and swab the sting. It will help soothe the pain.

➤ Take an ice cube and place it in a cloth and apply the cold towel to the bite for 10 to 30 minutes. Be sure to keep the ice from direct contact with the skin, to avoid the chance of freezing.

See also Insect Bites and Stings.

Bladder infection (urinary tract infection). To reduce the chances of getting a bladder infection, take 1 teaspoon of vinegar each day. The vinegar helps keep the urinary tract at the proper acid level.

Alternatively, you can drink a glass of cranberry juice daily to reduce the chances of getting a bladder infection. If you feel a bladder infection coming on drink 2 to 3 glasses of cranberry juice daily.

Body odor. Mix equal parts of baking soda and cornstarch. Pat or rub a small amount under arms or on feet for a natural deodorant.

Home Remedy for Boils

Try this homemade liniment for use on boils.

> 1 cup vinegar
>
> $1/4$ cup turpentine
>
> White of 1 fresh egg

Smart Solution

Need an emergency ice pack? Use a plastic bag of frozen vegetables from your freezer. Wrap the bag in a towel and apply to the bruise.

Combine the ingredients in a bottle, and shake until they are mixed. The mixture will have a white, creamy texture. Apply a small amount to boils on the skin, and allow to dry. Repeat twice daily. If your skin is sensitive, omit the turpentine.

Bruises. Dip onion slices into apple cider vinegar and rub on bruises immediately after they occur to prevent black and blue marks from forming.

You can also apply ice to bruises for 5 to 10 minutes. Place the ice in a cloth or use an ice-pack. The ice will help minimize swelling.

Burns. To alleviate the pain of minor burns, pat undiluted cold apple cider vinegar on the burned area every 15 minutes. Keep a bottle of apple cider vinegar in the refrigerator to use for this purpose.

Alternatively, keep a small bottle of very strong cold tea in the refrigerator for use on any sort of non-serious burn. The acid in tea is very beneficial in treating burns. Simply pour a small amount of the tea on the burn, or dip a clean cloth into the tea and hold on the burn.

Cool compresses also minimize minor burn pains. Apply a cool compress (using wet washcloths or paper towels) for 10 to 15 minutes.

Burn Cure Reliever

This formula will relieve some of the pain of a minor burn on the skin. It will also help the burn to heal.

   1 egg yolk

   1 tablespoons honey

   1 tablespoon olive oil

Mix all together well in a blender, food processor, or with a wire whisk. Spread some of the mixture on surgical gauze and place on the burn. Put any unused mixture in the refrigerator for up to 12 hours; then discard and make a new batch. Repeat the treatment twice a day until the burn is healed. This remedy helps aid the healing process and relieves some of the pain.

Canker sore relief. Canker sores are a result of viral infection, but an overlying bacterial infection causes the painful, whitish sore. Neutralize the bacteria by gently rinsing your mouth with a solution of 1 teaspoon baking soda in $1/2$ glass of warm water. This solution will also help relieve the pain.

Chapped lips. Wet your chapped lips several times a day with cool water, pat dry and apply a thick layer of petroleum jelly.

Colds. *See* Cold and Flu Prevention, and Cold Relief *at the end of this chapter.*

Constipation. This problem can almost always be solved with home remedies. Don't spend money on over-the-counter laxatives, which can irritate your bowels; eat some prunes or drink prune juice instead. Figs are another natural laxative to try if you don't care for the taste of prunes, and regular eating of bran and other high-fiber cereals and grains can be very effective in preventing constipation.

Corns and calluses. Use a vinegar compress to remove corns and calluses. Soak a slice of stale bread, cotton, gauze or small sponge in apple cider vinegar; tear off a piece of the bread large enough to cover the corn or calluses, and tape it in place with first aid tape. Leave the bread on the area overnight and in the morning you'll find that the corn is smaller.

Coughs. Put a dab of honey on the back of the tongue to bring relief from a nagging cough.

Cough Syrup

Here's a natural cough syrup that even tastes good. But the best news is, it quickly quiets your cough.

   1 teaspoon honey

   1 teaspoon lemon juice

Mix honey and lemon juice and use as needed to relieve a cough. To make a larger batch, mix equal amounts of honey and lemon juice. Take 2 teaspoons as needed.

Minor cuts, scrapes, abrasions, and burns. Break open a leaf of the aloe vera plant and apply the slick liquid directly to the afflicted area. Do not cover it up. The aloe stops swelling and speeds up healing.

Old Country Ointment

Use this ointment on cuts, wounds, or other skin troubles.

> 1 part flour
>
> 1 part honey

Mix together and apply to the cut, wound, or skin problem.

Dandruff. Eliminate dandruff and keep hair healthy by rinsing after each shampoo with $1/2$ cup apple cider vinegar mixed with 2 cups of water.

You can also make your own dandruff shampoo. Beat two egg yolks in $1/2$ cup of water. Massage into the hair and scalp well, and leave on for 5 to 10 minutes. Wash out with water and then rinse with a mixture of 2 tablespoons of apple cider vinegar and water.

Diarrhea. To prevent traveler's diarrhea, drink a mixture of 1 teaspoon apple cider vinegar, 1 teaspoon honey, and 2 cups water 30 minutes before each meal. (If traveling out of the country, be sure to use bottled water instead of tap water for this mixture—and also for all the water you drink and use to brush your teeth.) Start this treatment a few days before traveling, and continue during your stay away from home.

Douche. Regular douching is no longer recommended for women, but if you are prone to vaginal infections, you can prevent them by occasionally douching with a solution made of 2 teaspoons apple cider vinegar and 1 quart of warm water.

Earaches. To treat earaches and help prevent swimmer's ear, very gently dry the outside of the ear with a dry towel. Mix equal parts of vinegar and rubbing alcohol together, and use a drop or two in each ear right after swimming to help dry the ear canal.

Gas pains. To ease gas pains, drink a glass of very warm water with 1 teaspoon honey and 1 teaspoon vinegar added. *See also* Indigestion.

Hair, green from chlorine. The chlorine from a swimming pool can turn light hair green, but this is very easy to remedy. Just rub a little tomato juice on your hair, let it soak in for about two minutes, and wash as usual to remove the green tint. You may be able to avoid the green tint altogether simply by rinsing your hair in a quick shower as soon as you are finished swimming.

Headaches

Add $1/4$ cup apple cider vinegar to the water in a vaporizer and inhale the vapors for five to 10 minutes. Rest quietly, and the headache should go away in about 30 minutes or less. This also helps to relieve migraines.

Headaches (sinus). Drink a glass of water with 1 teaspoon of apple cider vinegar five times during the day to ease the pain and help clear the sinuses.

Headaches (sinus or a stuffy nose). Dip a washcloth in hot water, wring out only enough to keep it from dripping, and place it over the upper half of the face. Press around the nose and eye sockets. When the cloth cools, repeat. Continue doing this for 10 to 15 minutes. This will relieve the pressure that caused the headache. It is best done while lying down.

Headaches (tension). Ease a tension headache with a gentle massage of the facial muscles or by applying a heating pad or hot compress to the forehead and the base of the skull. The best solution for a tension headache, of course, is to avoid the source of the tension. (Easier said than done!)

Bet You Didn't Know

To make a reusable ice pack, simply mix one part rubbing alcohol to two parts water. The mixture will not freeze solid but will stay slushy so it can be shaped around knees or elbows and the like.

For a small pack, pour 1 cup rubbing alcohol and 2 cups water into a self-sealing quart-sized plastic storage bag. Squeeze out the air before pressing the bag closed. Store in the freezer until you need it. To make a large ice pack, use a gallon-size bag and double the recipe.

Hiccups. To get rid of a tough case of hiccups, sip a glass of warm water with 1 teaspoon of vinegar added. Drink the whole glass all at once, but slowly; the hiccups should disappear. Or swallow a teaspoon of sugar and quickly wash it down with water.

Indigestion

Sometimes referred to as heartburn, indigestion can be caused by any one of a number of things, including spicy foods, fatty foods, and sometimes just plain too much food. If you get occasional bouts of indigestion, any of these may help. (For severe and frequent stomach problems, see a doctor.)

Or take coke syrup (ask the pharmacist for it, no prescription needed). Pour a tablespoon or two over crushed ice and sip. Repeat every hour. You can also let a can of Coke go flat and use that, but it's not as concentrated as what the drugstore sells.

➤ Mix about an ounce of lemon juice in a glass of cold water, and drink it.

➤ Sip 1 teaspoon of apple cider vinegar mixed in $1/2$ glass of water throughout the meal.

➤ To calm an irritated stomach, take 2 to 3 teaspoons of honey. For chronic problems, take 1 tablespoon of honey at bedtime on an empty stomach.

Antacid Liquid

When you have a sour stomach or gas this remedy will help relieve the pain.

1 tablespoon baking soda

1 teaspoon sugar

4 drops peppermint oil

1 cup water

Mix well and store in an airtight bottle in the refrigerator for up to one month. When needed, take 1 or 2 tablespoons.

Insect Bites and Stings

The pain and irritation of most common insect bites and stings can be relieved by a quick application of one of these simple pastes. Both will help draw out the poison and prevent swelling.

➤ Mix baking soda with just enough water or witch hazel to form a paste. Keep the paste moist by covering it with a damp cloth or dressing.

➤ Make a paste of 2 tablespoons of cornstarch and a few drops of vinegar. Just pat the vinegar and cornstarch paste on the area and let it dry.

Insect repellent. Keep insects and bees away when outdoors by rubbing vinegar on your body. Rub full-strength on any exposed parts, such as arms, legs, wrists, ankles, and throat. Or dilute oil of citronella with a little vegetable oil and rub it on.

See Chapter 25 for more information on repellents for specific pests.

Insomnia

For relief of insomnia, add 3 teaspoons of apple cider vinegar to a cup of honey. Take 2 teaspoons of the mixture before going to bed each evening. This will help you go to sleep. If you wake up in the middle of the night and can't go back to sleep, take another 2 teaspoons.

It really is true that a glass of warm milk will help you fall asleep. The active ingredient in warm milk is tryptophan. Some people suggest that it is essential to eat a couple of cookies with the warm milk to help the body absorb the tryptophan!

Tranquilizer Tea

Chamomile and mint are natural relaxers. Either alone make soothing teas, but they're also good together, as in this recipe.

> 1 cup chamomile tea
>
> Fresh or dry mint leaves
>
> 1 tablespoon honey

Steep the mint leaves in the hot tea for three minutes. Drink the tea before going to bed, and you'll sleep like a baby.

Joint pain reliever. *See* Arthritis.

Kidney infections. To reduce the chances of getting a kidney infection, take 2 teaspoons of vinegar each day. The vinegar helps keep the urinary tract at the proper acid level. You can take the vinegar undiluted or mix it with 1 cup water and 2 table-spoons honey. Drinking a glass of cranberry juice daily also works.

Laxative

Prunes, either as juice, stewed or plain dried, are a very effective natural laxative.

Laxative Juice

Use this gentle solution when you are constipated. It's good for you and I think you'll even like the taste.

> 1 cup tomato or vegetable juice
>
> $1/2$ cup sauerkraut juice
>
> $1/4$ cup carrot juice

You can buy both sauerkraut juice and carrot juice at a health food store. Some grocery stores have carrot juice. Or you can drain a can of sauerkraut.

Mix together in a glass and drink all at once. You can pour this juice over ice or add Tabasco sauce for flavoring. You can use this solution twice a day without having to worry about cramping or other side effects. *See also* Constipation.

Leg cramps. Many find that cider vinegar relieves leg cramps. Keep a spray bottle with undiluted vinegar in it next to your bed; then when you have a sudden attack of cramps you can reach for the bottle. Nighttime leg cramps may be prevented by drinking a glass of water with 1 tablespoon of apple cider vinegar added to it before each meal, or apply a hot water bottle, soak in a warm bath with epsom salt ($1/2$ cup) or baking soda.

Menstrual cramps. Exercise regularly to relieve menstrual cramps. If exercise doesn't work, heat may soothe the pain. Use a heating pad, hot water bottle, a long soak in a warm bath, or a cup of hot tea.

Motion sickness. Drink a cup of ginger tea at the first sign of motion sickness. If you are prone to motion sickness, drink one cup of ginger tea before traveling. You can also try candied ginger as an alternative to over-the-counter motion sickness remedies. It has no adverse side effects and it really tastes good going down.

Nausea, vomiting. Relieve the discomfort of nausea or vomiting by soaking a cloth in warm apple cider vinegar, wringing it out, and placing it on the stomach. Replace with another warm cloth when it cools.

If you wake up with nausea or vomiting, drink a solution of water and 2 tablespoons of apple cider vinegar during the day. By evening you should feel like trying a light amount of food. Continue to take vinegar and water five times a day for the next three days to make sure the bacteria is completely out of your system.

A glass of Coca Cola is an old home remedy for nausea that has withstood the test of time. Serve it lukewarm and even a little bit flat. You can stir it with a spoon to make the bubbles disappear.

Night sweats. Before going to bed, rub full-strength vinegar on your arms, legs, chest, neck, and shoulders. Allow to air-dry. Do not wash off. Many people find that this prevents night sweats or decreases their severity.

Nosebleeds. Hold a clean cotton cloth or gauze that has been dipped into white vinegar over your nose whenever you have a nosebleed. The vinegar will help stop the bleeding and speed the healing process.

Perspiration on hands. If your hands are always moist use a weak solution of vinegar, rubbing alcohol, or witch hazel, which will act as an astringent. Mix one part vinegar with four or five parts water.

Ringworm. *See* Impetigo.

Scalp itch. Add 1 tablespoon of vinegar to a glass of water, and dip your comb into the mixture. Comb through the hair. Continue to do this until the hair and scalp are saturated with the vinegar water. This will help stop itching by returning the skin to its normal pH balance. Rinse with clean water.

Shingles. *See* Impetigo.

Skin Irritations

If you have a skin irritation, sponge the area with undiluted vinegar. If the itching stops, the condition is on the outside of the skin and the vinegar will quickly heal it. If the irritation persists, the condition may be internal; consult a doctor in that case. Applying vinegar to the skin helps normalize the pH balance of its surface.

Acne. Make a mixture of 2 teaspoons apple cider vinegar and 1 cup of water to dab on blemishes several times a day after washing. This vinegar treatment will help clear up the acne without drying out the skin.

You might also want to try dabbing toothpaste, a drying agent, onto a pimple at night and then using ice the next day to reduce swelling.

Age spots. Age spots (liver spots) can be faded or even eliminated with onion juice and vinegar. Mix 1 teaspoon onion juice (squeezed from a fresh onion) and 2 teaspoons vinegar together and rub on the spots once or twice a day. In a few weeks you should see the spots beginning to fade.

Blackhead treatment. To loosen blackheads, mix equal parts of baking soda and water, and apply to the area. Rub gently for two to three minutes, then rinse with very warm water. Do not squeeze.

Chapped skin. Skin hydrates from the inside out, so apply a bath oil directly on your skin after bathing. Bath oils work better than baby oil because they have ingredients that act as dispersants to make sure the oil gets into the top skin layer.

Freckles. Lightenfreckles on the body (not the face) by rubbing lemon juice on them. They will lighten over a period of several weeks. Freckles will not disappear completely, but you'll notice the difference.

Hives. Applying an ice pack or cold compress on the itchy area frequently brings relief. You can do this as often as necessary, for about 10 minutes each time. Be sure to wrap the ice-pack in a towel so that it doesn't directly touch the skin.

Impetigo, ringworm, and shingles. To help the skin heal, apply full-strength apple cider vinegar to the problem skin areas five or six times daily.

Irritated skin. In a small glass jar with a lid, place the two halves of an empty eggshell. Add enough apple cider vinegar to completely cover the eggshell. Tightly cover the jar. Bubbles will start to form on the eggshell, and within a day or two the eggshell will have dissolved into the vinegar. All the calcium and minerals from the eggshell will now be contained in the vinegar mixture left in the jar. Apply the liniment to skin irritations, itchy skin, and sore, aching muscles.

Itchy skin. Relieve itchy skin by patting undiluted apple cider vinegar on the area. If the itch is near the eyes or other delicate areas, dilute the vinegar to four parts water and one part vinegar. For large areas of skin that itch, a vinegar or oatmeal bath is the easiest way to get treatment. Simply add 2 or 3 cups of vinegar or oatmeal to the bath water.

Poison ivy. To stop the itch of poison ivy, mix $1/2$ vinegar and $1/2$ water; dab frequently on infected area to help stop the itching and promote healing.

Alternatively, mix 1 cup vinegar with 2 tablespoons salt in a saucepan. Boil until the salt is dissolved. Let cool. Apply liberally to skin. Let dry and leave on the skin for at least 30 minutes. Reapply several times a day.

Poison ivy, oak, and sumac. Take a warm (not hot) bath with either $1/2$ cup baking soda or 1 cup oatmeal. Use ground colloidal oatmeal (such as Aveeno) for best results.

Windburn protection. Protect skin from the chapping of windburn by applying a protective layer of olive oil and witch hazel. Mix half olive oil and half witch hazel. Rub a small amount on the face and other exposed areas of skin.

Snoring

If mucus is contributing to the blockage problem, you can flush it out with saltwater. Dissolve $1/4$ teaspoon of salt in 8 ounces of water. Bring the water to a boil to sterilize it. Then let the salt water cool down to body temperature before putting it in a nose dropper. Apply a couple of drops in each side of the nose.

Soreness

Apple cider vinegar works its magic on tired, achy muscles all over. Here are some ways to use it for relief.

Sore feet and legs. Fill the bathtub with several inches of warm water (enough to cover your feet). Add $1/2$ cup of baking soda or apple cider vinegar, and walk back and forth in the solution for five minutes. Do this twice a day, and your feet and legs will feel relaxed.

Sore muscles. Wrap arms, legs, shoulder, back, or whatever aches in a cloth dipped in apple cider vinegar. Leave the cloth on the area for five to 10 minutes, and repeat as often as needed. For even more relief, add a dash of cayenne pepper to the vinegar.

Liniment for stiff or sore muscles. Beat the yolk of one egg with 2 tablespoons of apple cider vinegar. Apply this mixture to the skin, rub in well, and allow to dry. Do this twice a day to relieve stiffness and soreness.

Bath for sore muscles. Add 2 cups of baking soda, Epsom salts or apple cider vinegar to your bath water. All 3 work for sore muscles and fatigue, and they work better than expensive bath additives. *See also* Backaches.

Peppermint Vinegar Rub

Nothing works better for sore muscles. Mix up a batch and rub it on them.

> 1 pint vinegar
>
> 1 pint water
>
> 1 teaspoon peppermint oil

Mix all together. Peppermint vinegar makes sore muscles feel better and adds a firmness to the texture of skin.

Sore Throat

A sore throat can have multiple causes. For severe and prolonged ones, see your doctor. For minor ones, try gargling with vinegar water or salt water, or try one of these:

Sore Throat Remedy #1

$^1/_4$ cup honey

$^1/_4$ cup lemon juice

Mix together and take 1 tablespoon every four hours. This remedy is also recommended for the flu.

Sore Throat Remedy #2

$^1/_2$ cup apple cider vinegar

$^1/_2$ cup water

1 teaspoon cayenne pepper

4 tablespoons honey

Mix together and take 3 tablespoons every four hours. This will ease the pain and speed healing.

Stomach problems. *See* Indigestion.

Stress relief. To relieve stress and feel energized, add $^1/_2$ pint vinegar to a tub full of bath water and soak for at least 15 minutes. The skin will absorb some of the vinegar, and the potassium in it will pep you up. Add some of your favorite herbs such as lavendar, sage, and rosemary for a refreshing stress reliever.

Stuffy nose. *See* Headaches (Sinus or stuffy nose), and Cold relief.

Sunburn Relief

Red, stinging sunburn is no fun. To cool it down, try one of these:

➤ Rub full-strength vinegar (white or cider) on the sunburned skin. If you rub the skin with vinegar before the pain starts, you will dramatically reduce the pain!

➤ Dip clean rags or washcloths in cold milk and place them over the sunburned areas. Leave the milk-soaked rags in place for about 15 minutes. Be sure to use whole milk because the fat content and the protein soothes irritated skin.

➤ Soak in a lukewarm bath with baking soda. Pour 1 cup baking soda into the water, and sprinkle some on the trouble spots after you get into the tub.

➤ Gently rub talcum powder on the sunburned skin. It can be quite soothing, especially before bedtime.

Swimmer's ear. *See* Earaches.

Toothache. Rub apple cider vinegar, oil of cloves, or oil of peppermint on the tooth and surrounding gums for temporary relief from the pain.

Urinary tract infection. *See* Bladder infection.

Varicose veins. Relieve and shrink varicose veins by wrapping the legs with a cloth wrung with apple cider vinegar. Prop up your legs, and leave the vinegar-soaked cloth on for 30 minutes twice a day (morning and evening). You should notice considerable relief within six weeks. To speed the healing process, follow each treatment with a glass of warm water with 1 teaspoon of apple cider vinegar added to it. If desired, add a teaspoon of honey to the mixture.

Vomiting. *See* Nausea.

Wound healer. Because honey is rich in sugar, enzymes, minerals, and vitamins, it can help heal wounds and sores. Not only does honey protect the wound from infections, but it also provides nutrients for the wound that encourage healing. Simply apply a thin layer of honey on the wound.

Cold and Flu Prevention

During the winter season, it seems like everyone catches a cold or the flu. With the cost of over-the-counter medications, doctor visits, prescriptions, and lost time from work, a cold or flu can put a strain on your body and wallet! Here are some solutions to stay well when everyone around you seems to be catching the flu bug.

➤ Wash your hands often. It is easy for someone to cough or sneeze on a phone, toy, or dish that is later picked up by someone else. If you touch your nose, eyes, or mouth with your hand, the germs you picked up can quickly spread. Washing your hands often when a member of the family or coworker is sick is one of the best ways to keep the germs from spreading.

➤ Keep your fingers off your face. You probably are not even aware of how often you touch your face. The eyes, nose, and mouth are easy places for bacteria or a virus to invade your body.

➤ Replace the hand towel in the bathroom often. This is another easy way for germs to spread from one person to another.

➤ The cotton in medicine bottles (cold remedies, aspirins, and vitamins) should be removed as soon as you open the container. It's only there to keep the pills from breaking during shipment. Germs are easily spread from your hands to the cotton, then from the cotton to the next person who touches it.

➤ Clean areas that are touched often. Bacteria and viruses can live many hours on faucets, doorknobs, counters, phones, and other frequently handled objects. Use rubbing alcohol or hot, soapy water to kill the germs.

➤ Avoid cigarette smoke. Smokers have twice as many respiratory infections as nonsmokers, and it takes them twice as long to get well. If you smoke, quit or cut back. Nonsmokers, stick to no-smoking areas to avoid secondhand smoke.

➤ Don't forget your flu shot. Flu shots are not just for the elderly. Anyone who wants to significantly reduce the risk of flu is a good candidate for vaccination—that includes healthy young people raising a family or working. Flu shots are bargain-priced compared to a doctor visit. Check with your local health department or walk-in clinics; many will give you a flu shot at a lower price than your doctor will. If you are a senior citizen, Medicare will pay the cost of your flu shot. Some supermarkets and drugstores now have flu shot days in the fall where you can get inexpensive flu shots.

Cold relief. Almost any herbal tea will help relieve the symptoms of a cold. Chicken soup helps make breathing easier and may help you get over a cold quicker.

Nighttime Cold Remedy

This remedy will help you get to sleep when you've got a cold just as well as store-bought products.

Juice from 1 lemon

$1/4$ cup maple sugar

$1/4$ cup hot water

2 tablespoons brandy

Stir the lemon juice into the maple syrup. Add the hot water and brandy. Drink the entire recipe while it is hot.

The Least You Need To Know

➤ While home remedies are not a replacement for sound medical advice, they can relieve pain and make you more comfortable.

➤ You'll want to keep a bottle of apple cider vinegar on hand for home remedies. It can be used for ulcers, weight loss, sunburn, varicose veins, and many other ailments.

➤ Baking soda can be used to remedy backaches, canker sores, gas pains, and insect bites.

➤ To avoid colds and the flu, wash your hands often, clean areas that are touched often, and avoid cigarette smoke.

Chapter 14

Holidays and Other Special Occasions

In This Chapter

➤ Sweetheart ideas for Valentine's day

➤ Easter egg decorating

➤ Pumpkin tips for Halloween

➤ Creative holiday gifts and wrapping solutions

➤ Natural holiday decorations

➤ Party-time ideas

Special occasions are only special when you or someone else makes them that way. In this chapter you'll find lots of ways to spice up your holidays—and inspiration for starting your own unique family traditions.

Fun Ideas for Valentine's Day

These fun suggestions are sure to please the one you love—and remember that Valentine's Day can be any time of the year!

Breakfast in bed. Get up early and surprise her with her favorite breakfast. Use the best china, and serve orange juice in a wine glass or champagne flute. Line a tray with a napkin—and don't forget a candle or flower.

Candlelight dinner. If you are too rushed in the morning for breakfast in bed, plan a special meal and eat by candlelight. Cook his favorite meal and bake a heart-shaped cake (see recipe below).

Tightwad Tip

Instead of spending several dollars on a store-bought Valentine's card, make paper hearts and write love messages on them. Hide several hearts in places where you know your love will find them—it will bring a smile to your sweetheart's face each time he or she finds one.

Chocolate-covered strawberries. Instead of buying the same old box of chocolates, buy a pint of strawberries and dip them in chocolate. First, wash the strawberries and let them dry. Then melt some regular or white chocolate in the microwave or in a double boiler; holding the strawberries by their leaves, dip them in the chocolate and place them on a piece of waxed paper to dry.

Picnic lunch or dinner. Weather permitting, pack a picnic basket full of goodies and go to a romantic spot to enjoy each other's company. Be sure to pack luscious finger foods (such as fruit cut into small pieces) that you can feed to each other.

Love poem. To really win some points, write a love poem or letter to your Valentine—the poem can be romantic or funny. Read it out loud.

Love coupons. Make up coupons for him to redeem at any time. Coupons can include anything from a body massage, to a favorite meal, to doing her chores. Use your imagination and tailor the gift to whatever your love will enjoy the most. Make your coupons on colored paper cut into heart shapes.

Bake cookies. First bake his favorite cookies, then buy a bag of balloons and have them inflated with helium at a party store. Deliver the cookies and balloons to the receptionist at his office. Be sure to include a sweet note with your sweet treat. You can even wrap each cookie individually with a love note inside. If you can't deliver the cookies yourself, send them to his office via the mail. A small package of cookies will be within the weight for priority mail, which costs $3.

Romance by the fire. If you have a fireplace, build a fire; grab some pillows and blankets, make some hot cocoa (perhaps add a chocolate peppermint candy to each cup), and roast marshmallows in front of the fire. Turn off all the lights and enjoy the warm glow. Remind your sweetie how much you love her.

Heart-Shaped Valentine Cake

This cake is very easy to make, but if you prefer, use a boxed cake mix instead. What makes it special is not the ingredients but its shape and trimmings.

2 cups self-rising flour*

1 $1/2$ cups sugar

$1/2$ cup shortening

1 cup milk

1 teaspoon vanilla

3 eggs

*Note: you may substitute 2 cups flour, $2/3$ teaspoon baking powder, and $1/2$ teaspoon salt if you do not have self-rising flour.

Preheat oven to 350°F.

Grease and flour one round cake pan and one square cake pan. Measure all ingredients into a large mixing bowl. Blend at low speed until ingredients are mixed. Beat on high speed for three minutes, scraping bowl occasionally.

Pour batter into pans. Bake at 350°F for 30 to 35 minutes, or until a wooden toothpick inserted in the center comes out clean. Cool. Cut round cake in half and use to make a heart shape, by abutting the cut sides of the two pieces against adjacent sides of the square cake.

Frost with cherry frosting (see following recipe) or vanilla frosting mixed with a few drops of red food coloring.

Cherry Frosting

Homemade frosting is so easy to make, and it tastes so much better than packaged frosting. (Besides, it's cheaper!)

3 cups powdered sugar

$1/3$ cup margarine, softened

1 $1/2$ teaspoons vanilla

about 2 tablespoons milk

2 tablespoons drained, chopped maraschino cherries

2 drops red food coloring

Smart Solution

If you do not have a serving plate large enough for the heart-shaped cake, cover a sturdy piece of cardboard with aluminum foil.

Mix powdered sugar and margarine. Stir in vanilla and milk. Beat until smooth and spreadable. If needed, add a few more drops of milk to make the consistency right for frosting. Stir in cherries and food coloring. Frost heart-shaped cake.

Easter Egg Decorating

Decorated Easter eggs make a fun tradition. With a little creativity and a few items from the kitchen, you can make some pretty nifty eggs. Here are some ideas to try.

For the best results, use only fresh, clean, unbroken eggs. The eggs should be hard-boiled and chilled before dyeing. (And if you make more colored eggs than your family will eat as boiled eggs, don't let them go to waste; make egg salad or deviled eggs out of them.)

Coloring Eggs

There's more than one way to dye an egg, as you can see here:

➤ Dye eggs with a powdered drink mix (such as Kool-Aid). Just mix one package of unsweetened drink mix with $2/3$ cup warm water. Place the eggs into the mixture for about a minute until they're the color you want.

➤ Add beet juice to the water when boiling eggs. This will color them pink.

➤ Lay a paper towel over a piece of aluminum foil. Drop some food coloring on the towel (about 8 to 10 drops) and gently wrap the foil around the damp egg. Then open and allow the egg to dry. You can use one or more colors on each egg for original designs.

➤ Decorate eggs with colored marking pens. Pick a few colors and draw any designs or pictures you like.

Nature's Patterns

To make beautiful and unusual decorated Easter eggs, gather some small leaves and flowers. Lay a few tiny flowers or leaves flat against an uncolored egg. Wrap the egg in a piece of old panty hose material, and tie the ends tight around the egg. Lower the egg into dye, and when it's the color you want, remove it from the dye to dry inside the panty hose. When dry, cut the fabric away and you will have a beautiful patterned egg.

You can also use fresh herbs such as parsley, rosemary, or any other herb you grow, the same way as you would leaves or flowers. Herbs make interesting prints on the eggs.

Halloween Pumpkins

If possible, pick your own, right from a pumpkin patch. You'll find the best pumpkin this way, and you'll have fun picking your own.

Seal your carvings. A fresh pumpkin will keep well outdoors for weeks if it doesn't freeze; but once carved, it's very perishable. Rub the cut areas of a jack-o'-lantern with petroleum jelly to help make it last longer.

Let there be (flash)light! Cut a hole in the bottom of the pumpkin just large enough to hold a small flashlight. Carve the pumpkin as usual, but instead of buying lots of candles, just flip on the light. A flashlight is much safer than candles, too; this makes it fun for small children to get to light the pumpkin.

Halloween candle holders. For inexpensive holiday candle holders, use tiny pumpkins, squash, or apples. Just carve a hole in the top in which to set the candle.

Cooked Pumpkin Pulp

Fresh pumpkins can be boiled or baked to prepare the pulp for use in pies, casseroles, breads, and the like. (Select small pumpkins, both for taste and for ease in cooking.)

To boil: Slice open the pumpkin. Clean out the seeds and the membrane. Cut the pumpkin into pieces, cover with water in a kettle or large saucepan, and cook until tender. Then drain and peel off outer skin. To bake: Slice pumpkin in half and clean out the seeds and the membrane. Place halves face down (cut side down) in a baking dish. Bake in a 325°F. oven for 45 to 50 minutes. Peel outer skin.

Bet You Didn't Know

Don't throw away the pumpkin seeds. They make a tasty, inexpensive snack. Just rinse them, mix with butter and seasonings (salt or cinnamon), and toast them in the oven. Let a few of the seeds dry, and try to grow your own pumpkins from them next year.

Watch Out!

If you would like to carve a pumpkin and also eat the meat, you must act quickly. You will need to wait until Halloween night to carve the pumpkin and quickly bring it inside after the kids have finished trick-or-treating. Use a small light or flashlight inside the pumpkin for light instead of matches to keep the pumpkin in the best shape. Wash the pumpkin thoroughly before baking or boiling it.

Whether boiled or baked, put cooked pumpkin meat through a food processor or blender, or mash it with a potato masher.

Refrigerate or freeze the prepared pulp until you are ready to use it.

Celebrating Christmastime

'Tis the season to overspend on gifts, wrapping, decorations, cards, foods and entertaining, travel, holiday clothing, and on and on. The list is endless! Financial experts say that during the holidays many people go overboard, without even realizing it (until it's too late).

Savvy Shopping

This list can help you keep the spending under control without feeling like Scrooge.

➤ Set a spending limit or budget. Know how much you can afford to spend, then decide how you want to spend the money. Make smart choices, and cut corners on things that are the least important to you and your family.

➤ Take an inventory of all your holiday items before you buy anything. This way you won't buy extra cards, bulbs, candles, or other items you already have on hand.

➤ Start holiday shopping early, and look for sales on the items on your list. If you are looking for a specific item, ask the department manager when it will be on sale. If he knows that the item will be on sale within, say, a few days, many times you can get the item at the sale price then and there, without having to wait for the sale. If not, then when you make your purchase, save your receipts and if the item goes on sale a little later, ask for a refund of the difference.

➤ Buy family members gifts they need. A step ladder or screwdriver set may not seem like a romantic gift, but if your loved one needs it, he'll probably enjoy it much more than a necktie or another pair of slippers.

➤ Pay cash or write checks for gifts. When you have to deduct the money from your checking account or hand over cash, you're less likely to overspend. If you charge all your purchases, you may be shocked when the bills arrive next year. Long after the gifts are forgotten, the credit card bills will still come due.

➤ Be creative with gift wrap. Use any wrap left over or saved from last year, and look for other low-cost ways to wrap gifts. It's crazy to spend almost as much money on the wrapping, bow, and tag as you paid for the gift!

➤ Whenever possible, exchange names with a group of people (at work, church, or school) instead of buying individual gifts. If you have a large extended family, suggest that you each pull one name from a hat and buy just for one person. You can even agree to spend a little more on that gift because you're saving by not buying for everyone.

Postcard Greetings

Save on postage by mailing holiday postcards instead of cards—you'll still have plenty of room to write a holiday message. Make homemade postcards out of Christmas cards from last year. Cut the front of the cards (the part with the picture) to postcard size (4 inches by 5 1/2 inches), and use the back to write the address and a holiday message.

Cookie Exchange

Cookies are one of the most fun and least expensive ways to celebrate the Christmas holidays. Start an annual cookie exchange with friends, relatives, or coworkers. Here's how it works: Each person makes three dozen of the same kind of cookies (or any amount you decide) to give away, and each person gets three dozen different kinds in return.

Gourmet Chocolate Chunk Cookies

Here's a good cookie recipe you might like to use for your cookie exchange.

2 1/4 cups unsifted flour

1 teaspoon baking soda

3/4 teaspoon salt

1/2 cup margarine, softened

1/2 cup shortening

1 cup firmly packed brown sugar

1/2 cup sugar

2 eggs

1 teaspoon vanilla extract

12 ounces chocolate (plain eating chocolate, broken or chopped into chunks*)

1 cup chopped nuts (optional)

* Buy discounted chocolate after Christmas, Valentine's Day, or Easter.

Preheat oven to 350°F.

In a small bowl, sift together flour, baking soda, and salt; set aside. In a large mixing bowl, beat margarine, shortening, and sugars until creamy. Beat in eggs and vanilla. Add flour mixture; mix well. Stir in chocolate chunks and nuts. Drop by rounded teaspoonfuls, two inches apart, onto ungreased cookie sheets. Bake 9 to 12 minutes or until lightly brown.

Makes about six dozen cookies.

Christmas Decorations, Naturally

Homemade holiday decorations are not only fun to make—they also get you into the festive mood.

Scented Pine Cones

For a beautiful holiday centerpiece, make a basket of scented pine cones. All you need is a basket, ribbon, pine cones, spray paint, glue, and ground cinnamon or cloves.

Spray-paint the basket green or red, and tie a matching bow around it. Spraypaint the pine cones gold or silver, or leave them natural. Using a cotton swab, dab the inside edges of the pine cone with clear-drying glue. Sprinkle with cinnamon or ground cloves. Tap off the excess spice and let dry. Arrange the pine cones in the basket.

If you prefer pine scent over a spice, you can buy pine-scented oil from a craft store to scent the cones. Just put them in a large plastic bag and sprinkle with the pine-scented oil. Close the bag tightly and allow them to sit for at least a week.

These baskets make nice gifts to give to unexpected guests. Make a few extra to keep on hand. The spice scent will last for several months.

Smart Solution

Always save artificial wreaths for next year. Even ones that look really ragged can be made beautiful with the trimmings from your tree. Just poke in large springs of holly or pine and add a pretty bow. The greens will last a long time (probably all holiday season) without water, especially outside.

Twig Candle

Collect small, straight twigs from the yard to make an unusual holiday candle. Start with a thick 8-inch candle. Arrange the sticks vertically, side by side, around the outside of the candle; secure them with a rubber band or hot glue. Trim them, if necessary, so they're all the same length. Tie a colorful or plaid ribbon around the twigs, and you have a wonderful and useful holiday candle. Keep a few for yourself and give some as gifts.

Orange Idea

A bowl of orange pomander looks beautiful and adds a wonderful scent to the house. First pierce several holes (a few dozen at least) in fresh oranges to form a simple design. Poke whole cloves into the holes. Tie a few thin ribbons around the orange to add more color.

Holiday Scent

Nothing makes your home feelmore like the holidays than this wonderful scent. When guests are coming over, heat it up and enjoy the aroma.

   1 cinnamon stick

   3 bay leaves

   $1/4$ cup whole cloves

   $1/2$ lemon (halved)

   $1/2$ orange (halved)

   1 quart water

Combine the ingredients in a kettle or pot. Bring to a boil, reduce heat and simmer as long as needed to fill the house with the aroma. One batch can be used for several days; just keep adding additional water as needed. This is an inexpensive way to set the mood for the holidays.

Salt Clay Christmas Ornaments

This is a fun project to entertain your children or grandchildren during the holidays.

   $1/2$ cup salt

   $1/2$ cup water

   $1/2$ cup cold water

   $1/2$ cup cornstarch

   food coloring, if desired

Mix the salt and water in a large pan, and bring to a boil. Place the cold water in a small bowl, and stir in the cornstarch. Add the food coloring, if desired.

Tightwad Tip

For inexpensive decorations, wrap pictures you've got hanging on the walls in colorful holiday wrapping paper. Tie a pretty bow around them. You can also wrap empty boxes and place them around the room. Spray-paint bare branches and pine cones, and place them in baskets.

Add the cornstarch solution to the boiling salt water, and stir continually to keep the mixture from forming lumps. Cook over low heat until the mixture is stiff.

Remove from heat and allow to cool slightly. Before it is completely cool, turn onto a cutting board. Let cool and knead until it is the consistency of clay. Store in an airtight container if you will not use it immediately.

To make Christmas decorations, roll out the dough and either cut it with cookie cutters or shape it freehand. Use a toothpick or drinking straw to make a hole in the top for hanging. Bake at 200°F. for two hours. Decorate and hang with string or bread twist-ties.

Post-Christmas Sales

You can save a bundle next holiday season buying leftover holiday merchandise. Look for these bargains after Christmas; stock up and save.

Artificial Christmas trees. Ask the store manager to hold one of the fully decorated display trees for you until after Christmas. You should get the tree at 50 to 80 percent off the retail price. Be sure to ask for the box that the tree came in so you have somewhere to store it. Other Christmas decorations are good buys now, too.

Chocolate for baking. Buy marked-down Christmas chocolate (packages of foil-wrapped bells and other holiday shapes) and freeze to use later in cookies, cakes, and all your baking. Chip the chocolate into pieces to make delicious chocolate chunk cookies (see previous recipe). Use a vegetable peeler to make elegant chocolate shavings.

Butter cookies in tins. Drugstores and grocery stores usually have tins of cookies left over, for sale at considerable discounts. Buy some and put the tins in the freezer to use throughout the year for lunch box treats and snacks. When empty, save the tins to fill with homemade goodies next year.

Plasticware and kitchen linens. So what if forks, knives, spoons, paper plates, cups, and napkins are red or green? You can buy a year's supply at 50 percent off or more. Use them all year long for picnics and parties and in lunch boxes. Stock up on kitchen towels, pot holders, and place mats. The colors will be red and green, but the price will be right.

Tablecloths. Buy a few extra disposable paper tablecloths on sale to use to wrap large packages next year. They can be much cheaper than wrapping paper and easier to work with.

Cards. Buy your boxed Christmas cards after the holidays for next year.

Clothes. Don't forget to look for holiday clothes after Christmas, too. Why not buy a party dress for next year, if you can get it at a real steal?

Many stores have appliances on sale after the holidays, too. January is the traditional appliance sale month, so look for markdowns from 10 to 40 percent.

Clever Gifts, Year 'Round

They say it's the thought that counts. And if you put a little thought into your gift giving, you can save money and, at the same time, give a very special gift. Here are some ideas for you to try for any gift-giving occasion.

Family Memories

Family tree. Go to the library and trace your family tree. Many large libraries have a genealogy department that will help you in your search. Make several copies of the tree you make, frame them, and give to your immediate family members. You'll have put a good amount of time into the project, but the gift won't cost much and it will be the talk of the holidays.

Heirloom gift. I'll bet you have something you would like to have handed down from generation to generation. Why not surprise your daughter, son, or grandchild this year so they can enjoy it sooner rather than later?

Photo album. Give a photo album full of special pictures. Everyone loves to look at pictures. Be creative; include baby pictures or pictures from past generations. Be sure to write names and dates on the back of each.

Calendar. Buy or make a pretty calendar for the new year. Put important family dates (birthdays, anniversaries, and so on) on the calendar.

Food and Cookery

Homemade goodies container. Cover an oatmeal box with wrapping paper to hold homemade goodies. This works great for mailing cookies, taking goodies to work, or delivering to nursing homes. The container is sturdy and looks pretty, and the recipient does not have to worry about returning it when empty.

Care package. Buy several small inexpensive items instead of one large gift. A kitchen care package might include pot holders, dish rags, paper towels, salt and pepper, and other miscellaneous kitchen gadgets.

Homemade recipe book. Make a family cookbook of all the favorite recipes that you treasure. Ask family members for the best recipes that everyone enjoys, and include them, too.

Give of Yourself

Coupon book. A coupon book is a thoughtful, inexpensive gift for the holidays. Children can even make them for their parents or grandparents. The coupons are limited only to your imagination: A teenager can make coupons to mow the lawn or clean out the gutters, garage, or attic for a parent or grandparent. Many times this type of gift is remembered long after the holidays have passed.

Manicure and facial. Offer to give your friend, mother, or sister a manicure or facial. Everyone loves to be pampered!

Bedtime stories. Make a cassette tape of fairy tales (in your voice) to give to a child or grandchild. This is especially fun for a faraway relative to send to a child.

Baby sitting. Every parent of a young child will *really* appreciate getting free baby-sitting services!

Firewood. If trees are plentiful on your property and you have the time and energy, deliver some cut and split fire wood. This would make anyone with a fireplace happy.

Gifts of Special Interest

When possible, create or buy gifts that appeal to the special interests, talents, or collections of the recipients. They will know the gifts were intended just for them.

Music lover. Frame an old piece of sheet music in a pretty gold or black frame. A song with special meaning will be remembered for years to come. Antique and junk stores usually have a box of old sheet music, and the average cost is a dollar per song.

Collectibles. Search antique stores, flea markets, and garage sales for unusual items for someone with a special interest. Find an old cookbook for someone who loves to cook. Kitchen gadgets, old bottles, and buttons are just a few of the inexpensive items that make nice gifts when given to the right person.

Wrap it Up!

Buy wrapping paper after the holidays when it's marked down to "give-away" prices. If you wait long enough, you can find it for 75 to 80 percent off the original price.

Smart Solution

Small gifts can be wrapped together by dropping them in a paper towel or toilet paper tube. Wrap the tube to look like a piece of candy by rolling paper around the tube and tying the ends with a ribbon.

If you don't have any paper left over from last year, use some of these creative wrapping ideas.

Gift bags. Use the brown paper bags from the grocery store for gift bags. Let kids paint or color them to mark the occasion. Tie the tops together with colorful ribbon or string. This is a lot cheaper than buying gift boxes and wrapping paper.

Gourmet gift. Save large and small bottles throughout the year. Wash them out and fill them with someone's favorite coffee, potpourri, or even homemade spaghetti sauce. Tie a ribbon around the neck, and it's wrapped and ready to go.

Bottle it. If you really want to drive someone crazy, wrap a small gift in a large bottle. Wrap the gift in crumpled up paper and place it inside the jar. Put a ribbon around the jar. You can even put confetti made from a hole punch in the jar for decoration.

Trash or treasure? Wrap packages in any colorful paper you have. Some ideas are newspapers (the comics, coupons, or stock listings), old calendars, travel posters or brochures, computer paper, magazines, or even colorful junk mail.

Basket wrap. Be creative—use an inexpensive basket to wrap small gifts. Wrap the gift in tissue paper or newspaper, and place in the basket.

Chocolate kiss. Wrap up a gift to look like a chocolate kiss. Place the gift on a sturdy paper plate or cardboard circle. Fold a large sheet of aluminum foil up around the gift to create the kiss shape. Make the tag out of a long strip of white paper and tuck it in the pointed top. The process is easier if you have a chocolate kiss on hand to use as a guide.

Plain beautiful. Make an elegant-looking package by wrapping the gift in white or light-colored tissue paper, then use a rubber stamp or stickers to dress up the package.

Dip and dot. Use a pencil eraser to make polka-dot paper. Just dip the eraser in gold, red, or green paint, and dot on tissue paper. You can even carve a simple design into the eraser, such as a star or tree.

Box it. Instead of plain old gift wrap for small gifts, cover a sturdy little box with a piece of beautiful fabric. Simply cut out the fabric and glue it to the box. If you can get your hands on cigar boxes, they really turn out beautiful—and the box itself is another gift worth keeping.

More freebies. Collect free sample products all year long, and add as decoration with a bow (or instead of a bow) when gift wrapping. For example, add a sample baby powder or baby oil bottle to a baby gift, or add a sample of any type of cosmetic to a teenage girl's gift.

Tightwad Tip

Always ask for boxes when shopping at stores that still give away boxes. If the store offers free gift wrapping, let them wrap your packages as you finish shopping.

Tightwad Tip

Don't throw away all the crumpled Christmas wrapping paper; use it to pack up the ornaments and decorations for next year.

After-Any-Holiday Bargains

The biggest sales will fall after the biggest buying season, and that's Christmas. But don't overlook other post-holiday sales.

At the supermarket. Turkeys and hams are usually on sale around Christmas, but look for good buys on turkeys right before and after Thanksgiving, and on hams around Easter as well. Buy and freeze extras to enjoy later.

Seasonal items. Drug stores and some discount stores are notorious for marking down seasonal items. Look for 50 percent off wrapping paper and other supplies the day after Christmas and Hanukkah. A week or two after holidays, many stores will substantially discount seasonal merchandise—Easter candles, 4th of July napkins,

Bet You Didn't Know

When you get out the good silverware to use for the holidays and find it needs polishing, use plain old white toothpaste instead of buying an expensive silver polish. Coat the silver with toothpaste, dip it in warm water, work the toothpaste into a foam, and rinse off. For stubborn stains or for silverware with an intricate design, use an old soft-bristled toothbrush.

Smart Solution

Start making extra ice cubes several weeks before a party. Store ice cubes in paper or plastic bags in the freezer. You'll have plenty of ice, and you won't have to waste money buying bags of it from the store. Make large cubes, either of plain water or fruit juice, in plastic margarine containers to use in the punch bowl. The large blocks will keep the punch cold longer, so guests will not need to add ice cubes to their punch. You can also freeze grapes to float in punch.

Valentine's Day cards, and more. If you've got the storage room, stock up on nonperishables for next year.

Gift-wrapped goodies. Look for special packages of beauty products that were Christmas, Valentine's, Mother's Day, or Father's Day gift items. Department and drug stores will mark them down to clear them out. You can usually find colognes and toilet water, bath salts and oils, and other assorted beauty products for women and men.

White sales. While linens might be on sale any time of the year, January is traditionally the big white sale month. Stock up on sheets and towels while they are on sale. Look for advertised sales, and compare prices. For many stores this will be the lowest price of the year on sheets and towels.

It's Party Time!

Here are ideas for making the most of holiday gatherings or party any time of the year.

China. You can mix china from various patterns you own. The effect is appealing, and you avoid buying expensive (often quite expensive!), one-time-only paper products. Use a solid color tablecloth to tie the different colors and patterns together.

Silverware. If you don't have enough sets of matching silverware, wrap what you've got in colorful cloth napkins and tie a ribbon around each set. Guests won't even notice that you have used several different patterns together. If you are serving buffet-style, stand the wrapped silverware up in a large flower vase at the end of the line so guests can pick up a set.

Edible centerpiece. A simple bowl of red apples and mixed nuts makes a pretty centerpiece. Add a candle to the middle of the centerpiece. Your apples will sparkle if you shine them with a banana peel; rub the inside of the banana peel over your apples, and buff with a soft cloth. The best thing about this centerpiece is that you can eat it during or after the party (there's no waste).

A dessert party. Entertaining costs add up quickly. Plan get-togethers after dinner, and serve just desserts and coffee. A party can be festive and fun without being expensive.

All chip in. For a big family meal, have each family bring a different side dish or dessert. Everyone will enjoy the variety, and you'll cut your costs.

The Least You Need to Know

➤ You can make Valentine's Day very special by giving your love a creative gift, such as breakfast in bed or a hand-written love poem.

➤ To make jack-o'-lanterns last longer, seal the carved parts with petroleum jelly and light them up with flashlights, not candles.

➤ Some of the best gifts cost nothing, or next to it. Scrapbooks and family trees, coupons for services, and found and free things items can mean more to the recipient than something store-bought.

➤ Wrap gifts in hand-decorated paper bags, boxes, and baskets; wrap with scraps of fabric or even the comics!

➤ After Christmas, the best times to stock up on holiday foods and seasonal sale items are Valentine's Day, Easter, and Mother's and Father's Days. Look for bargains on things you can use all year long—or that will keep until next year's holiday.

Chapter 15

On the Go: Travel Tips

In This Chapter

➤ How to plan your vacation and get information about your destination

➤ Getting the lowest airfare

➤ Tips for lodging and car rentals

➤ Packing smart

➤ Saving on road food

Taking a trip? What fun. Where are you going? When? With whom? What do you want to see and do? How much is it gonna cost? Whoa!

A vacation or weekend getaway is certainly something to look forward to, but before you can start having all that fun, you've got a lot of decisions to make and some organizing to do.

Planning the Get-Away with an Agent

If it's a big trip you're taking, or if you're going some place you've never been before (and even if it's not), you'd be wise to get an expert's help before you make your plans. A good travel agent can save you money by searching for bargain destinations and looking out for good deals. Usually their fees are paid by the hotels, airlines, and tour companies, not by you. And an agent who's experienced should be able to make travel suggestions that will get you the most for your travel dollars. Let her know where you want to go, who's going, and about how much you'd like to spend, and see what she suggests. You may be pleasantly surprised.

Planning on Your Own

Some people like to research their own trips—to find the most perfect places to stay and discover their own delightful things to see and do. If this is you, then roll up your sleeves and start looking! Lots of resources are there just for the asking.

Smart Solutions

Check with AARP (American Association of Retired Persons) if you're a senior, or contact AAA (American Automobile Association) for travel advice, discounts, maps, and other services. Both have lots of valuable information.

Tourism Offices

If your trip is within the United States, contact that state's department of tourism or the city's chamber of commerce for more information. Most tourism bureaus have a toll-free number. Many will provide you with a lot of useful material at no charge. You may even find discount coupons from local restaurants, hotels, and attractions in the information these agencies send you.

Traveling outside the country? Then don't forget to contact that country's United States-based embassy or tourist office. Also try overseas-based airlines; they usually have general tourist information that you can get by contacting their United States information or reservation number.

Videos

Travel videos are plentiful; check your library and local video rental stores, and even ask travel agencies for suggestions. Some of these videos are, frankly, not worth a flip, but if you get a good one, it's going to be full of interesting information. Seeing the place you're going to visit can give you a good overview, tell you about the terrain and climate, and maybe even provide some cultural and historical background that can add another dimension to your visit. And, of course, all those picturesque views can be a great trip appetizer!

Keep in mind that the videos you borrow from a travel agency are usually distributed by a tour company, hotel chain, or airline, so they might be just a *little bit* biased in favor of the provider!

Guidebooks

Before buying a travel guide, check it out first. Borrow it from the library or browse through it at the bookstore to make sure it has the practical information you want, such as what days and hours museums are open and how to get around town from one attraction to another. Ask friends or relatives that have visited the area what guides and maps they found most helpful. Who knows, they may even have one that you can borrow.

National Parks

For vacations that take you to a national park or forest, write ahead for information about sights, lodging, hours, facilities, reservations, and fees. The addresses are listed here:

➤ National Park Service, Department of the Interior, Washington, D.C. 20240. Internet address: www.nps.gov

➤ U.S. Forest Service, U.S. Department of Agriculture, Room 3008 South Building, Washington, D.C. 20250

Tightwad Tip

Travel during off-season if possible to avoid crowds and save the most money. October to April is generally the off-season for most areas, except those that feature winter sports. Call ahead to find out when the off-season rates begin, and find out how much you will save.

Renting A Car

When renting a car, these tips will save you a bundle.

Get a compact. Reserve the lowest rate you can find on a compact car. You can almost always upgrade the car when you arrive, and often the upgrade will be free. Most car rental companies have many more mid-sized and large cars than small ones. If the compact car you reserved is not available when you check in, ask to be upgraded to a larger car for free.

Car insurance. Call your insurance agent before renting a car to find out if you are insured while driving a rental. The insurance rental agencies try to sell you is very expensive—and, in most cases, it is not necessary because your own insurance already has you covered driving any car.

Fill 'er up. Don't opt for the rental car company to refill the gas tank. It may sound like a bargain, but in reality you'll be charged for a full tank of gas even if you turn in the car with some gas in it. Fill the gas tank up yourself before returning the rental car to make sure you don't overpay.

Fly For Less

Flying saves so much time, and with some planning it can be affordable, too. Here are some tips to get you in the air.

Good Deals

Post-holiday flights. Look for airfare bargains right after a major holiday (such as Christmas, Thanksgiving, or Easter).

Summertime travel. This is also a great time to search for airfare bargains because business travel falls off. Scan your local newspaper for special deals such as buy one, get one free offers. Airfares drop significantly during off-season travel, too.

Try to be flexible. Staying over a Saturday can drastically reduce your fare. When making reservations, tell the operator that you are looking for a bargain fare, and ask what you have to do to get the lowest rate.

Avoid high-traffic times. These are early mornings, late afternoons, and Fridays. Ask the reservation agent if the airline offers lower fares for off-peak travel.

Work Smart with the Agents

Make friends with a travel agent; they can let you know in advance when bargain fares will be offered.

Do some research, too, before blindly having a travel agent book your airline tickets. Travel agents receive special bonuses from the airlines, so they may try to book all customers on one particular airline when possible to increase their bonuses from the airline. A few phone calls can make you prepared so you know whether to jump on the rate the agent offers or book the flight yourself.

Tightwad Tip

Plan ahead. To get most of the bargain airfares, you need to buy tickets 21 days in advance.

Bet You Didn't Know

If you are flying to attend a funeral or family medical emergency, ask the airline about their bereavement policy. You'll need some paperwork, such as funeral notice or a letter from the doctor, but if you qualify, it could save you a bundle.

Know All Your Fare Options

Call twice to each of the airlines that flies to your destination. Don't settle for what one representative quotes; call a second agent. You're likely to discover that each quotes you a different fare for the same trip—even if you ask them for the lowest price possible.

Consolidate and Save

An easy way to save money on travel is to use a consolidator. Consolidators buy airline tickets, hotel rooms, or tours that are projected to not sell out at the full retail price. The company selling the tickets, tours, or rooms figures that selling to a consolidator at a deep discount is better than leaving some rooms or seats empty.

Airline Consolidators

These people buy seats on regularly scheduled flights at rock-bottom prices. Then they add a markup and sell the tickets to the general public at a savings of 20 to 50 percent off the regular fares. Many consolidators advertise in the travel section of large-city newspapers; or you can call UniTravel, a well-established consolidator, at 800-325-2222. Always pay consolidators with a credit card so you'll have a record of the transaction.

Hotel Consolidators

If a consolidator has a room you want, you can save as much as 40 percent on your stay. After you've called and negotiated your best price with the hotel, call the hotel consolidators and see if you can get a lower rate. Call Hotel Reservations Network at 800-964-6835, or call Quikbook at 800-789-9887. Both list lodgings in more than 20 large American cities that are frequent travel destinations.

The Low-Down on Lodging

Lodging can be one of your biggest travel expenses—sometimes the biggest. Here are some ways to get the most for your money.

Plan ahead. Book reservations at least three weeks in advance; rates are often 40 to 50 percent lower if you call way ahead.

Book directly with the hotel. Central reservation services that answer calls for all their hotels may not know about special deals available at the particular hotel where you will be staying.

Condo or cottage. If you will be staying for a full week at your destination, try to find a condo or vacation cottage to rent instead of a hotel room. The rate will probably be cheaper and you'll have much more space—as well as the added benefit of a full kitchen.

Always bargain for rates. Ask about senior citizen discounts, a corporate rate, a weekend rate, or a group discount offered to members of clubs or associations; also ask if the hotel has any special promotional rates. When they find out that you are insistent about saving money, they will work harder to find you the lowest rate.

Hi cousin! Visit relatives for free overnight lodging. Don't impose on them for too many days, but a night or two shouldn't wear out your welcome.

Bet You Didn't Know

Stop at the state welcome center and pick up a discount hotel booklet. Many states offer a discount booklet for rooms that would otherwise go empty. Most of the time the rates in these booklets are really a bargain.

Double-check bills. Always review your lodging, car rental, or any other travel bill closely. Frequently, you can find errors. Also ask about any charges you are not certain about.

Pack It Up

Taking the time to carefully organize and pack your belongings can make your trip go more smoothly. These ideas should help.

Emergency needs. Pack a small carry-on suitcase with one change of clothes, cosmetics, medications you must have, contact lens solutions, and anything else you'll really need if your luggage gets lost.

Smart Solution

When you unpack your clothes and find that they are wrinkled, hang them up in the bathroom when you take a hot shower; the steam will loosen the wrinkles.

Jewelry. Put your small jewelry, such as rings and earrings, in a small plastic container; a pill jar or an empty film canister works just as well as anything special you could buy. Your jewelry will stay organized and be less likely to get lost. Put larger pieces of jewelry into socks, and tuck them into shoes. This will protect them from getting broken and will make them easy to find.

Shoes. Pack your shoes inside plastic bags to keep any dirt on the bottom off your clean clothes.

Plastic Bags

Self-sealing plastic storage bags work great when traveling. Put anything that might leak or soil other items into a plastic bag, and zip it shut. The bags work particularly well with these items:

Smart Solution

Take several clip-style clothespins with you when you travel. Use them for clipping bags shut and clipping slacks and skirts to regular hangers.

➤ Pantyhose, socks, and other small items. This keeps them organized and keeps your hose from getting snagged.

➤ Dirty clothes. They'll stay together and away from your clean clothes.

➤ Wet towels, face cloths, and bathing suits. The bags will keep water spots off your clean clothes.

Sewing kit. Take a small sewing kit with you whenever you travel. If you don't have one of the freebies that hotels and businesses give away, make your own. Take an empty film canister and insert a needle or two, some thread, buttons, and safety pins.

Rx. Pack a small first-aid kit. Include aspirin, medicated cream, antiseptic, antacid, adhesive bandages, prescriptions, and any other over-the-counter drugs you may need.

Laundry. Even if you don't plan on doing laundry during the trip, take a small bottle of liquid laundry detergent with you. You can pour some into a trial-size bottle so you don't have much to carry. Use the detergent to hand-wash anything you need to wear again, or to wash a spill off before it becomes a stain.

Packing Toiletries and Makeup

When buying essential toiletries such as toothpaste, deodorant, and lotions, choose the smallest size available. If you travel often, save the little bottles and refill them. Save the "ends" of toothpaste to take on trips.

Toothbrush holder. Make your own toothbrush container out of a clean plastic pill bottle. Cut a slit in the top, slide the toothbrush handle through it, and snap it back on the bottle with the bristles inside.

Keep it simple. Just take the bare essentials. Your favorite lipstick color, a light foundation, powder, blush, eyeshadow, and mascara should get you through. And leave some of your bottles behind. Simply moisten cotton pads or balls with eye makeup remover and astringent, and pack them in separate self-sealing plastic sandwich bags.

Toiletries bag. If you don't have a toiletries bag, a child's plastic lunchbox makes a great organizer for your cosmetics and beauty aids. The lunchbox will keep lotions and cosmetics together so you can find them quickly.

Cotton swabs and balls. Pack a small plastic bag full of cotton swabs and cotton balls. You'll find many uses for both.

Tightwad Tip

Send away for free samples of products, and save them to use when traveling.

Fresh-Smelling Suitcases

To keep suitcases smelling fresh when not in use, place any of these inside them:

➤ A bar of scented soap.

➤ A fabric softener sheet.

➤ Crumpled newspapers.

➤ Or make your own mini air freshener out of a film canister or pill bottle. Poke some holes in the top of the lid, and fill the container with baking soda or activated charcoal. Place the container inside your suitcase. Replace the baking soda as needed.

Smart Solution

When traveling, keep in mind that shampoo can be used as laundry soap for hand-washing, and conditioner can be used as shaving cream.

Suitcase Spotter

Many travel bags look alike; make yours stand out so you can spot it easily. For examples, you can place a bright-colored ribbon or piece of yarn on the handle, or put a large, bright sticker (such as a bumper sticker) on the side of the bag.

Tightwad Tip

When flying, pack a few things to keep you busy if there is a delay. Some good items to have on hand are a book, magazines, a deck of cards, crossword or word search puzzles, and some food. The prices for these items in airport shops are out of sight.

Road Food

Food is another big expense when traveling. Here are some ways to save on food on the road.

Big breakfasts. Eat a big breakfast when traveling, and go lighter on lunch or dinner. Breakfast is typically the least expensive meal of the day.

Bring your own. Take a cooler filled with drinks, snacks, and even quick meals such as sandwiches (especially if you have children) to keep your food costs under control.

Lunches on the go. For a quick travel lunch, pack a sandwich, carrot sticks, fruit, and a cookie or other snack. Arrange the lunch on a clean Styrofoam tray, and cover with plastic wrap. Make one for each person traveling. You can stop almost anywhere and enjoy the quick lunch—the tray makes it easy to eat anywhere, even if you can't find a roadside table.

Equip your room. Take your own coffee pot and supplies to make fresh coffee in the hotel or motel each morning. You can even take it a step further and take items such as a toaster and an electric skillet. Some families really economize on meals and then spend the bulk of the vacation budget on special attractions or take a longer vacation.

Note: Some hotels may discourage cooking in their rooms; when possible, stay in rooms with a kitchenette to make cooking easier.

Restaurants, not hotels. Don't eat at the hotel restaurant where you are staying. You can usually get a better meal at a local restaurant close by for much less.

Beverages. Order ice water to drink with restaurant meals. Water should be free, and it will really make a difference in the total tab. Buy a pack of soft drinks at the grocery store, and keep them in your cooler.

Is Your Car as Ready as You Are?

Check your car before heading out on a trip. If needed, tune it up and change the oil. Also make sure your spare tire is filled with air. Check fluids, air pressure in tires, belts, and any other problem areas to help avoid an expensive out-of-town breakdown.

Charting your car trip. Save time—and possibly gas—by writing down the major cities you will travel through. Post the notes on the dash so you can quickly look to make sure you are headed in the right direction. One wrong turn can lead you miles out of the way.

First aid kit. A small first aid kit will come in handy when traveling. You can buy one with the supplies already in it or use an old lunch box to organize bandaids, gauze, and other first aid items.

Traveling with kids. If traveling with children, start planning early and put aside small games, toys, books, and other items to entertain them on the road. Let each child pack a small tote bag or backpack to carry inside the car with their favorite goodies.

> **Smart Solution**
>
> Fill a plastic liquid detergent bottle (without rinsing it out) with water, and keep it in the glove compartment of the car. Also keep some paper towels on hand. When you need to wash your hands or tackle a quick clean-up, you'll be all set!

What to Keep in a First Aid Kit

- Box of individually wrapped adhesive bandages
- Large absorbent bandages—assorted sizes from medium to extra large
- Elastic bandages for strains and sprains
- Open weave bandages
- A triangular bandage to make a sling
- Gauze dressing
- Skin closures for gaping wounds
- Roll of sterile cotton
- Tweezers
- Assortment of safety pins
- Small pair of scissors
- Hydrogen peroxide
- Mild antiseptic cream

Do Sweat the Small Stuff

These little ways to save while traveling can quickly add up.

Stamps. Take along postcard stamps; they're cheaper than sending first-class letters. Trying to find postcard stamps on vacation wastes valuable time.

Film. Always buy more film that you think you'll need when it is on sale at home. You can spend double or even triple the amount if you wait and buy while on vacation.

Watch Out!

When flying, carry your film in your purse or in a carry-on bag to avoid it being destroyed. Some new scanning equipment for checked luggage at airports will ruin your film.

Telephone calls. Use a pay phone to make calls rather than pay the hotel fee to have your phone turned on. Some hotels have extremely high phone rates for long-distance charges, and you never know what the rate will be. Use a calling card with your regular long-distance company to save the most.

Use rest areas for breaks. These places have free water and clean rest rooms—and no restaurants or gifts to tempt you to spend more money.

Travel reading material. Buy books and magazines to read on vacation at used book stores or garage sales. A new book bought at the airport will cost at least $5 for a paperback. Be prepared with your own magazines and books to read during any layovers or delays.

The Least You Need to Know

➤ A travel agent can be a big help—and a moneysaver—when planning a vacation. Talk to a few before making reservations.

➤ Find out as much as you can about your destination before leaving, whether you're using a travel agent or not. Read books, watch videos, and call for maps and guide books to get you acquainted with the area and what it has to offer.

➤ Book your airplane flights and lodging well in advance, if you can, for the best chances of getting special discounts and promotional rates.

➤ Don't skimp on the time it takes to organize and pack your luggage; being prepared for the weather, all activities, and emergencies can make your trip a real success.

➤ You can save lots of money on your food bill when traveling by packing a cooler and by making breakfast and lunch your big meals of the day.

Chapter 16

The Home Office

In This Chapter

➤ How to find office space in your home

➤ How to set up and organize your workspace

➤ Convenient ways to buy office supplies

➤ Handling mail and reducing junk mail

➤ Ways to save on postage and writing letters

Whether you use your home office just to pay bills or to run your own business, you can use the tips in this chapter to help you set up and get organized.

Finding Office Space

If you will use the office space daily and plan to leave work out, a separate room is usually the best place for your office. For example, you may want to turn the spare bedroom into a work room. Simply take down the bed and replace it with a fold-out sofa bed for guests if you still need sleeping arrangements. Even space in the garage, attic, or basement can work if you can get the proper temperature and lighting.

Nooks, Crannies, and Corners

If you don't have a separate room at your disposal, look around for nooks and crannies that could serve as an office. A friend of mine has the coolest office I've ever seen— right under her stairs. She converted what had been wasted space into a pleasant and efficient home office nook.

A corner of a room is another good spot to tuck away a little office. I like the corner idea because you can use a three-panel screen to cover the area when you aren't working. Simply leave out all your papers, and close off your office!

The formal dining room also works well as a home office. Think about it: How often do you actually eat in the dining room? Buy a plastic tablecloth to protect the dining room table, and convert the table into your desk—you'll have plenty of room to spread out. While you probably don't want to put metal cabinets into the dining room, you still need some storage space. Keep papers and other supplies in plastic milk crates so you can move them out of the dining room easily if you need to use the area as a dining room.

Office Furniture

If you can afford to buy a new piece of furniture for your office, you can find beautiful computer work stations with doors that close to cover the clutter. Everything pulls out for easy access and can be pushed back inside afterward behind doors that close. These items look like just a beautiful piece of furniture—it's only when you open it up that can you see a whole home office inside.

When most of us set up a home office, we don't have a lot of money to spend on the project, so we've got to be clever. Try your hand at these substitutions and innovations.

The Desk

One of the most expensive furniture items can be the desk. If you buy a small, inexpensive desk, you may find you actually have no room at all after you get it home and put the computer on it. For a larger desk, consider using an old dining room table. If you don't have one at home, check around at garage sales and thrift stores. If the table looks rough, put a plastic tablecloth over it.

You can also make your own large "desk" by setting a prefinished hollow-core door on top of two short (two-drawer) file cabinets. You can stain or paint the wood, or even put a plastic tablecloth over the top. Another item that makes a perfect desk is a commercial quality folding table. These usually have a fake walnut finish over a melamine top, and you can usually buy them from an office super store (such as Office Depot or Staples) for $30 to $40 each. These tables are very sturdy and are big enough to hold a computer, printer, and all the other goodies you'll have on your desk.

Shelves

You can never have enough bookshelves—always keep your eyes open for these at garage sales. Even if the shelves you find aren't in perfect condition, you won't notice scratches and nicks after you loaded them up with books and papers. In the meantime, you can make some bookshelves just like the college kids do: Stack bricks on each side, and put boards on top. They look rustic, but they do the job and can be arranged as your needs change.

Cabinets

When buying a filing cabinet, consider how much stuff you are going to put inside it. A lightweight file cabinet might seem like a good deal—until you load it up and find that the drawers are hard to open and close with all that weight. You're better off buying a little better quality cabinet that will hold up when you load it up.

Most new file cabinets have sides that are ready-made to accept hanging file folders. Before you buy a file cabinet, make sure this is the case. If not, you'll have to buy special racks to hold the file folders.

The Chair

When you are selecting a chair for your office, make sure it's comfortable to you. An uncomfortable chair will make your back hurt, give you a headache, and give you an excuse not to use your home office. A decent chair is a good investment, and a basic typist chair that will adjust up and down is the bare minimum you should consider. If your budget allows, spend a little more and get the most comfort you can afford. You'll appreciate your investment in the months and years to come.

Super Saver Supplies

Office supply "super stores" (such as Office Depot and Staples) are popping up all across the country. These stores carry a large selection of office supplies and very low prices—and unlike food warehouse stores, office supply super stores don't force you to buy in large quantities to get the lowest prices. They have most anything you'll need for your home office, and very few other office supplies stores will be able to compete with their high-volume discount prices. As with any shopping, you always should compare prices from time to time, just to make sure you are getting the most for your money.

House Brands

The office super stores also offer their own brand of basic office supplies that will save you even more. Their private label brand is usually of a high quality comparable to national brand quality, but at a lower price. For a comparison of prices, take a look at this table:

Office Super Store Prices vs Office Supply Store

	Office Super Store	Office Supply Store	Dollar Savings	Percent Savings
Envelopes	3.99	12.99	9.00	226%
Copy paper	3.19	8.39	5.20	163%
Pens	1.99	4.99	3.00	151%

Prices on the same brand and size package of supplies.

Mail Order Office Supplies

If you buy more than $50 in office supplies from a super store and live within the delivery area, you may be able to get your supplies delivered to your door free of delivery charge. Office super stores usually offer free delivery to encourage small (and large) businesses to buy all their supplies from them. This makes it very convenient and saves you time and gasoline. To get a free office supply catalog, call the following toll-free numbers. I like to keep the catalogs on hand and compare them before making an order—they're very competitive on prices, but each carries different items. You'll have to consider how fast you need the supplies, too. One vendor might deliver to your area the next day, while two other companies might deliver in about three to four business days.

Office Depot: 800-685-8800

Staples: 800-333-3330

Viking: 800-421-1222

Computers

When organizing your office space, place the computer so that the screen won't get a glare from windows or lights. If you can't completely eliminate the glare, you can buy a glare-reducing screen for your computer. Measure your monitor to find out the size you need.

It's better to turn your computer on in the morning and leave it on all day instead of turning it on and off several times. Each time you turn on your computer, a surge of power goes through it, so the fewer times you turn it on and off, the longer it will last.

If you want your computer to go blank (for privacy) while you're away from your desk, don't turn it off—just adjust the brightness so your screen goes dark. Your computer will look like it is turned off to anyone passing by. You can also turn off your monitor or utilize a built-in screensaver.

Clean Screen

Clean your monitor frequently to reduce eye strain. Usually a quick wipe with a clean dry towel will do the job. Never use window cleaner on the screen; a waxy film will slowly build up and will attract dust, which in turn will eventually yellow your screen. You can buy commercially prepared solutions to clean your monitor, but washing it with a slightly damp rag (dipped in warm water and wrung out completely) is the most economical way to get it clean. Do not spray water or any commercial cleaner directly on the monitor—instead, spray the liquid sparingly on a lint-free cloth, and then use the cloth to clean the screen.

Recycled Disks

When buying computer disks, be sure to consider using recycled ones. Made by several major manufacturers, recycled disks perform the same as new disks, cost less, and, as a bonus, help save precious landfill space. The disks are typically made from obsolete or unsold software programs. They're magnetically erased, reformatted, and re-labeled.

Handling the Mail

The post office delivers literally tons of mail every day. And if you're like me, you're probably overwhelmed with junk mail some days. Some people love getting lots of mail, and others hate it all. Even if you're one of the former, your mail can get the better of you unless you keep the clutter under control.

Sorting

When you open a piece of mail, first decide whether to keep or toss it. Try to handle each piece of mail just once. If you're going to keep it, put it in the proper place (such as the bill box or magazine rack).

Throw away any junk mail you don't want right away. If you're not interested in it now, you probably won't be later, either, when you've got a mound of it! Quickly browse coupons as they come in, and clip the ones you plan to use. Throw away the others, or give them to someone who may be able to use them.

Keep a basket to store catalogs. When you're in the mood, flip through them and keep the ones that you like or plan to order from. Toss the rest.

Watch Out!

Cut up any unsolicited credit cards, and throw them away. Throw part of the credit card into one trash bag, and throw the other pieces into a different trash bag so that anyone digging through the trash cannot piece the numbers together.

Minimizing Your Junk Mail

To cut down on junk mail, you can send a request to the Direct Mail Marketing Association. This service will be able to take your name off the mailing lists of its member organizations. Write to:

> Mail Preference Service
>
> Direct Mail Marketing Association
>
> PO Box 9008
>
> Farmingdale, NY 11735-9008

Enclose a note that says something like this:

I am concerned about the amount of resources being wasted on unwanted mail. Please remove my name from the mailing lists being sold to the major mailing list companies. Thank you.

Be sure to include your name and address. Also take a look at how mail is addressed to you, and include any ways your name is spelled and any address variations.

Oh, Those Bills!

When bills arrive, write the amount and due date on the outside of the envelopes, then put them in order so the ones due first are on top. You can write the due date and amount in the spot where the stamp goes so that when you put the stamp on, it will be covered.

Smart Solution

Always use the envelopes provided in your bills. They're specially coded to speed delivery to the correct department.

It's important to keep all your bills in one place so that when you sit down to pay them, you won't miss any. Keep your unpaid bills together in a special drawer, file box, napkin holder, or whatever you like. Don't mix together paid and unpaid bills; it'll just add to your confusion!

Quarterly or yearly bills that arrive early should be filed with the unpaid bills. Keep them in the stack until they are due. Write the due date and amount on them just like any other bill, and file them at the back.

Organize your paid bills in a file. A folding file with a pocket for each month works great, and you can use the same file each year—just clean it out in January and start over. When bills are organized, it's easy to look back and compare them month to month. If anything looks out of line, call the customer service department and see if an error has been made. It can happen, you know.

When a magazine subscription renewal form comes in the mail, either fill it out right away or file it with your regular bills. Make a note of the ones you recently paid—if the company sends another notice shortly after payment, you can assume that the two crossed in the mail.

Letters and Stamps

While a postage stamp truly is a bargain (you can mail a letter a thousand miles or more for just 32¢), it's a waste to put on more postage than required. Weigh an envelope instead of just guessing. Many people will put two first-class stamps (64¢) on a letter that feels heavy. Even if the letter is over the weight for one first class stamp, the next ounce is cheaper by 9¢. If you mail very many letters, overpaying adds up quickly.

Post offices have weight scales in the lobby that you can use even if you can't get to the post office during regular business hours. When you buy your first class stamps, buy some 23¢ stamps to keep for the additional ounces.

If you do a lot of mailing, buy yourself a postage scale. Over time, it will probably pay for itself in the postage you save and the trips to the post office you don't have to make.

Watch Out!

When you clean out your personal records and files, be careful what financial papers you discard. Thieves known as "dumpster divers" dig through garbage cans looking for financial information such as old checks, credit card receipts, bills, bank statements, pre-approved charge card applications, or anything else they can use for fraudulent transactions. Fraudulent transactions end up costing everyone more in higher fees and interest rates.

Protect yourself by tearing all sensitive documents into tiny pieces, and scatter the pieces among several trash cans; if you have a fireplace, burn any unwanted papers containing financial information.

Don't Overpay the Post Office

	Two First Class Stamps	Proper Postage	Money Savings	Percent Savings
2-ounce letter	64¢	55¢	9¢	14%

Return address. Buying a rubber address stamp and an ink pad is cheaper in the long run than buying address labels—unless, of course, you get free mailing labels sent to you by charities wanting a contribution. Keep in mind that if a company mails any sort of "gift" (such as mailing labels, greeting cards, or gift tags) the "gift" is yours to keep. You are not obligated or expected to return the item if you do not make a contribution.

Postcards. For a short note, send a postcard instead of a letter. You'll save 12¢ per card on postage. You can also get free postcards from the U. S. Postal Service—that's right, postcards with 20¢ postage on them cost a mere 20¢ each, so that means when you buy the postage, the card is free!

Greeting cards. Always keep a few birthday cards and all-occasion note cards on hand. Send out your special greetings when you pay the bills instead of making this a separate job.

Sticky stamps. Most stamps are now the self-stick type, but when the lick type get stuck together, a few minutes in the freezer may be enough to loosen them apart. If this doesn't work, take them to the post office for replacement.

Sticky envelopes. Don't throw away envelopes that stick together; instead put them (the ones without metal clasps, that is) in the microwave on high for about a minute, and they will open right up.

The Least You Need to Know

➤ Home offices can go almost anywhere: under the stairs, in a corner—even in a cabinet that unfolds into a desk with shelves.

➤ If money is tight, be creative: Use an old door for a desk top or computer stand, use pieces of wood and bricks for shelves, and buy recycled furniture that can be upgraded later. But don't scrimp on the chair; a good one will last long and treat your back right.

➤ Office supply superstores can save you big bucks—and many deliver for free if you spend $50 or more.

➤ Work on the mail when it comes in to keep it from mounting up; try to handle each piece of mail just one time.

➤ If in doubt, weigh those packages and letters rather than just slapping on an extra 32¢ stamp; each additional ounce costs only 23¢.

Part 5
Eating Smart and Cheap

Shopping, cooking, and eating take a big bite out of our time and money budgets. But you can save time, cut costs, and even enjoy preparing the meals for your family, etc.

You'll find out where to food shop to get the most for your money, how to use coupons and rainchecks, and even ways to stop impulse spending. Looking for creative ways to use leftovers? You'll find hints, tips, and recipes for them that taste so good, your family won't even realize they're eating leftovers! There's good advice for storing all kinds of food, as well as ideas for microwaving, grilling and other cooking techniques. And you'll find homemade baking mixes that are easy and very tasty.

Chapter 17

Food, Glorious Food

> ### In This Chapter
>
> ➤ Tips for buying fruit at its peak of freshness
>
> ➤ Secrets for longer life for vegetables, milk and cheese, and breads
>
> ➤ Some of the best and easiest desserts you can make
>
> ➤ Leftovers for great (second) eating

It's Fruity

Fruit tastes good—and it's so good for you. Use these tips to make the most of it.

Bananas. If bananas are starting to turn brown before you can eat them, put them in the refrigerator. The cold air will turn the skin brown—but the fruit inside will stay fresh for several more days.

Grapes. Buy grapes when they're on sale, and freeze them. Frozen grapes are a fun and nutritious snack that both children and adults will enjoy. Add frozen grapes to any type of punch to keep the drink cold without diluting it.

Citrus fruit. When lemons or limes are bargain-priced, buy extras, squeeze them, and freeze the juice in ice cube trays. Then when citrus is out of season and the price is very high, you can use the juice cubes instead. You will be surprised at how fresh the frozen juice tastes.

Bet You Didn't Know

To keep fresh fruit from discoloring, keep a spray bottle filled with half water and half lemon juice in the refrigerator. Whenever you cut up fresh fruit, spray it with the lemon water. This is quicker and easier than dipping the fruit into lemon juice, and you'll use less lemon juice with better results. The lemon spray will keep for about one month in the refrigerator.

Tightwad Tip

Don't throw away citrus rinds! Simmer them in water on your stove for an inexpensive air freshener. The clean, fresh aroma will make your house smell wonderful.

More juice. Submerging a lemon, lime, or other citrus fruit in hot water for 15 minutes before squeezing will yield almost twice the amount of juice. Or, you can place the citrus in the microwave for about 15 to 20 seconds before squeezing to get more juice.

Citrus zest. Freeze a few citrus rinds whole. Then when a recipe calls for a zest of lemon or orange, you can use the frozen skin. Use a potato peeler to peel off small pieces of the rind. The frozen rind will be much easier to make into zest than a fresh one.

How to Buy Fruit at the Peak of Freshness

Apples. Look for apples with bright colors and no bruises. Apples should be firm or even hard to the touch.

Apricots. Look for a soft yellowish to orange color and a firm texture. Refrigerate when you get them home; for best results, use them within five days.

Bananas. For bananas that you plan to eat or use in a fruit salad, choose ones that are slightly underripe, and let them finish ripening at home. These will be bright yellow, will have no bruises, and will be slightly green at the stem end. If you are going to use the bananas one at a time, cut off the end of the connecting stem and separate them gently.

If you plan to make banana pudding, a cake, or muffins, look for very ripe bananas with brown spots on them. You may be able to find them marked down because they're past the prime for eating whole.

Berries. Look for bright color when picking berries. Ripe berries should be stored in the refrigerator, covered and unwashed. For best flavor and texture, use berries as soon as possible.

Cherries. You'll find that the sweetest cherries are dark in color. Refrigerate and eat them as soon as possible.

Grapes. Pick grapes that are plump and that have flexible stems. Avoid those with dried-out stems. Refrigerate and eat as soon as possible.

Grapefruit. Both white and pink grapefruit are the sweetest when their skins turn a greenish-yellow. Grapefruits should feel slightly heavy (packed with juice) when picked up. When they're past their peak and drier inside, they'll be lighter in weight. Refrigerate and use all fruit within two to three weeks.

Melons. The sweetest melons will be the most fragrant. Let your nose be your guide.

Cantaloupes. Ripe cantaloupes are yellowish, with thick, course veining. Avoid ones that are too soft (mushy) when you pick them up.

Honeydew melons. The best honeydew melons have creamy or yellowish-white smooth skin. If a honeydew melon is very white or greenish-white and has a very hard feel, it probably will never ripen properly.

Watermelon. Pick a watermelon that is firm and smooth. The underside should be yellowish or creamy white. To test for ripeness before cutting, gently tap on it. You should hear a deep, hollow thump.

Nectarines. When nectarines are at their best, they will be orange, yellow, and red. Store at room temperature until they soften and become ripe. When ripe, refrigerate and eat as soon as possible.

Oranges. Choose oranges that are firm and heavy with juice. Navel oranges are delicious for eating, while Valencias, Temples, and Kings make the best orange juice. Refrigerate and eat within about two weeks.

Peaches. Peaches will get softer but not any sweeter after they are picked. Choose a firm peach with bright color for the best flavor. Refrigerate and use within five days.

Pineapples. A ripe pineapple has a wonderful smell, a small compact crown, and richly colored leaves. Pineapples store best at room temperature (70°F is ideal). Do not store in direct sunlight.

Plums. Choose plums that are soft but not mushy, shriveled, nor brown. Refrigerate and use within five days.

Summer Ice

This wonderful warm weather recipe makes an inexpensive substitute for ice cream. Make it with fruit that's in season, or look for ripe fruit that has been marked down for quick sale. Some of my favorite fruits for this dish are peaches, cherries, and all kinds of berries. I have even made summer ice out of fresh orange sections.

> 2 pints strawberry halves (or other fruit in season)
>
> 1 package (10.5 ounces) miniature marshmallows
>
> 1 tablespoon milk
>
> 1 tablespoon lemon juice

Blend the strawberries until smooth in a food processor or blender. Melt the marshmallows and milk in the microwave or on the stove. You don't have to melt the marshmallows completely; some small pieces of marshmallows make the ice look and taste good.

Gradually add the strawberries to the marshmallow creme. Mix with an electric mixer until well blended. Add lemon juice.

Freeze two hours or until almost firm. Break up the mixture with a spoon. Beat the ice until smooth with an electric mixer. Refreeze until firm.

Smart Solutions

Don't throw away limp carrots or celery. Soak them in ice cold water for 30 minutes, and they'll be crispy again. (If you trim the ends first, they'll soak up more water and crisp better.)

Tightwad Tip

Don't toss leftover mashed potatoes. Freeze dollops of them on a cookie sheet and when they're frozen, lift them off the sheet and store them in freezer bags. While they're not good to eat as is, they're fine for making potato cakes or to use for thickening soups, stews, gravies, and sauces.

Veggie Good Ideas

Make the most of vegetables with these creative tips.

Steaming. You don't need a special steamer for vegetables—just steam them the easy way. Simply place the vegetables in a metal colander, then place the colander over (not in) a saucepan of boiling water. Cover and steam on medium heat.

No-fat mashed potatoes. Save some of the cooking water and add it back to the potatoes as you mash them instead of using milk and butter.

Keep those peels. Unpeeled potatoes make healthy, delicious mashed potatoes. Just wash and trim thoroughly, boil, and mash as usual.

Speedy oven-baked potatoes. To speed baking time, cut baking potatoes in half and place them cut side down on a baking sheet. Bake as usual in the oven, but for about half the normal time. For added flavor, place a pat of butter or margarine under each half.

Mushrooms. Store fresh mushrooms in a brown paper bag in the refrigerator. If you buy mushrooms in a plastic bag or package, take them out of the wrapping and place them into a paper bag to make them last longer. The paper bag absorbs some of the moisture and prevents spoilage.

Onions. To make onions last longer, don'tstore them near potatoes. Moisture from the potatoes will cause onions to sprout, and onions will give your potatoes a strange flavor. One of the best ways to store onions is to hang them in old pantyhose. Drop the onions in the hose, and tie a knot between each one. Hang in a cool, dry, dark place, and snip off onions one at a time as you need them.

Fried Green Tomatoes

Slice the green tomatoes and dip them in milk. Then dip them in flour seasoned with salt and pepper. Let the tomatoes sit for five minutes, and dip them again in the flour mixture. Fry over medium heat until brown, about two minutes, on each side. Serve hot from the grill. Not only are these different and delicious, but this is a great way to use up all those extra tomatoes!

Smart Solution

Get together with friends and neighbors and buy fruit and veg-etables from a wholesaler (see the *Yellow Pages* for one in your area) by the case. It's much fresher and lower in cost than what you can get at the grocery store.

Frozen Assets

Frozen foods are so handy to have on hand. Here are some ideas to get the most from your frozen foods.

Vegetables. When you buy frozen vegetables, you should be able to feel the indi-vidual vegetables inside the bag. Don't buy a bag if you can't; the package probably has thawed at some point before being re-frozen. The re-frozen vegetables can have an off taste, and they won't be as nutritious.

Ice cream. To make ice cream last longer, place a piece of waxed paper, plastic wrap, or aluminum foil on top of the ice cream after the container is opened. This will prevent ice crystals from forming on the ice cream and will keep it fresh-tasting longer.

Popping corn. To make inexpensive popping corn pop bigger and stay fresh longer, store it in the freezer. You don't even have to thaw the popcorn before popping it.

The Wet Stuff: Beverages

Gourmet coffee. Make your own inexpensive flavored coffee by adding 1 chocolate covered mint, 1 tablespoon cocoa, 1 cinnamon stick, 1 teaspoon chopped almonds, or 1/2 teaspoon vanilla flavoring to 1 cup of coffee. Be creative and make up your own flavored gourmet coffee.

Frothy frozen juice. To make low-cost frozen juice more appealing, mix it in the blender. This mixing method turns it into a light and frothy drink.

Flavored fizzy water. Instead of buying expensive flavored sparkling water, you can make your own. Buy inexpensive store brand or generic club soda or seltzer, and add a small amount of juice or a few drops of fruit extract (such as strawberry or lemon) to make a low-calorie, inexpensive drink.

Tightwad Tip

After opening a can of fruit (pears, pineapples, peaches, or cherries), don't pour the juice it's packed in down the drain. Instead, add the juice to whatever store-bought juice you have in the refrigerator.

Bet You Didn't Know

Not all bottled water is spring water. If the label on the bottle doesn't specify that it comes from a natural spring, it is usually tap or well water that has been chemically treated and purified. In some supermarkets, you can buy purified drinking water from a machine for about 25 cents per gallon when you fill your own containers.

Smart Solution

Instead of buying buttermilk for recipes, use regular milk and add a tablespoon of vinegar to each cup of milk. Let the mixture stand for half an hour before using.

Flavorful cubes. Freeze leftover tea or any other drink your family likes in ice cube trays. Then use these cubes for a drink that does not get diluted as the ice melts.

Flavored teas. To make your own flavored teas, make a pitcher of iced tea and add about half a cup of lemonade, punch, or orange juice to it.

Wine substitutes. When a recipe calls for wine, you can substitute cranberry or red grape juice. For white wine, substitute apple or white grape juice.

Stretch that coffee. If you prefer an expensive brand of coffee, try mixing your favorite brand half-and-half with a lower-priced brand. The rich flavors of your favorite brand will still come through, and you probably won't be able to taste the difference.

Keeping coffee hot. After coffee has perked, pour the hot coffee into a thermos bottle or an insulated coffee carafe (which has been warmed with hot water). The coffee will stay hot without getting bitter.

Got Milk?

Safe longer. You can extend the shelf life of milk for about 10 days past the expiration date. Before the expiration date (and if it's not spoiled), microwave milk (in the carton or in a microwave container) on high until the temperature reaches 160°F. (One cup of milk takes about $1^1/_2$ minutes.) Don't let the milk boil. Refrigerate immediately.

To make milk last several days past the expiration date, add a pinch of salt. The salt will not affect the taste of the milk, but it will keep it from spoiling as fast.

Instead of pouring away milk that is about to go out of date, pour it into an ice cube tray and freeze it. Then use the milk cubes to cool down hot coffee or hot cocoa, or thaw the cubes and use them for baking, cooking, or making pancakes.

Soon sour. When milk just starts to go sour, there's no need to throw it out. Don't drink it, but it's safe to use in cooking. Use it right away in cake batter, cookie dough, or pancake batter. You can also use it in recipes calling for buttermilk.

Chocolate milk. When you think the chocolate syrup container is completely empty, fill the container with milk and shake. You'll get every last bit of syrup out of the container. You can drink the chocolate milk cold or heat it for hot chocolate.

Cheese, Please

Cheese is so versatile. Here are some ways to make the most of your favorite cheeses.

Longer-life. To prevent cheese from drying out, wrap it in a moist paper towel with a few drops of cider vinegar. Store the cheese in a sealed plastic bag or airtight container. You may need to add water or a drop or two of cider after a use or two.

Too hard? Instead of throwing away cheese that's hardened, grate it and use it in omelets, soups, or casseroles; on baked potatoes or other vegetables; or for grilled cheese sandwiches. Or mix it with stale bread crumbs for a delicious topping for vegetables and casseroles.

Topsy-turvy. Partially used cottage cheese will stay fresher longer if you store the carton upside down in the refrigerator. Just make sure the lid is on tight!

Here's The Beef

Beef is many people's favorite meat. Here are some ideas and hints to make your beef taste great.

More tender. Meat fibers are broken down and tenderized by acid, such as that in vinegar and citrus juice. So to tenderize meats, soak them in a cup of vinegar or lemon or orange juice overnight. If desired, rinse off the vinegar or juice before cooking.

It's in the bag. Marinate meats in a plastic bag instead of a pan. By placing the meat in a bag, you will be able to use about half the usual amount of marinade with the same results. Turn the bag several times during the marinating process.

Plan to save. Plan your weekly menus around the meats that are advertised on sale by your local grocery stores. Next week something else will be on sale, so your menus will vary from week to week.

Grocery Items

Before you shop, consider these suggestions to save some money.

Homemade syrup. Make your own inexpensive flavored pancake and waffle syrup: Stir 1 cup of corn syrup and 4 tablespoons of your favorite jam or preserves in a saucepan over low heat. Store any leftover syrup in the refrigerator.

Oatmeal. Don't buy expensive instant oatmeal packages. Regular oatmeal cooks just as fast in the microwave and costs less than one fourth the price. Add your own spices and fruits to make flavored oatmeal.

Tightwad Tip

Bread crumbs can be used in casserole and meatloaf recipes to substitute for oatmeal. This is a great way to use up crusts; grind them in your food processor.

Keep it Fresh: Bread Tips

Bread makes the meal. Here are some hints to help you make the most of your bread.

Thrift bakeries. Buy bread and other bakery items from bakery thrift stores that sell day-old bread. You'll save at least half the price—and probably more.

Making bread fresher. Place a rib of celery in the bag with day-old bread that has dried out to make it fresh again, since the celery will add moisture to it. Leave the celery in the bag to keep the bread fresh longer.

The Sweet Stuff

Don't be tempted to buy individual sugar packets for convenience. One packet of sugar costs about 500 times as much as the same amount of sugar bought in a 5-pound bag.

To moisten a dry cake, poke holes in the top with a toothpick and pour a small amount of fruit juice in the holes. Start with 1 tablespoon and continue to add juice until the cake is moist.

If honey has crystallized, set the bottle in a pan of hot water. Heat on the stove over low heat until crystals disappear. You can use the same process for jelly and syrups. Watch the water closely and don't let it get too hot; very hot or boiling water could crack glass jars or melt plastic ones, so be careful. You can also melt the crystals in a microwave; see Chapter 19, "Cooking, Baking, and Grilling."

Pudding cups. Pre-made pudding in individual containers is very expensive per serving. To save money, make your own (see following recipe) and pour it into small plastic containers. Use custard cups or small margarine or cream cheese containers for individual servings. Cover with plastic wrap or the container lids so that the pudding top doesn't develop a crust. Somehow, pudding always seems to taste better in individual servings.

Homemade Pudding Mix

Pudding mix is easy to make and is about 50 percent cheaper than the lowest-priced boxed kind in the stores.

$3^1/_3$ cups dry milk

$2^1/_3$ teaspoon salt

1 tablespoon corn starch

$1^2/_3$ cups sugar

246

Combine dry ingredients and store in a tightly closed container. This recipe makes four batches of pudding.

Vanilla pudding. Combine $1^1/4$ cups of dry pudding mix with $1^3/4$ cups water. Cook over low heat to a boil, stirring constantly. Boil gently for two minutes. Add 1 teaspoon vanilla. Chill until set.

Chocolate pudding. Add 4 tablespoons cocoa to dry pudding mix. Then measure $1^1/4$ cups of this chocolate mix and combine with $1^3/4$ cups water. Cook over low heat to a boil, stirring constantly. Boil gently for two minutes. Chill until set.

Homemade Desserts

Nothing tastes better than a homemade dessert. Here are a few sweet recipes that are quick and easy to make, that taste great, and that are low in cost.

Wacky Chocolate Cake

This cake is so moist it doesn't need to be iced; just sprinkle some powdered sugar on top. It's a chocolate lover's delight.

> 1 teaspoon baking soda
>
> 1 cup sugar
>
> 2 tablespoons cocoa
>
> $1^1/2$ cups flour
>
> $1/4$ teaspoon salt
>
> 1 tablespoon vinegar
>
> 1 tablespoon vanilla
>
> 1 tablespoon vegetable oil
>
> 1 cup water

Preheat oven to 350°F.

Mix baking soda, sugar, cocoa, flour, and salt together; sift into an 8-by-8-inch cake pan. Make three holes in the mixture and pour the vinegar into one, vanilla into another, and oil into the last. Pour the water over the whole mixture, then mix well until there are no lumps, about three minutes.

Bake at 350°F for 30 to 35 minutes, or until toothpick comes out clean.

No-Pecan Pecan Pie

This tastes like pecan pie without the cost (or calories) of pecans.

1 stick butter ($1/2$ cup), melted

$3/4$ cup sugar

2 eggs

$3/4$ cup dark corn syrup

1 teaspoon vanilla

1 cup uncooked oats

Unbaked 9-inch pie shell (fresh or frozen)

Mix together butter, sugar, eggs, syrup, and vanilla. Add oats and blend. Pour into the uncooked crust and bake for 50 to 55 minutes, or until knife inserted near center comes out clean.

Vinegar Pie

Vinegar pie may not sound too good, but wait until you sink your teeth into this! It tastes very much like chess pie.

$1/2$ cup margarine, melted and cooled

3 eggs, slightly beaten

$1/4$ cup vinegar

$1^1/4$ cup sugar

2 tablespoons flour

1 tablespoon vanilla

1 9-inch pie shell (fresh or frozen)

Preheat oven to 325°F.

Mix the margarine, eggs, vinegar, sugar, flour, and vanilla in a bowl until well blended. Pour into the uncooked pie shell and bake for about one hour at 325°F.

Check it a few minutes before the hour is up so that the top doesn't burn; the pie should be light brown when done. Allow the pie to cool before cutting it into slices. It's also delicious cold or warmed up in the microwave.

The Art of Leftovers

Sometimes the best meal is one made out of leftovers. Many dishes (soups, stews, and casseroles, for starters) actually taste better after they've sat in their own juices for a day or two). And all you have to do is heat 'em up!

Keeping Track of Them

Tape a piece of paper on the refrigerator to keep a list of leftovers inside. This way you will remember to eat what is inside before it turns into a science experiment!

If you don't plan to eat the leftovers right away, put them into the freezer. Write the contents and date on a piece of masking tape, and attach it to the freezer container so you'll know what's inside and how old it is. (Don't use freezer tape for marking because it's hard to remove from containers; it's designed to seal freezer paper.)

Homemade TV Dinners

Use leftovers to make TV dinners. Put the leftovers on a microwavable plate (wash and save the ones that microwave frozen foods come in). Then freeze. When you don't feel like cooking, you've got a supply of ready-made dinners right in your freezer to heat up and serve.

This method is handy if you have older children working after school. When they get home from work, they can pull out a TV dinner and have a quick, hot meal that is inexpensive for both the parent and the teenager. Homemade TV dinners sure beat paying $2 to $5 for a prepackaged frozen meal (that's probably not as good as yours).

Keep a large container in the freezer, and add leftover meat, gravy, rice, and any vegetables. When you have enough meats and vegetables, add them to broth or tomato juice to heat up for a delicious soup that is a little different each time (see recipe below).

Soup Supreme (a.k.a Leftover Soup or Garbage Soup)

When serving this yummy soup to your family, it's best to call it Soup Supreme instead of leftover soup or garbage soup. (It just seems to go down better.)

> One large container or freezer bag of frozen leftover vegetables and meats
>
> 3 to 4 cups broth or tomato juice
>
> Water
>
> Salt and pepper
>
> Any fresh vegetables in the refrigerator that may be a little past their prime

Thaw the frozen container of vegetables and meats, and pour the mixture into a large pot. Add tomato juice or broth a cup at a time until it's as thick as you like it. (Add water if the broth is too thick.) Cut up fresh vegetables, trimming off any brown spots. Add to the pot. Add salt and pepper to taste. Heat soup over medium heat until fresh vegetables are tender (approximately 20 to 30 minutes).

Tightwad Tip

Save the cookie crumbs left at the bottom of the cookie jar and the cereal crumbs left in the bottom of the box. They make one of the best (and certainly the cheapest) toppings for ice cream.

A Leftovers Buffet

Plan a "leftover night" when you notice that the freezer is getting full of them. Heat up all the different leftovers and serve them buffet-style. Each family member can pick and choose which ones they like best. And then the family dog or the compost heap gets the leftovers!

The Least You Need to Know

➤ Stay flexible, and plan your fruit buying around what's in season. The fruit will usually taste fresher and cost less.

➤ How you store veggies makes a difference in how long they keep.

➤ Leftovers make great TV dinners, soups, and even dinner buffets.

➤ Vinegar prevents cut fruit from browning, tenderizes tough cuts of meat, keeps cheese from getting moldy, turns milk into buttermilk, and is the secret ingredient in a great chocolate cake and a surprisingly good pie.

Chapter 18

Food-Shopping Strategies

In This Chapter

➤ Types of food stores: What's the difference?

➤ Stopping impulse spending

➤ How to lose weight without buying expensive diet food

➤ Getting the most for your money when shopping for food

➤ Strategies for using coupons and rain checks

Shopping is very time consuming, and, of course, you've got to spend all that money! You'll find hints and ideas in this chapter that will save you time and money and may even make shopping fun for you.

Where to Shop

Food stores come in all shapes and sizes—convenience stores, box stores, super stores, discount stores, thrift stores, and warehouse stores. You can find bargains at each if you know what to look for.

Supermarkets

We all know what these are: full-service food stores. They're usually owned by a large corporation and buy in such high volume that they get significant price breaks that can be passed on to shoppers. Supermarkets will also carry a "house brand" of merchandise that usually is priced lower than the national brands. Most supermarkets have a weekly flyer of advertised specials; each week one or more items on the flyer will be priced low enough to entice folks to do their weekly shopping there.

Super Stores

Super stores are like supermarkets, only much bigger with many more departments. Some of the newest have a full-service discount drugstore (such as WalMart) and a full-sized food store under one roof. They also may have a branch bank, a fast food restaurant, and many other special services inside—it's almost like a mini mall.

Such super stores can be hard to shop because there's so much territory to cover. You'll find low prices on most food items and many drugstore items. But you'll find higher prices in special departments such as a gourmet shop or an imported wine and cheese shop.

The Price of Convenience

Convenience stores (such as 7-11 and Circle K) are not for the frugal-minded; for the most part, their prices are extremely high. What you're paying for is the convenience of a small neighborhood store that stocks all kinds of things that you just ran out of. And you're paying for being able to shop there most any time, day or night (many are open 24 hours a day). Some offer low prices on gasoline to get you inside the store, hoping you'll pick up a few impulse items while inside. Other convenience stores offer one or two low prices per week on items such as ice cream, soft drinks, or milk.

Box Stores

Box stores are so called because you shop, quite literally, out of boxes. Talk about a "no-frills" shopping experience! The merchandise is usually very limited. You'll have few choices when it comes to brands and sizes, but the prices are low—perhaps the lowest you'll find anywhere. If you don't mind bagging your own groceries, and if your family is not too picky about brands, you can save quite a bit here. Most box stores will accept personal checks and coupons.

Thrifty Is Nifty

Thrift stores are frequently called day-old bread stores. You can save about 40 percent on whatever they've got on the shelves, which is usually whatever was on the other food store shelves yesterday and was pulled on their expiration dates. The merchandise is usually limited to bakery items such as bread, buns, sweet rolls, cookies, cakes, muffins, and doughnuts. If you have a large family (or a teenager or two) that quickly eats everything you buy, a thrift store can really stretch your food budget. Most thrift stores will accept personal checks, but they *will not* accept coupons. They expect you to use the coupons for full-priced merchandise.

The $100 Club: Membership Warehouse

Why do I call them $100 clubs? Because it's hard to get out without spending $100. One of the great dangers of warehouse shopping is that you assume everything is cheaper and go on a shopping spree!

If you have a small family, warehouse shopping probably will not save you money. But if you can use larger quantities and have room to store the extra goodies, you can find *some* bargains at the warehouse store.

Compare Prices

Don't assume you're buying the lowest prices just because you're buying it from a warehouse store. Always compare prices to your regular food store. Many times you can find the same items at the food store for the same price—and you don't have to buy three boxes to get that low price. Beware of the tendency to overbuy at warehouse stores. Go in with a list, and stick to it.

Recently I compared food prices at our local membership warehouse to those at the supermarket. I was surprised to how many items were very close—or even cheaper—at the supermarket! Many basics such as peanut butter, jelly, spaghetti sauce, pasta, and potatoes were priced within cents of each other. Meats were as much as 69 cents per pound less at our local food store!

Bet You Didn't Know

Before you spend the money to buy a membership to a warehouse store, ask for a one-day free pass to shop and compare prices.

Tightwad Tip

You may be eligible for a free membership through your work, a credit union, or some other organization.

Stock Up on Staples

The warehouse did have the local supermarket beat on sugar, flour, milk, eggs, coffee, coffee filters, and hot dogs. But you must be able to use the large quantities. You can also save on condiments such as ketchup and mustard, but once you open the large cans you need storage containers and the space in your refrigerator to keep them.

Another big warehouse saving: individual boxes of juice for the kids. It's cheaper, but still it's no bargain per ounce when you compare it to larger-sized cans, bottles, or cartons.

Watch Out!

If you shop with coupons, keep in mind that most discount membership warehouses *do not* accept any coupons.

Bet You Didn't Know

Don't pay extra for fancy packaging. You may actually be paying more for the package than the contents! Individual serving packages of juices or puddings cost double or triple the price per ounce because of the extra packaging. Ditto little individual boxes of cereal and juices. In the fresh produce department, look for loose vegetables instead of those are dressed up in plastic trays and shrink-wrap.

Let's Go Shopping

No matter where you shop, here are some things to look for and think about.

Do it alone. Leave your children at home, and don't take a spouse with you when food shopping unless he or she is a thrifty shopper. Children and spouses often encourage extra spending.

Once is enough. Limit your food-shopping trips to once a week, or even once every two weeks. How many times have you just run into the store for milk and spent $50 or more? If you must go to the store for just an item or two, resist the temptation to walk all the aisles to see if you can find something else you might need.

Starvin' Marvin. Grab a snack before you food shop. You've probably heard it before, but it's worth saying again: Don't food shop when you are hungry. You'll spend more money on junk food than you normally would. Everything looks good, especially the high-priced snacks and convenience foods that are ready to eat. Eat an apple, a peanut butter sandwich, or some other healthy snack before shopping if you are hungry.

Kick the habit. Avoid habit buying. Most people (including you?) buy practically the same items each week. Always look for new or different alternatives that may be cheaper and better. Even products that were once the least expensive may be high-priced when compared to other brands and sizes.

Stop Impulse Buying!

It pays to plan ahead when food shopping. Without a list and at least a general menu plan, you'll spend more money at the store than you bargained on.

➤ Keep a list on the refrigerator, and write down items as they are used up. Train your family members to add to the list.

➤ Take an inventory before going to the store. Check the pantry, refrigerator, and freezer for staples. Add any items you're low on to your list.

➤ Make a master list of items that you regularly buy. Then you can quickly go down the list, check off the needed items, and add any other items to the bottom of the list.

➤ Make a weekly menu and review recipes to include any needed items on the list.

➤ Review supermarket advertised specials. Plan your menus around the low prices to save.

The high and low. Look up and down, high and low. The most expensive (and profitable) items are placed at eye level. The generic items, store brands, or other good deals are frequently placed high on the upper shelves or on those at the bottom.

Non foods, not a bargain. Basically all non-food items such as kitchen gadgets, health and beauty aids, cleaning supplies, seasonal items, and other miscellaneous items are very high-priced at the food store. These are considered convenience items, so the store will increase the price. These items should always be purchased at a discount store. Don't give in to temptation, even if the item seems reasonably priced. Unless you know *for sure* the item is on sale at a really low price, skip these aisles and make a trip to a discount store.

Sweet deal. Stay away from anything pre-sweetened. If you are going to buy sugar any-way, why pay four or five times more for the sugar? You can also better control the amount of sugar added. Some examples of pre-sweetened items are instant tea, cereal, and packaged soft drinks.

Watch Out!

Check containers and packages carefully. Manufacturers change products all the time. A can of vegetables may contain 16 ounces one week and 15 ounces the next. The price will be the same (or maybe even more), but it usually looks exactly like the old product so most people won't even notice that they are getting less for their money. Always compare prices per ounce!

Watch Out!

Beware of "sale" items on the ends of aisles. Many times these items are not on sale at all. Manufacturers have found that a product can increase by as much as 600 percent when it's placed at the end of an aisle. Know your prices and be sure it is a "bargain buster deal" before you stock up.

Is bigger better? Bigger is not always better—or cheaper. Large "economy" sizes many times are the best buy, but don't assume they are always the cheapest per ounce or serving. Sometimes buying two small boxes or bags is cheaper than one large one!

Let's look at some examples. Take, for instance, coffee cans. Two cans may be the exact size, but when you look closer, one contains 16 ounces and the other only 10. Even the bricks of coffee vary greatly in size, but they're shaped to look as big as the larger bricks. Always look for the price per ounce on the shelf; if your food store does not list the cost per ounce, take a calculator with you when shopping so you can figure the cost per ounce or serving.

Store Brands and Generics

Don't be afraid to try store brands or generics; most are high-quality products. Start with the least expensive product (per ounce) and work your way up if the quality doesn't meet your standards. The store brands—and even some generic brands—are often the same products, supplied by the same companies that make the national brands, at much lower prices. So what's the difference? Store brands don't have advertising costs that jack the prices way up!

You can't lose on these generic products—they have the same chemical makeup no matter whose label is on them. Why pay extra only for a name brand?

➤ Baking soda

➤ Cooking oils (except olive oil)

➤ Cornstarch

➤ Extracts (flavorings)

➤ Herbs

➤ Honey

➤ Lemon or lime juice

➤ Molasses

➤ Orange juice

➤ Salt

➤ Spices

➤ Sugar

➤ Unbleached flour

➤ Vinegar

It Pays to Weigh

In the produce department, look for the best buys on in-season produce; it should be at the peak of freshness and at the lowest price of the year. Always weigh any produce bought by the piece or sold in a 5-, 10-, or 20-pound bag. You will be surprised at the weight difference in a bag of fruit or vegetables. Look for a bag that seems to be a little fuller than the others. Also, weigh produce sold by the piece (lettuce, broccoli, cauliflower, and so on) to get the most for your money.

Buys From the Butcher

In the meat department, don't be fooled by large packages. Sometimes large "family packs" are the same price per pound as the smaller packages. And don't be afraid to ring for the butcher. Most meat departments will repackage items for you at no additional cost. Don't buy a package of four pieces of meat when you know your family will just eat three.

The service you get from butchers will vary from store to store. Check out local meat markets; you may be able to buy better quality meats, packaged to order at a cheaper price per pound, from a local meat market. Look for a busy market that is able to offer better prices and fresher meat due to the high volume of customers.

Smart Solution

Make it a habit to keep your pantry and freezer filled with basic items for a quick, easy meal so that you don't have to run out to a fast-food place because you don't have the things you need to cook up a quick meal at home. Even going out once in a while for an unplanned fast food dinner can make your food budget see red.

Clipping Coupons: It Makes Cents

Keeping track of coupons may seem like a bother at times, but it can really save you money if you use them wisely. Think of your coupon savings as a hobby, and make a game out of it. Whether you are a serious "coupon keeper" or just an occasional clipper, the savings can add up: $5 saved per week is $260 saved in a year.

Tightwad Tip

Don't buy expensive freezer tape; use ordinary masking tape. It works just as well as the freezer tape at a fraction of the price, and you can easily write on it with a permanent marker.

Top 10 Ways to Get Coupons

1. Sunday newspaper inserts.
2. The food section of the newspaper.
3. Magazines.
4. Store circulars and shopper newspapers delivered to your door.
5. Food store bulletin boards. Some stores have an exchange table where you can pick out the coupons you want and leave the rest.
6. In-store flyers. Always ask for a store advertising flyer at the service desk if you don't get one in the mail. Sometimes you can get super bargains, such as a dozen eggs for 20¢ with a $10 purchase.

Bet You Didn't Know

Send away for free recipe booklets or calendar offers. Even if you have to send in a few proofs of purchase, it's worth the effort because with most offers you'll get several dollars' worth of free coupons.

Smart Solution

Always take your coupon file with you when shopping. You may run across a terrific unadvertised special, and you can go ahead and buy now when the price is low. You can buy inexpensive coupon organizers at the grocery store or discount store, or if you have more coupons than will fit in a small organizer, you can use a recipe box, a small shoebox, or a plastic storage container. Make your own dividers out of cardboard to keep the coupons organized.

7. Contact the manufacturer. A little-known way to get coupons is by calling the toll-free numbers listed on the back of products, or by writing to the manufacturers of your favorite items. Most companies are happy to send coupons and other promotional items, such as recipes, rebate offers, and maybe even a free sample product.

8. Food packages. Look carefully on food packaging (boxes, bags, and so on) inside and out for coupons that may be printed on them before you recycle or discard them.

9. Junk mail. Don't throw anything away before checking for coupons.

10. A coupon network. Trade coupons with friends, neighbors, relatives, or coworkers.

Double dilemma. In some areas of the country, not as many stores offer double coupon discounts as they did a few years ago. If you like to use coupons, call all the local food stores and discount drug stores and ask if and when they offer double coupons. Some stores will offer them on a slow day of the week (such as Tuesday or Wednesday); others on the first Tuesday of the month. If you take a few minutes to find out when and where the double coupons days are, you can really increase your savings.

Stock up on supplies. Use coupons to stock up on items such as toilet paper, shampoo, detergent, and any other non-perishable items when the store has a special price and you have several coupons. If you can get them for practically nothing, it's worth stocking up and storing them for a while—you know that your family will eventually use them.

Economy Size May Not Be the Cheapest

You may think buying in large quantities is the cheapest way to go, but when shopping with coupons, many times the smallest size is the cheapest per ounce. Getting several small bottles for just a few pennies—or even for free—is better than using the same coupons to buy several large bottles that will cost $1 or $2 each. Always take a calculator with you when shopping with coupons so you can figure out the cost per ounce *after* deducting the coupon. (But read the fine print; some coupons require a minimum-sized purchase.)

Coupon Comparisons

	Retail price	Price per ounce	50¢ coupon doubled	Net price after coupon	Net price per ounce
8-ounce shampoo	$1.09	$0.14	$1.00	S0.09	$0.01
32-ounce shampoo	$2.59	$0.08	$1.00	$1.59	$0.05

In this example, it is more economical to buy the 8-ounce bottle of shampoo. The net price after deducting the coupon is just 9¢, or about a penny an ounce.

Don't get locked into brand loyalty. To save the most money, be flexible when shopping. Compare prices of the name brand to store brands. Many times the store brand will be cheaper than using the coupon on a name brand. Give the store brands a try, and note which ones are as good as the name brands—and which ones your family doesn't like.

Don't be afraid to let them expire. Coupons now tend to have a much shorter expiration date than they did years ago. But usually as soon as one expires, you will be able to find another coupon.

Don't buy something just because you've got a coupon. A bargain is not a bargain if it is wasted. Many coupons are printed for highly packaged convenience foods that will not be bargain-priced even with the coupon. Don't even bother clipping these.

Bet You Didn't Know

Coupons are built into the advertising budgets of companies. If they don't spend the money on coupons, you can be sure that it will be spent on television, radio, or print advertising. At least with coupons you have a chance to save some money—provided you're willing to clip 'em and use 'em.

Look for bonus items. When shopping for health and beauty aids, look at the back of the shelf to see if any of the products have some sort of bonus. A bonus can be in the form of an instant coupon attached to the product, more of the product for the same price, or a "freebie" such as a toothbrush or razor attached to the package. Many times these bonus packages are pushed to the back of the shelf so the store can get rid of the regular-sized products first.

Tightwad Tip

Ask the food store manager if he or she will accept another store's coupons or advertised specials. Many stores do this, even though they don't advertise the fact.

Let it rain! Lower your food bill by taking advantage of rain checks. Stores frequently run "door buster" sales, and often by the end of the sale they have sold out of the item. Stop by the store at the end of the sale and see if it's indeed out of the item; if so, drop by the service desk and ask for a rain check. Most stores have liberal policies for cashing in rain checks (some will give you up to a year to use it). So buy the limit on the tuna fish when it is advertised for 29¢, then check back later in the week and either buy more at the low price or get a rain check and buy it whenever you need it at the "door buster" price.

Not satisfied? If you buy a product and there's a problem with it or it just doesn't meet your standards, call the company at its toll-free number (look on the back of the product for the number. If it's not there, call long distance information at 800-555-1212 to get the number), or write the firm a letter to explain the problem. Most companies are very customer service–oriented and will want to keep you happy; they'll likely send you a refund or replacement coupons for almost any reasonable complaint. When making a complaint, always be upbeat, but let them know you were disappointed with the product.

Lose Weight, Not Money!

By planning ahead you can save calories *and* money. When most people start a diet, they go to the food store and stock up on all sorts of diet products. Many of these diet products are very expensive, and some may have very little nutritional value. Here are some tips to help you take off the weight without spending lots of money on fancy low-fat and low-calories foods.

Homemade Frozen Meals

Frozen diet meals can be very inexpensive if you make your own from leftovers—and they'll have more flavor than the ones you can buy. If you do not have enough leftovers to make an entire meal, save what you have in a plastic dish, wrap it, and store it in the freezer. Then add to it the next time you have leftovers.

If you don't have any plastic compartment dishes for saving leftovers, you might want to invest in a couple. You can also save the trays from some types of frozen dinners and reuse them. If the carton does not say *not to* reuse the trays, you can assume that you can safely reuse them. And maybe you can persuade some neighbors and relatives to save some of their store-bought frozen dinner trays for you.

Small is beautiful. Most diet foods are usually just over-priced versions of their regular product with *slightly* fewer calories, but there are enough natural low-calorie foods in season to keep you satisfied. If you are craving something sweet, why not eat a small portion of a homemade brownie instead of spending big bucks to buy a "diet" frozen brownie that costs twice as much as an entire pan of homemade ones?

Take food to work. Take low-calorie snacks such as fruit and raw vegetables to work to keep yourself from being tempted at the expensive (and fattening) vending machine. If you have a friend at work that is also dieting, take turns bringing in the diet snacks. Have you ever noticed how much better carrot sticks taste if someone else cuts them up?

Smart Solution

When dieting, cook extra meat and slice it for a low-calorie lunch. Most packaged sandwich meats are loaded with fat and preservatives. Your fresh meat will taste delicious, have fewer calories, and be cheaper in the long run than prepackaged lunch meats.

Drink lots of water. Not only will water help make you feel full before meals, but it's also good for you. It cleans out your system and moisturizers you from the inside out. Another economical low-calorie drink is unsweetened iced tea. Make a pitcher of tea to take with you to work. If you must have diet sodas, buy them by the case and take them to work instead of buying them from the money-hungry vending machine.

Check the Checker

Don't lose all your savings at the checkout! Pay close attention to prices as you shop, and watch closely as the cashier is ringing up your groceries. Some stores give you the item free if you find that the item scans the wrong price. Don't assume that the scanner is perfect. (Many times it's not!) If you pay attention. you can find errors—and you can bet that they are not usually in your favor. In most cases, the pricing clerk will increase the price in the computer before the shelf price has been changed.

Also watch when produce is being rung up. One wrong code entered by the cashier can cost a bundle. For example: One type of red apples may cost 99¢ per pound and another type of red apples may cost $1.19 per pound. Check the price per pound on each produce item purchased. Write down the price per pound on your food list if you cannot remember them all.

The Least You Need to Know

➤ Knowing the best buys at each type of food store—supermarkets, super stores, box stores, and membership warehouses—can really save you money.

➤ Coupons can save you a bundle, as long as you don't get sucked into buying things you don't want and don't need.

➤ If you want to keep your food budget trim while you're getting slim, look for foods that are naturally low in calories and high in nutrition; don't give in to prepared diet meals.

➤ Always check your cash register receipt for errors before leaving the store. Watch the prices as they are being rung up.

Chapter 19

Cooking, Baking, and Grilling

In This Chapter

➤ Cooking techniques: Do you know the differences?

➤ Dice, slice, mince—and other cutting methods made clear

➤ Microwaving hints and tips

➤ Best baking shortcuts

➤ Homemade baking mixes that are quick and economical

➤ Ways to making grilling food fun and easy

Cooking Techniques

Boiling vs. simmering; poaching vs. steaming: Is there much difference? You bet there is—and it can make the difference between a great dish and a disappointment. If you don't know these techniques, read and find out before you open a cookbook again.

Baking. Cook food in the indirect heat of an oven. The food may be covered or uncovered.

Boiling. Heat liquids until bubbles form and rise in a steady pattern, breaking the surface.

Broiling. Cook food a measured distance from the direct dry heat of the heat source.

Deep-fat frying. Cook in enough melted shortening or cooking oil to cover the food. The fat should be hot enough (365°F to 375°F) that the food cooks without absorbing excess grease, but not so hot that the fat smokes or food burns.

Grilling. Broil food on a gas, electric, or charcoal grill.

Poaching. Cook food partially or completely submerged in simmering liquid.

Sauté. Cook food quickly in a small amount of fat.

Simmering. Heat liquids over low heat until bubbles form slowly and burst below the surface.

Steaming. Cook food in the steam given off by boiling water. Place the food in a perforated metal basket, a bamboo steamer, or on a wire rack set just above, but not touching, boiling water. Cover the pan and steam until the food is done.

Bet You Didn't Know

Place a slice of dry bread in the broiler pan to soak up the dripping fat. This will prevent splatters and keep the fat from catching fire.

Stir-frying. Cook foods quickly over high heat in a lightly oiled wok or skillet, lifting and turning the food constantly.

Steamed Vegetables Timetable

Steaming vegetables takes a little longer than boiling but it's a healthier way to cook—and it really brings out the flavor of fresh veggies.

Vegetable	Steaming Time
Asparagus	8 minutes
Beets, medium	40 to 45 minutes
Broccoli	10 to 12 minutes
Brussels sprouts	8 to 10 minutes
Carrots, sliced	20 minutes
Cauliflower, florets	6 to 10 minutes
Corn on the cob	6 to 10 minutes
Green beans, whole	20 to 25 minutes
Onions, small white	15 minutes
Peas	15 minutes
Potatoes, new	20 to 25 minutes
Spinach	5 minutes
Squash, summer, sliced	10 minutes

Cutting Techniques

You'll run across several different cutting techniques when preparing food. Here are the most common cuts.

Chopping. Cut the food into small, irregular pieces about the size of peas.

Finely chopping. Cut the food into small, irregular pieces smaller than peas.

Cubing. Cut the food into strips $1/2$ inch wide or more. Line up the strips; cut crosswise to form cubes. The recipe will generally tell you what size cube to make (such as a 1-inch cube).

Dicing. Cut the food into strips $1/8$ to $1/4$ inch wide. Line up and stack strips; cut crosswise to form pieces.

Grating. Rub food across a grating surface to make very fine pieces.

Julienne strips. Cut the food into slices about 2 inches long and $1/4$ to $1/8$ inch thick. Stack the slices, then cut lengthwise again to make thin, matchlike sticks.

Mincing. Cut into tiny, irregularly shaped pieces. For garlic, a garlic press can be used.

Shredding. Push the food across a shredding surface to make long, narrow strips.

Finely shredding. Push the food across a fine-shredding surface to make very thin strips.

Slicing and bias-slicing. To slice, cut food crosswise, making cuts perpendicular to the cutting surface. To bias-slice, hold the knife at a 45-degree angle to the cutting surface.

Microwave Mastery

No one needs to tell you why microwave ovens are so popular (but I will anyway!). They're big time-savers, and they conserve energy. A recent study conducted by a power company found that for about 87 percent of your cooking tasks, a microwave oven can cut energy costs by at least 50 percent.

Small batches work best. Microwaves are most efficient heating small to medium quantities of food. For example, to bake four potatoes, a microwave uses about 65 percent less energy than an electric oven. Plus, during the hot summer you get the added bonus of not heating up the kitchen.

Tightwad Tip

It's not worth it to boil water in a microwave. To bring 4 cups of water to a boil, a microwave uses 10 percent more energy than an electric range top.

Watch Out!

While some of today's microwave ovens are metal-tolerant to some degree, this does not mean that food can be cooked in conventional metal pots and pans. You *should not* use metal pans in microwaves because metal reflects microwave energy. Use a metal pan, and you'll get either a cold meal or a damaged oven.

What Containers Can You Use?

A microwave oven is deceptively powerful. Metal and some plastics and ceramics (and even some paper) don't belong inside it.

Safe cookware test. To test whether cookware is microwave-safe, place the item in question in the microwave oven next to a glass measuring cup half full of water. Heat on high (100 percent) power for one minute. If the dish you're testing is hot, it shouldn't be used in the microwave. If it's slightly warm, you can use it for reheating. If the dish is room temperature, it is safe to use for all microwave cooking.

Common containers. Many common kitchen containers and other utensils work fine in the microwave. You can defrost foods right in their plastic freezer containers (with the lid off). Just be careful not to overheat the food, which can melt the plastic containers. You can heat bread or other items in straw serving baskets. In addition, some frozen vegetables can be cooked in their plastic packaging, if placed on a microwave safe plate. However, self-sealing plastic bags can melt if heated for very long.

Ceramic and glass cookware. Before you go out and buy a special set of microwave cookware, consider this. Most ceramic or glass pots, pans, casseroles, and baking dishes work just fine in the microwave oven. These types of cookware are more versatile than the plastic types designed specifically for the microwave. You'll save money and storage space, because you can use the same cookware in the regular oven and in the microwave.

Avoid metal and pottery. Don't use your best china or any dishes with metal trim in the microwave. Pottery may also be a poor choice to use in the microwave because it can have metal in the glaze or impurities in the clay.

Round containers. Your food will cook more evenly in a round container. When cooking with rectangular pans in the microwave, food in the corners tends to overcook.

Microwave Magic

What can you do besides defrost and cook in a microwave oven? Plenty!

"Grilling" bacon. Cook bacon the easy way without even buying a special microwave bacon pan. Place a layer of clean paper towels on top of a brown grocery bag or several thicknesses of newspaper, and place the bacon on top. Cook the bacon for 45 seconds to one minute per slice (or until done). The paper towels and the paper bag beneath will absorb most of the grease without wasting a bunch of paper towels. You'll end up with crisp bacon every time.

Softening brown sugar. If your box of brown sugar is hard, don't throw it away; you can soften and freshen it by placing the entire box in your microwave and heating it on high (100 percent) power for about 20 seconds. (Time will vary slightly, depending on the amount of sugar in the box.)

De-crystallizing honey. When honey starts to turn to sugar, just place it in the microwave oven in a microwave-safe container. Insert a food probe (if your microwave has one) or a microwave-safe food thermometer, and microwave on high (100 percent) power to 120°F. Watch the thermometer closely because the honey will heat up quickly.

Dry, tough bread. Heating leftover bread or rolls too long in the microwave can make them tough and dry. To eliminate the problem, heat bread or rolls for about 15 seconds on high. Then heat for an additional five seconds if they're not hot. To prevent muffins or pastries from getting soggy on the bottom, heat them on a paper towel—or, if you prefer, you can heat them on a paper (not foam) plate that can be used several times.

Microwave popcorn. You can buy regular popcorn (instead of microwave bags) to pop in the microwave if you use microwave-safe containers made especially for popping corn.

Drying Herbs in the Microwave

A number of herbs—such as dill, basil, parsley, sage, celery leaves, chives, mint, oregano, tarragon, and thyme—can be quickly dried in your microwave oven. Here's what you do: Take one small bunch of fresh herbs (about four or five stalks). Discard any discolored or decayed leaves. Rinse herbs in cold water, and shake off excess. Pat dry completely.

Watch Out!

Don't use recycled paper towels in your microwave because there might be small metal pieces in the recycled material.

Watch Out!

Always remove bread from the thin plastic wrapper before heating it in the microwave. This plastic melts easily, and some of the paint used on the bags may contain metal.

Watch Out!

Don't try to make microwave popcorn in a brown paper bag. Kernels can scorch and cause a fire inside the microwave oven if brown bags or other improper containers are used. You can find a microwave popcorn popper at discount store (such as WalMart or K-Mart), and even some grocery stores sell them.

267

Then place a double layer of paper towels in the microwave. Spread herbs on paper towels. Place another paper towel over herbs. Microwave on high (100 percent) power for two to three minutes. Check leaves for dryness by rubbing between paper towels to crumble. If leaves are not dry, microwave for additional 30-second intervals until dry. Remove from the microwave and allow to cool.

Crumble herbs, discard any tough stems, and store in an air-tight container.

Smart Solution

When cooking, always measure ingredients. This way you will get consistent results with your recipes, and you'll also save money. Most people wind up adding about twice as much as needed when they don't take the time to measure. The difference could affect the end results—and you'll end up buying twice as much as you really need.

Smart Solution

To decorate a cake with ease, put colored icing in clean, squeeze-type catsup and mustard containers. The narrow spouts make it easy to write a message or draw a picture.

Baking

Here are some ideas you'll find helpful when you put on the apron and get out your mixer.

Getting ready. Place all the ingredients on the counter on one side of the mixing bowl, then after using an ingredient put it on the other side of the bowl. This way you will know what you added and what you have not if you're interrupted.

Measuring hint. Measure dry ingredients first, then use the same spoons or cups for liquids. This will cut down on the cleanup.

Clean-up helper. Fill the sink with hot sudsy water before starting, then slip each utensil into the water when finished (except for sharp knives and food processor blades—ouch!). Soaking makes cleanup easier.

Sugar sprinkles. Sprinkle frosted cookies with packaged gelatin to add color instead of buying expensive colored sprinkles. You can also make your own colored sugar sprinkles by shaking a little granulated sugar (2 to 3 tablespoons) and two or three drops of food coloring in a self-sealing plastic bag.

Burnt cookie remedy. Don't throw away cookies that are burnt on the bottom. Instead, scrape off the burned parts (or use a food grater to grate them off), and they'll taste just fine. If the cookies crumble when you scrape off the burned part, save the good crumbs to use as ice cream topping.

Chocolate saver. When baking a chocolate cake, add a little flour to the container in which you melted chocolate. The flour will get the last bit of chocolate out of the pan so you can transfer it into the cake batter. (I hate to waste anything, especially chocolate!)

Chocolate dust. Dust the pan of a chocolate cake with cocoa instead of flour; it is dark instead of white, so your cake will look better, and it also adds flavor.

Dry cake. To "save" a dry cake, poke holes in the top with a toothpick and pour 1 to 3 teaspoons of fruit juice in the holes. Use a light colored juice, such as apple, for a white cake, and any type of juice for a chocolate cake.

Fresh cake. To keep a cake fresh longer, put a slice of fresh apple into the cake container.

Stuck cake. To prevent a cake from sticking to the bottom of the cake pan, line the bottom with waxed paper. To remove one that's stuck, place the hot pan on a wet towel.

Smart Solution

To keep a recipe card handy, slip it between the tines of a fork and stand the fork in a glass. You'll be able to read it and turn it over without having to pick it up with your messy hands.

Low-fat substitute. When baking a cake or brownies, you can substitute apple sauce for some or all of the oil. The goodies taste great without all that fat and calories.

Eliminate lumps. To keep granulated sugar from lumping, put a few soda crackers, such as Saltines, in the container.

Eggs first, then oil. When making a cake, crack the eggs in the measuring cup first and then pour them into the mixing bowl. The eggs will coat the cup so that when you measure out the oil it will slide out easily.

Wet first, then dry. Put the water in the bowl before putting in the cake mix or dry ingredients. This way you won't have unincorporated dry mix on the bottom of the bowl.

Goodies to go. Save the pieces of cardboard from frozen or delivery pizzas to use as disposable plates-to-go for cakes and other baked goods. Cover the cardboard with aluminum foil and place the cake, brownies, or batch of cookies on top. You can leave the goodies and the plate when it's time for you to leave the party.

Shiny pie crust. Take the pie out of the oven when it is almost baked, and brush the top with white vinegar, then place it back in the oven for a few minutes. You'll have a beautiful pie crust—and don't worry, you won't be able to taste the vinegar.

Greasing pans. Use butter or margarine wrappers to grease baking pans. The wrappers make a handy wipe, and you're not wasting any butter or margarine. Place unused wrappers in a plastic bag in the freezer until you need to grease a pan.

Sticky solution. To avoid a sticky mess when measuring honey, molasses, or corn syrup, rinse the measuring cup in very hot water right before using it.

Rx for Cooking Disasters

You try your very best—but darn it, something goes wrong. Don't despair! Many times you can save a dish if you know what to do.

Bland Dish

Sprinkled in some salt and/or pepper, and it still lacks pizzazz? Try adding one of these before you give up on it:

➤ A little hot pepper sauce, mustard, or Worcestershire sauce

➤ Your favorite herb or spice

➤ Minced or powdered onion or garlic

➤ Lemon juice

➤ A dollop of sour cream, butter, yogurt, or cottage cheese added to soup

Reduce salty taste. Bread crumbs, yogurt, cream, and parsley can help save a salty dish. You can also add a teaspoon of cider vinegar and a teaspoon of salt to eliminate the salty taste.

Salty soup or stew. Add cut raw potatoes to soup or stew and discard them once they've cooked and absorbed the salt.

Too much sugar? If you add too much sugar to a main dish or vegetable recipe, add a teaspoon of cider vinegar to save the dish.

Heavy on the garlic? Place parsley flakes in a tea ball and set it in the stew or soup pot to absorb some of the excess garlic.

Curdled hollandaise sauce. To rescue hollandaise sauce, place a teaspoon of lemon juice and a tablespoon of the curdled sauce in a bowl. With a wire whisk, beat vigorously until the mixture is creamy and thickened, then gradually beat in the remaining sauce, a little at a time, making sure that each addition has thickened before adding the next batch. You can also put hollandaise sauce in a saucepan over hot water in a double boiler and add sour cream by the teaspoonful until the sauce is smooth.

Burned stew solution. Don't stir a burned stew; you'll only loosen scorched bits from the bottom of the pot if you do. Instead, pour the unburned part into another pot.

Burned rice. To remove burned flavor from rice, place a heel of fresh white bread on top of the rice and cover the pot to let it sit. In about five minutes, the bad taste should disappear.

Sticky pasta. If drained pasta is glued together, reboil it for a minute or two in hot, fresh water.

Gravy Recovery

Even the best cooks don't always get the gravy right, but they know what to do when they've got a problem on their hands. Now you will, too:

➤ Burned gravy? You can cover up a burned flavor in brown gravy by adding a teaspoon of peanut butter to it.

➤ Pour lumpy gravy into a mixing bowl, and use your hand mixer to break up the lumps—or pour the gravy through a strainer to remove them.

➤ To thicken thin gravy, mix water and flour or cornstarch into a smooth paste. Add gradually, stirring constantly, and bring to a boil. You can also try adding instant potato flakes instead of flour.

➤ Gravy too greasy? Add 1/4 teaspoon baking soda.

➤ To give pale gravy a rich, dark color, add a few tablespoons of dark coffee; it won't affect the taste.

Homemade Baking Mixes

Some things are just better when they are made from scratch. These recipes are easy to make, taste great, and are low-cost to boot!

Sweetened Condensed Milk

Here's a homemade version to use when baking.

1/3 cup plus 2 tablespoons evaporated (canned) milk

1 cup sugar

3 tablespoons butter

Place the ingredients in a saucepan, and cook over medium heat, stirring all the while, until butter is melted and ingredients are blended. Let cool to room temperature, and use as you would a can of sweetened condensed milk. Refrigerate any leftover milk. The taste and consistency is similar to Eagle Brand and other brands of canned sweetened milk.

Egg Substitute

This recipe is similar to Egg Beaters brand and other low-cholesterol egg substitutes, and it can be used just as they are used.

6 egg whites

1 tablespoon oil

1/4 cup powdered milk

Combine all ingredients in a mixing bowl and blend smooth, or use a blender. Store in a jar in the refrigerator, where it will keep up to one week. The mixture also freezes well. You can add a drop of yellow coloring to make it look more like real eggs. About $1/4$ cup equals one whole egg.

All-Purpose Baking Mix

Whip up a batch of this mix and keep it on hand to make pancakes, dumplings, biscuits, and muffins.

> 10 cups sifted flour
>
> $3^1/3$ cups powdered milk
>
> 5 tablespoons baking powder
>
> $2^1/2$ teaspoons salt

Combine well and store in an airtight container. This makes about five batches.

Pancakes. Combine $2^1/4$ cups baking mix with a mixture of one egg, $1^1/2$ cups water, and 2 tablespoons vegetable oil. Stir until moistened; batter will be slightly lumpy. Cook on a hot, greased griddle. Flip when bubbles form on the surface and the edges start to turn brown.

Dumplings. Combine 2 cups baking mix with 1 cup water. Stir until mixed. Drop by spoonfuls into simmering soup, water, or gravy. Cover and cook for 20 minutes. Add spices or shredded cheese, if desired.

Biscuits. Combine $2^1/4$ cups baking mix with $1/4$ cup shortening and $2/3$ cup water. Mix lightly until dough forms a ball. Turn onto a lightly floured surface. Knead and roll dough out to about $1/2$ inch thick. Cut into rounds with a biscuit cutter or small glass. Bake on an ungreased baking sheet at 450° for 10 to 12 minutes. For drop biscuits, use 1 cup water instead and drop by tablespoons onto baking sheet.

Muffins. Combine $2^1/4$ cups baking mix with $1/4$ cup sugar. In a separate bowl, combine one egg and $3/4$ cup water with $1/3$ cup vegetable oil. Add to dry ingredients. Add nuts, raisins, cinnamon, chopped fruit, or even shredded carrots or squash for variety. Mix only enough to moisten flour; batter will be lumpy. Grease muffin tins and fill two-thirds full. Bake at 400° for 45 minutes.

Hot off the Grill

Backyard barbecues during the summer can be lots of fun—and food always seems to taste better when it's hot off the grill. Here are some ideas to help make your backyard barbecuing easier and cheaper.

Briquettes

If you use charcoal briquettes, don't let them continue to burn after you finish grilling. Remove the charcoal (with tongs) and put them into a large tin can with holes punched in it. Pour water over the coals and let them dry out. To reuse the pieces of leftover charcoal, simply mix them with a few new ones for your next barbecue.

Starting. An easy way to get charcoal briquettes started is to put several into a paper bag and light the bag. You can also use a dry pine cone or two under the briquettes to get it started fast.

Instead of using lighter fluid, fill empty cardboard (not plastic) egg cartons with charcoal briquettes. Place them in the grill and light with a match; when they catch on fire, your charcoal will be spread out evenly.

Smart Solution

You don't have to replace the lava rocks in gas grills every year just because they get dirty and filled with grease. Instead of buying new ones, turn them over and turn the grill on high for about five minutes. Turning the rocks upside down allows the grease to drip out, which will clean the rocks and make them as good as new!

Cleaning the Grill

Here's an easy way to clean that messy grill: Dip newspapers in water, and place them wet on the top of the rack while the grill is still warm. Close the lid, and let the newspapers stay on the rack for about 20 to 45 minutes. When you come back, you'll find that the newspapers have steam-cleaned your grill. Just rub the newspapers across the rack, and it will be clean and ready for the next barbecue. This method is quick, easy, and practically cost-free.

Note: Don't let the newspapers stay on the grill for more than an hour; if they dry on the grill, they will be hard to remove!

Where's the sauce? Use barbecue sauce only during the last 20 minutes of grilling. If you put it on too early, it will burn. To make your barbecue sauce go farther, add $1/3$ water and $1/4$ sugar to 1 cup of barbecue sauce before brushing it on your meat. The result will be a sticky, yummy coating.

Grill once, eat twice. Grill enough meat for more than one meal. Microwave or steam the meat for another quick and easy meal. No hot oven required!

Smart Solution

When grilling hamburgers, take a straw and poke a hole through the middle of each burger. The patties will cook quicker and more evenly throughout.

Emergency water. Keep a water bottle close at hand to keep your barbecue fire under control. Don't waste your money on a special water bottle for the grill. You can use a clean liquid detergent bottle or any type of spray bottle. Even one of the kid's squirt guns will do the trick!

Easy Barbecue Sauce

This recipe makes the best sauce for all your summer barbecues. It tastes great and is much cheaper per ounce than buying individual bottles.

Watch Out!

Don't squirt water on a gas grill to cool it down. Adjust the dial or move the food to the cooler corners.

1 pound brown sugar

1 #10 can catsup (see note)

2 oz. coarsely ground pepper

1 5-oz. bottle Worcestershire

1 4-oz. bottle liquid smoke

Mix together all the ingredients, and pour them into a large glass jar (or jars). Refrigerate and enjoy! This should make enough barbecue sauce to last most of the summer. Homemade barbecue sauce also makes nice gifts. Pour into smaller bottles and make a label for each jar.

Note: A #10 can is the large industrial-size can that holds about 7 pounds, 2 ounces. You can find the large cans of ketchup at many regular grocery stores, and any warehouse-type store will carry the large cans.

The Least You Need to Know

➤ When cooking, just knowing what the terms (such as poaching, sautéing, and simmering) mean will help make your recipes a success.

➤ Baking can be so much fun, but it can also be time-consuming. A few shortcuts will make the job quick and enjoyable.

➤ Microwaves are big time-savers,—and they can be used to do so much more than just heat up leftovers.

➤ Many times you can save a cooking disaster (such as too much salt, lack of flavor, or lumpy gravy) by adding something to the pot, such as spices, lemon juice, or even peanut butter!

Food Storage

A well-organized kitchen makes it easier (and quicker) to cook. Use the many suggestions in this chapter to get yours in top shape—and to pick up some tips on storing foods in the pantry, refrigerator, and freezer.

Stocking Up on Staples

You can keep your kitchen running smoothly by always having an ample supply of commonly used staples—such as flour, sugar, eggs, and milk—on hand. Although you shouldn't buy more than you can use in a reasonable period of time, buy enough to avoid having to make extra trips to the food store.

Some ingredients, such as sugar and flour, can be bought in quantity and stored in canisters or any type of airtight containers for several months. Herbs and spices can lose their flavor in about a year, though, so purchase smaller quantities. Just what ingredients you want to stock up on will depend on the foods you regularly use. Here's a basic rundown of the more common ones.

Flour	Sugar, brown sugar
Shortening	Vegetable oil
Baking powder, baking soda	Cornstarch
Salt, pepper	Spices, herbs
Vanilla	Cocoa
Mayonnaise or salad dressing	Mustard, catsup
Honey	Vinegar
Worcestershire sauce	Bottled hot pepper sauce
Bouillon cubes or granules, or canned chicken and beef stock	Coffee, tea
	Soy sauce
Pasta	Rice
Beans	Cereals
Bread	Bread crumbs
Eggs	Milk
Margarine or butter	Cheese

Organizing Your Kitchen

Even if you have a large kitchen, before you know it, you're tight on space. Use some of the hints here to make the space you have, no matter how big or small, go further.

Keep them where you use them. To save time and make your kitchen more efficient, keep in mind where, what, and how you cook. Place food supplies and cooking utensils as close as possible to the area in the kitchen you'll use them. Save easy-to-reach shelves and cupboards for the items that you use most often. Store less frequently used items in top shelves and out-of-the-way places.

Watch Out!

Avoid storing foods near appliances that give off heat (such as stoves, ovens, refrigerators, and freezers), or in damp areas. Heat and moisture shorten the shelf life of canned and packaged foods.

The pantry. Arrange canned goods and packaged mixes on shelves by types of food (grains together, baking items together, and so on) so that you can find them quickly and easily. Rotate your pantry stock by using, for instance, the oldest can of green beans first. When you buy groceries put the new cans or boxes behind the ones that are already in the pantry. Periodically check for expiration dates, and try to use them up before those dates.

Skinny shelf. Add a narrow shelf along one wall for spice jars, sauce bottles, salt and pepper shakers, and all the other little things you'd like to be able to see and have quick access to.

Basket storage. Attach small wire baskets to the insides of lower cabinet doors to hold cleaning items. This works especially well for the cabinet under the sink.

Glass jar storage. Use glass jars to store dry foods such as sugar, flour, beans, popping corn, and cornstarch. These items look pretty sitting on a shelf or on the counter. If possible use colored glass instead of clear; it will give the food more protection from deterioration.

Metal boxes. Metal boxes and tins are also wonderful for storage. They keep items such as crackers and cookies fresh. You may even be able to stack several boxes or tins to save storage space. Use masking tape and a black marker to list the goodies inside.

Cup hooks. Hang cups or mugs from cup hooks under upper kitchen cabinets or shelves. They'll be out of the way and look decorative at the same time.

Utensil holder. Large mugs or jugs are handy for storing kitchen utensils on the counter or a shelf. If you are short on drawer space, this will help tremendously.

Food Storage

Many foods can be kept a long time if they are stored properly in a dry, ventilated cupboard, refrigerator, or freezer.

Canned Goods

Canned foods will retain their quality for at least a year. Canned rhubarb and prunes are the exceptions to this rule; they should be eaten within six months. After a can is opened, transfer any uneaten food to a covered dish in the refrigerator, and eat the food within a day or two. If you keep your pantry full of canned goods, be certain to rotate your stock. Put the oldest cans in front so you'll use them first.

Watch Out!

Foods in cans with deeply dented seams or swollen ends should not be eaten. They may be loaded with bacterial toxins that can cause severe illness.

Bread, Cakes, and Cookies

Keep bread in a bread box or a cabinet that allows some air to circulate; otherwise mold will develop and spread quickly. If you have a bread box that does not have any holes to circulate air, you may want to cut some small holes into the box yourself. Also, breads can be stored in the freezer. Slices thaw very quickly in a toaster or microwave oven.

Cakes and pies. Cover cakes, and refrigerate cream or custard cakes or pies.

Cookies and snacks. Use a spring-type clothespin or a large binder clip to close packages of cookies and snacks, or put them in airtight containers to keep them from becoming stale.

277

Watch Out!

Don't store bread in the refrigerator. The cold temperature will break down the starches and actually make it stale quicker.

Watch Out!

Spices will lose their flavor quickly if stored on top of the range or stove-top because the heat from the range speeds the deterioration process.

Dried and Packaged Foods

Store foods in their original package or in a tightly sealed container in a dry place. Unless the package has an expiration date, packaged foods will retain their nutritional value for as long as six months. After that, they'll gradually deteriorate in quality.

Coffee. Coffee beans can be kept in airtight jars for up to three months; vacuum-packed coffee lasts up to a year. After the vacuum seal is broken, coffee should be refrigerated or frozen.

Beans and grains. Keep dried beans, rice, flour, and dried fruits in a cool, dry place out of direct sunlight. After you've opened a package of dried fruit, store it in the refrigerator or freezer.

Herbs and spices. Store herbs and spices in dark, airtight containers, or in jars in a cool, dry cupboard, to keep them fresh. Ground spices will keep for about six months. Whole herbs and spices will keep their flavor for up to a year. You can also freeze herbs and spices to extend their lives.

Having trouble keeping annoying pests out of your pantry and kitchen? See Chapter 25 to get your pests under control.

Vegetables and Fruit

Keep fresh fruits and vegetables inthe crisper section of the refrigerator, or in a loosely closed bag elsewhere in the fridge. Never wrap them tightly because they'll spoil faster that way. Except for salad greens, do not wash produce before storing; the water can destroy some of the vitamins.

It's best to wash salad right before using, not ahead of time. Washing can bruise some leaves, which promotes spoilage. And you shouldn't cut or tear leaves until you're ready to serve them for the same reason.

Allow fruits—especially, grapes, plums, and pears—to ripen at room temperature before refrigerating to improve their flavor.

Before refrigerating fresh vegetables, remove any leafy tops because they deteriorate faster than the rest. Rinse and drain all leafy greens. Leave corn in the husks, and leave beans and peas in their shells.

Allow tomatoes to ripen on the counter instead of in the refrigerator. They lose flavor quickly in the fridge, a fact even the Tomato Growers' Association advertises. If you prefer a cold tomato for a salad, place it in the refrigerator about an hour before serving.

Onions, potatoes, and other tubers and root vegetables can be stored in separate baskets or wire racks that allow air to circulate. Place them in a dry, cool, well-ventilated, and dark place.

Onions and garlic and sweet potatoes like 60-75 percent humidity, and potatoes, carrots, beets rutabagas, turnips, and other root vegetables need about 95 percent humidity, so they are best not stored in the same baskets.

Bet You Didn't Know

Don't put potatoes in the refrigerator; the cold makes the starch change to sugar. Also, don't store potatoes with onions; moisture from the potatoes can cause onions to sprout. One of the best ways to store onions is to hang them in old pantyhose. Drop the onions in the hose and tie a knot between each one. Hang in a cool, dry, and dark place, and snip off onions one at a time as you need them.

Freezing Fruits and Vegetables

Whether your garden provides a bumper crop or you buy a bushel from a local farmer's market, if you freeze fruits and vegetables when they are fresh and in good condition, they should last up to one year. Always store them in freezer bags or plastic freezer containers for the best results. Here's how to prepare your frozen assets:

➤ Select top-quality foods. The freezing process can only retain the quality of the food; it cannot improve it.

➤ Cool cooked foods quickly.

➤ Freeze in family-size or individual portions.

➤ Use good packaging or wrapping materials. Freezer wraps and containers need to be air-tight and moisture- and vapor-proof. Some of the best freezer packaging is heavy-duty aluminum foil, heavy-weight plastic wrap, freezer bags, and sturdy, reusable plastic containers (not the thin ones used for takeout food). If you want to use plastic wrap, use a heavy-duty one, or wrap your food in several layers of it.

➤ Seal wraps and containers. Fill freezer containers to within an inch of the top. You want to leave some expansion space, but not so much that there's a lot of air trapped inside, which promotes deterioration through oxidation. Squeeze out air in plastic bags before you seal them. Wrap freezer paper and aluminum foil securely to create an airtight package—unless directions specify otherwise.

➤ Label each package with the date, contents, and the number of servings.

➤ Do not freeze any foods that look off-color or have a bad odor.

➤ Keep the freezer temperature set at 0°F or lower for most frozen foods.

➤ Do not refreeze foods. This increases the risk of contamination by harmful bacteria.

➤ Rotate food in the freezer, and use it before the expiration date.

What Not to Freeze

Some foods simply do not freeze well:

➤ Cottage cheese and cream cheese; they separate and break down when frozen.

➤ Hard cheese tends to crumble when thawed. (Which means you can't use it as sliced cheese, but it's fine for melted cheese dishes.)

➤ Mayonnaise, sour cream, and yogurt all separate when frozen.

➤ Hard-cooked eggs will become rubbery or leathery if frozen.

➤ Cream and custard pie fillings may separate, and meringue topping will shrink.

➤ Never store carbonated drinks in the freezer because they may explode. Never freeze anything canned, for that matter. Juice boxes, however, can be frozen.

➤ Be wary about freezing fish and shellfish unless you know for sure that it's fresh; it may have been frozen already on its way to the store.

➤ Cooked potatoes will turn brown in the freezer, and although they're safe to eat, they're unappealing. Mashed potatoes will separate and are not good reheated (although they can then be used to thicken foods such as soups and stews or for potato cakes).

➤ Garlic gets bitter in the freezer. It's best to add garlic to a dish after it's defrosted.

➤ Cucumbers and lettuce go limp when frozen and are pretty useless. Ditto for celery, although it can be used in casseroles and soups.

➤ Although pears can be frozen; they brown quite readily and aren't recommended.

Smart Solution

To prevent peaches, nectarines, and apples from browning, pack them in fruit juice or a syrup made from 1 part sugar and 3 parts water. You don't have to heat it, but you can use warm water to speed the sugar dissolve.

How to Freeze Fruits and Vegetables

Berries, grapes, cherries, peeled and sliced nectarines, plums and peaches. Lay prepared fruit in a single layer on a cookie sheet, and freeze until firm. Then transfer the fruit into plastic freezer containers. By doing this you'll be able to thaw out just the amount you need because the fruit pieces will not be stuck together. Use without thawing in muffins, breads, cakes, and pies. Eat frozen cherries or grapes as a frozen snack or to chill fruit punch.

Tomatoes. Freeze whole, unpeeled, in a freezer container. Before using, drop in boiling water for a few seconds, then peel. These tomatoes are perfect in cooked sauces, soups, and stews.

Green beans. Rinse; trim ends and cook in boiling water for one to two minutes. Cool quickly, pat dry, and pack into a freezer container or bag. Use as a cooked vegetable or add to soups, stews, or casseroles.

Corn. Cook on the cob in boiling water for three minutes; cool and drain. Cut corn from cobs and freeze in bag or container. Serve as a cooked vegetable, or stir into chowders, soups, fritters, or muffins.

Onions and peppers. Chop onions and peppers into small pieces, and freeze on a cookie sheet (same method used for berries and other fruits). Transfer into a freezer container. Use frozen in recipes.

Herbs. You can freeze herbs either in small bunches wrapped in foil or chopped up in an ice cube tray covered with water.

Smart Solution

Place unpeeled tomatoes on a cookie sheet so they freeze individually before you put them in a freezer bag. You'll find it easy to remove just one or two to thaw and use.

How to Freeze Bread, Cakes, and Pastries

Bread, cakes, pastries, and other foods can be frozen successfully, so long as they're well-wrapped and not kept in the freezer too long.

Loaf bread. Freeze whole loaves of bread in their original wrapping. When you thaw them out, place a paper towel on top of the loaf to absorb any moisture. Store in the freezer for up to six months.

Uncooked pastry. Freeze balls of uncooked pastry, freezer-wrapped, up to two months; or roll pastry into circles 3 inches larger than your pie plates, stack them with two sheets of waxed paper between layers, and then wrap and freeze. Store in the freezer for up to six months.

Pie crusts. Freeze baked or unbaked pie crusts in their metal or freezer-to-oven pie plates, then wrap and stack with waxed paper between crusts. Store in the freezer for up to six months.

Unbaked fruit pies. To freeze unbaked fruit pies, prepare as usual but do not cut slits in the top crust. Use a metal or freezer-to-oven pie plate. Cover with an inverted paper plate to protect the crust. Place in a freezer bag. Label and freeze. Store in the freezer for two to four months.

To thaw and bake: Unwrap and cut slits in the top. Cover edge with foil. Bake frozen pie in a 450°F oven for 15 minutes, then in a 375°F oven for about 15 minutes. Remove foil and bake for about 30 minutes more, or until the crust is brown and the pie is done.

Bet You Didn't Know

To freeze a frosted cake, put it in the freezer without any wrapping. Once it is frozen, wrap it and put it back into the freezer. This way the frosting won't stick to the wrapping. Remove the wrapping before thawing the cake. Store in the freezer for up to six months.

Watch Out!

Do not partially cook food, stop, then finish the cooking later. Harmful bacteria can grow between the cooking steps.

Watch Out!

Bacteria live all around us, so always wash your hands with soap and dry them with a clean cloth before you begin to cook.

Baked pies. To freeze a baked pie, bake it in a metal or freezer-to-oven pie plate and let it cool to room temperature. Cover with an inverted paper plate to protect the crust. Place in a freezer bag. Label and freeze. Store in the freezer for six to eight months. Do not freeze cream or custard pies.

Cookie dough. Pack unbaked cookie dough in freezer containers, or shape them into logs that you can slice and bake. Wrap tightly in foil or several layers of plastic wrap. Store in the freezer for up to six months.

Food Safety

Keeping food safe to eat is as simple as keeping hot foods hot, cold foods cold, and all foods clean. The following hints and food storage charts will guide you.

Cook thoroughly. To prevent the buildup of harmful bacteria, cook foods thoroughly, especially meat, poultry, and dishes containing eggs.

Don't leave sitting out. Bacteria can grow at room temperature, so discard any cooked or chilled food that has been left out longer than two hours.

Reheat carefully. Cover leftovers to retain moisture while reheating. Be sure, too, to reheat the food completely.

Check temperatures. Keep your refrigerator at about 36°F to 40°F, and your freezer at 0°F or below. Check them both from time to time with an appliance thermometer.

Thaw carefully. Thaw meat and poultry in the refrigerator overnight, when time allows. For faster thawing, place frozen packages in a watertight plastic bag in cold water. Change the water often. You can also defrost food in your microwave oven. Do not thaw meat on the kitchen counter.

When shopping. When food shopping, pick up the perishables last. Be sure frozen foods are solid and that refrigerated foods are cold. If you live more than

30 minutes from the store, or if aren't heading straight home, you may want to put frozen, refrigerated, and other perishable foods in an ice chest for the trip home.

Storing Meats

Raw meat, poultry, and fish. When working with raw meat, poultry, and fish, wash hands, counters, and utensils in hot, soapy water between each recipe step. Bacteria on raw meat and poultry can contaminate other foods.

Never put cooked meat or poultry on the same plate that held any of the raw food, and never use the same utensil with raw and then cooked food.

Wrapping. Chill meat and poultry in the store's packaging if you plan to use it in a day or so. For longer storage, remove the packaging; wrap tightly in moisture- and vapor-proof material such as heavy foil, freezer paper, freezer bags, heavy-duty plastic wrap, or freezer containers. Then freeze.

Meat compartment. If your refrigerator has a special compartment for meat, use it. Your meat will stay colder and fresher longer when stored in the compartment.

Wrapping for freezer. To freeze meat, wrap it in a moisture-proof wrapping, such as heavy plastic wrap, freezer wrap, or a self-sealing plastic bag. Be sure to force all the air possible out of the plastic bag before freezing meat. If you know when you buy the meat that it's going into the freezer, have the butcher at the store wrap it in freezer wrap.

Always remember to label your meat and put the date on it. Masking tape and a black marker can be used to mark almost any container.

Meat Storage Chart

Use this chart as a guide when determining whether meat is still safe to eat.

Meat	Refrigerate	Freeze
Beef steaks	3 to 5 days	6 to 12 months
Beef roasts	3 to 5 days	6 to 12 months
Pork chops	3 to 5 days	3 to 4 months
Pork roasts	3 to 5 days	4 to 8 months
Fresh pork sausage	1 to 2 days	1 to 2 months
Veal cutlets	3 to 5 days	6 to 9 months
Veal steaks	3 to 5 days	6 to 12 months
Lamb chops	3 to 5 days	6 to 9 months
Lamb steaks	3 to 5 days	6 to 9 months
Lamb roasts	3 to 5 days	6 to 9 months

continues

Meat	Refrigerate	Freeze
Stew meat	1 to 2 days	3 to 4 months
Ground beef or veal	1 to 2 days	3 to 4 months
Ground lamb or turkey	1 to 2 days	3 to 4 months
Ground pork	1 to 2 days	1 to 3 months
Variety meats (liver, kidney, brains)	1 to 2 days	3 to 4 months

Watch Out!

Never freeze poultry with stuffing inside. Freeze both the poultry and the stuffing separately.

Storing Poultry

Refrigerator storage. Remove giblets from poultry, and wrap and store them separately. Store poultry loosely wrapped (or in the original wrapping) in the coldest part of the refrigerator. If the whole chicken won't fit into the meat compartment, scoot it to the back of a shelf so it does not get a blast of warm air every time the door opens.

Freezing. To freeze poultry, wrap it in moisture-proof wrapping, such as heavy plastic wrap, freezer wrap, or a self-sealing plastic bag. Be sure to force all the air possible out of the bag before sealing. Label and date it.

Poultry Storage Chart

To keep poultry fresh, use this chart as a guide.

Meat	Refrigerate	Freeze
Whole chickens	1 to 2 days	12 months
Chicken pieces	1 to 2 days	9 months
Chicken giblets	1 to 2 days	3 months
Whole turkeys	1 to 2 days	6 months
Turkey pieces	1 to 2 days	6 months
Whole ducks or geese	1 to 2 days	6 months

Storing Fish and Seafood

For the refrigerator. Rinse fish thoroughly in cold water. Pat dry with paper towels, and cover with waxed paper. Store in the coldest part of the refrigerator.

To freeze fish fillets. Wrap in a moisture-proof wrapping, such as heavy plastic wrap, freezer wrap, or a self-sealing plastic bag. Be sure to force all the air possible out of the plastic bag before sealing.

Shrimp. This shellfish will keep longer if it is frozen uncooked.

Freezing crab and lobster. Cook without any salt, cool in the refrigerator, and remove the meat from the shell before freezing.

Freezing oysters, clams, and scallops. Shell and pack them in their own liquid. Add a little water, if needed, to cover them.

Don't forget to label and date your fish and seafood.

Fish and Seafood Storage Chart

Use this chart as a guide for keeping fish and seafood fresh.

Fish and seafood	Refrigerate	Freeze
Clams	1 to 2 days	3 to 6 months
Crabs	1 to 2 days	1 to 2 months
Fresh fish	1 to 2 days	6 to 9 months
Lobster	1 to 2 days	1 to 2 months
Oysters	1 to 2 days	3 to 6 months
Scallops	1 to 2 days	3 to 6 months
Shrimp	1 to 2 days	2 months

Storing Leftovers and Processed Meats

Cool or freeze leftovers quickly. Always put leftovers and cooked meats into the refrigerator or freezer quickly. Keep them covered with a lid, foil, or plastic wrap.

Refrigerating processed meat. Keep loosely covered in the refrigerator. Unopened vacuum-sealed packages of meats can be stored in the refrigerator for two weeks. After the seal is opened, use them within three to five days.

Freezing processed meat. Wrap tightly in a moisture-proof wrapping, such as heavy plastic wrap, freezer wrap, or a self-sealing plastic bag. Be sure to force all the air possible out before sealing. Processed meats don't keep their high quality for long when frozen because the seasonings added in the curing process speed rancidity.

Freezing smoked meat. Take extra care to wrap well so the odor won't make everything else in the freezer taste like smoked meat.

Leftovers and Processed Meats Storage Chart

Use this chart as a guide for storing leftovers.

Cooked meats and leftovers	Refrigerate	Freeze
Leftover roast (beef)	3 to 4 days	2 to 3 months
Leftover beef stew	3 to 4 days	2 to 3 months
Gravy or meat broth	1 to 2 days	2 to 3 months
Meat sauce (spaghetti sauce)	3 to 4 days	6 to 8 months
Meat loaf	2 to 3 days	3 months
Fried chicken	1 to 2 days	4 months
Cooked chicken	1 to 2 days	1 month
Chicken salad	1 to 2 days	Do not freeze
Leftover fish	2 to 3 days	1 month
Leftover canned or cured ham	4 to 5 days	1 month
Leftover fresh ham or pork	3 to 4 days	2 to 3 months
Cooked pork or lamb	3 to 4 days	2 to 3 months
Tuna salad	1 to 2 days	Do not freeze

Use this chart when refrigerating or freezing processed meats.

Processed meats	Refrigerate	Freeze
Bacon	1 week	2 to 4 months
Corned beef	1 week	2 weeks
Frankfurters	1 week	1 month
Ham, whole	1 week	1 to 2 months
Ham, half	3 to 5 days	1 to 2 months
Canned ham (unopened)	1 year	Do not freeze
Ham slices	3 days	1 to 2 months
Lunch meat	3 to 5 days	1 to 2 months
Sausage, smoked	1 week	1 to 2 months

Storing Dairy Products

Always look for the latest expiration date when buying any type of dairy product. If a store rotates its merchandise properly, you'll find the latest date in the back of the shelf.

In the fridge. Store cheese, milk, cream, sour cream, yogurt, margarine, and butter tightly covered in the refrigerator.

Cheese, please. Refrigerate cheese in its original wrapping, if possible, or cover the open side with plastic wrap or aluminum foil. If you put cheese into a plastic bag, be sure to squeeze out as much air as possible before closing the bag. Chill strong-flavored cheese in a tightly covered glass container.

To freeze cheese, put it in a self-sealing plastic bag and force out the air, or keep it in the original package. Shredded cheese freezes nicely. Do not freeze cheese in packages larger than 1 pound each.

Eggs. Refrigerate eggs in their own cartons.

To freeze eggs, you must remove them from their shells. For whole eggs, stir in 2 tablespoons sugar for each pint of lightly beaten eggs. Pack eggs in freezer containers, filling only half full to allow room for expansion.

Dairy Products Storage Chart

Use this chart as a guide to keep dairy products fresh.

Dairy products	Refrigerate	Freeze
Butter, salted	2 weeks	3 months
Butter, unsalted	2 weeks	6 months
Margarine	6 to 12 months	1 year
Eggs, whole	4 weeks	9 to 12 months
Eggs, whites	2 to 4 days	9 to 12 months
Eggs, yolks	2 to 3 days	9 to 12 months
Milk	1 week	1 month
Cream	1 week	1 month
Cheese spreads, opened	1 to 2 weeks	1 to 2 months
Hard cheeses, wrapped	3 to 4 months	Not recommended
Soft cheeses	2 weeks	4 months
Cottage cheese	5 to 7 days	Not recommended
Cream cheese	2 weeks	Not recommended
Ice cream		1 to 3 months

The Least You Need to Know

➤ If you take the time to organize your kitchen, you'll be much more efficient when you cook and bake.

➤ The most important things to remember about food safety are to keep hot foods hot, cold foods cold, and all food clean.

➤ Many things—not just fresh fruits, vegetables, and meats—can easily be frozen with good results. Baked goods, soft cheeses, and butter are some other foods that freeze well.

➤ Of all fresh meats, poultry, and fish, beef can be frozen the longest; lamb, veal, and fish the shortest; and, as a general rule, the bigger the cut, the longer its freezer life.

➤ Processed meats have a short freezer life—a few weeks to a month or two, depending upon the meat.

Part 6
Keeping the House in Tip-Top Shape

Our homes are our castles, but even castles require improvements and fix-ups from time to time. You can tackle many maintenance and repair projects around the house yourself, even if you're not particularly handy with a hammer, a paintbrush, or a screwdriver. Painting (and maybe some wallpapering), taking advantage of simple energy-saving strategies and products, and controlling bothersome pests in and around your home are within your reach, as the chapters here prove.

Chapter 21

Paint and Paper

In This Chapter

➤ Painting doesn't have to be messy!

➤ Shortcuts for painting windows

➤ Prepping is the key for painting the exterior

➤ Keeping paint brushes as good as new

➤ Storing leftover paint

➤ Wallpapering tips

Professional painters and paper hangers know many little tricks of the trade to make their jobs go quicker and easier. Read this chapter and you'll know many of them, too.

Drip-proof Solutions

Painting can be a messy business, with drips all over the place if you're not careful. Here are some ways to keep them to a minimum.

Ladle it in. Use an old soup ladle to transfer paint from the can to the paint tray without dripping. Stretch a large rubber band over the top of the can and under the bottom. Wipe the bottom of the soup ladle across the rubber band to scrape off excess paint into the can below.

Smart Solution

When stripping paint off a table, chair, or bench, place small bowls under each leg. The bowls will catch the excess paint stripper and protect your floors. You can also reuse the excess stripper.

Smart Solution

On the back of the light switch plate in the room you just painted, write down the paint color, where you bought it, and approximately how much paint was used. Then when you need to touch up a spot or repaint the entire room, you have the information you need right there.

Protect shoes. Slip an old pair of socks over your shoes when painting to protect them from drips and splatters.

Clean hands. Keep a few plastic bags (such as sandwich bags or grocery store bags) to slip over your hands so that you can grab the phone if it rings without getting wet paint all over it. You can also wrap a small towel around the telephone receiver and fasten it with rubber bands.

Preventing ceiling drips. When painting a ceiling, you can prevent drips from running down your paint brush by sticking the brush through the middle of a small paper, plastic, or foam disposable plate. Use some tape to hold the brush in place—if the plate is too large and bulky, cut it down to a smaller circle with a pair of scissors.

Light fixtures. To prevent drips of paint from falling on your light fixtures, tie plastic bags around them. But be careful not to turn on the fixtures when you have a bag over them; the plastic will melt and make a big mess. If you think you or someone else might turn them on by mistake, place a piece of tape over the light switch to keep it in the off position.

Furniture legs. Before painting a table, chair, or bench, place jar lids under each leg to catch any paint drips.

Instead of throwing away an old shower curtain or liner, save it for your next painting project. These make perfect drop cloths.

Keeping Paint Cans Clean

One of the messiest things about painting is the paint can itself. Here's how to keep it from driving you crazy.

Watch How You Wipe That Brush!

Don't use the side of the can to remove excess paint from your brush. Use a straight piece of wire across the opening of the can so that the sides and top of the can stay clean. To hold the wire in place, bend it at right angles and insert the end in two nail holes punched at opposite sides of the rim. The wire from a coat hanger works perfectly. Use wire cutters to snip off a straight piece of wire.

You can also stretch a large rubber band over the top of the can and under the bottom. Wipe the paint brush across the rubber band to remove any excess paint; the paint will drip back into the paint can.

Another solution is to cut an old paint can lid in half, put it on the new paint can, and use the cut edge for dabbing the excess paint off your brush.

Mess-less Pouring

Before pouring paint from a can, cover the rim with masking tape. After pouring, remove the tape. The rim will be clean and the paint lid will fit tightly without making a big mess.

Smart Solution

You can make a portable, light-weight paint bucket out of an empty, clean plastic milk or bleach bottle. Cut a hole for the paintbrush to fit through easily on the side opposite the handle. Use a funnel to pour the paint into the bleach bottle.

You can also poke several holes around the inside rim of the paint can with a hammer and nail. The holes will allow paint in the rim to drip back into the paint can.

Paint Odor

Some people like the smell of fresh paint, but if you're not one of them, here are two ways get rid of the odor:

➤ Add 2 teaspoons of vanilla extract per quart of paint. It will mask the smell without affecting the paint.

➤ Place a large pan of water that contains a tablespoon of ammonia in the freshly painted room. Close the door and leave it there for several hours or overnight.

Painting the Little Things

When it comes to painting, the so-called "little" jobs can be the worst. These ideas can help.

Drawer pulls and knobs. Remove these from the furniture and set them screw-end down into empty soda bottles. Then spray-paint them or paint with a brush. You'll be able to get all sides and edges of the hardware painted at one time this way, without making a mess.

Radiators. When painting radiators with enamel paint, it's best to have them warm. Warmth tends to bake paint on the metal, and your finish will last longer. Be certain that the paint you're using is recommended for use with radiators.

Smart Solution

To prevent white paint from yellowing, stir a drop of black paint into it.

Smart Solution

Add a few drops of citronella to a gallon of paint to keep away flying insects such as black flies and mosquitoes. The citronella won't affect the paint, but it will keep the bugs from messing up your fresh paint job.

Screens. Use a sponge or tack a small piece of scrap carpeting to a small block of wood. Dip the sponge or carpet into the paint, and dot it onto the screen. You'll use less paint this way than you would with a brush, and it will spread quickly and evenly.

Stairs. Painting stairs can be tough because as soon as they're painted you'll need something that's upstairs (or downstairs)! Here's how to solve that inevitable problem: Paint every other step on one day, and the rest on the next.

When painting outside or basement steps that you want to make less slippery, mix a little sand (add 1 cup per gallon) with the paint. Buy clean sand at a lumber yard or home improvement center.

Wrought iron. Paint wrought iron tables, chairs, railings, plant stands, and the like with a smooth piece of sponge. When the piece starts to get sticky, toss it and use a fresh one. You can cut one large sponge into many pieces to do this job.

Windows

Before painting windows, clean out all the hard-to-reach dirt in the corners and other nooks and crannies with an old paintbrush or toothbrush; then wipe the frame down with a damp cloth or go over it with a vacuum cleaner.

Keeping Paint Off Glass

Scraping paint off window glass after you've painted the frames is very time-consuming. To eliminate having to remove paint from the glass, try these tips:

➤ **Newspapers.** Dampen strips of newspaper or any other straight-edged paper with warm water. Spread the strips around each windowpane, making sure that the paper fits tightly into the corners and edges. The paper will cling to the window long enough for you to finish the paint job.

➤ **Bar soap.** Rub a bar of softened soap around the windowpanes. To soften the soap, dip it into warm water for a few minutes.

➤ **Liquid soap.** Use a clean paintbrush to paint liquid soap on the windowpanes around the corners and edges. When the soap dries on the windows, you are ready to paint. When the paint is thoroughly dry, wash the soap off the windows.

➤ **Petroleum jelly.** Smear it around the edges—you don't have to cover all the glass. Remove with warm soapy water after the paint dries.

Removing Paint Splatters

No matter how neat you try to be, you'll end up with some paint splatters. To get rid of them, try these solutions.

New splatters on glass. Wash freshly dried paint off glass with hot cider or white vinegar. To heat vinegar, pour some into a small container and microwave on high until it's warm. Watch it carefully so that it doesn't boil.

Older splatters. Use nail polish remover to get rid of paint splattered on window glass. Allow it to soak for a few minutes, then rub it off with a cloth and wash with warm soapy water. The paint splatters will usually disappear, even if they have been on the window for a long time.

You can also soften paint stains that have already dried on glass with turpentine and scrape off the paint with a single-edge razor blade. This method also works on putty stains.

Woodwork. Gently rub with very fine, dry steel wool to remove the splatters. Don't rub too hard, or you'll remove all the paint on the woodwork!

Tile and porcelain. To remove paint splatters from tile or porcelain, use an expired credit card and some warm cider or white vinegar. First apply the vinegar, then use the credit card to scrape off the splatters.

Door knobs, pulls, or hinges. To take off paint and varnish, remove the hardware and simmer them for a few minutes in baking soda and water, then wipe off the solution with a cloth.

Smart Solution

Before painting the wood, coat door hinges, doorknobs, lock latches, and other hardware with a thin coating of petroleum jelly. This will eliminate a lot of scraping later.

Smart Solution

Looking at a small paint sample or chart doesn't help you much in visualizing how a new color will look on your walls. To get a better idea, buy a small amount of the color and paint a poster board with it. Move the poster around to various spots in the room and see how it looks under different lighting.

No Lumps

Please, don't automatically throw away paint that has become lumpy. First stir or shake it up, then strain it. The best strainer is old pantyhose. Stretch one leg of the hose over a container, and slowly pour the paint over it.

You can also cut a circle from an old screen, slightly smaller than the paint can lid. Sit the lid on top of the paint. As it sinks, the lid will press all the lumps to the bottom of the can.

Exterior Painting

Painting the outside can be a big job, so prepare yourself with this advice.

Choosing the Paint

Just picking out what type of paint to use on the exterior of the house can be confusing. Here are some guidelines to steer you in the right direction.

Exterior paints are either latex or oil-based and come in various grades of glossiness, with or without enamel. Generally speaking, you use exterior latex paint for wood siding and exterior oil-based enamel on the trim. Because exterior paint must protect your house from the weather, using a good-quality paint is even more important on the exterior of your house than on the inside.

If the house has been painted before, flat latex house paint is the easiest to work with and it holds up well, too. It's a good choice if you don't know what paint was used before, because it works well over old latex or oil-based paint. Latex paint breathes better than oil-based paint and therefore allows some of the moisture that collects in the walls in the winter to pass through. This lessens the chance of peeling. Of course, if you apply latex over an old oil-based paint, you won't have this advantage.

For trim, most experts recommend an oil-based exterior paint. The oil-based products don't dry as fast as the latex paints, and, therefore, they hold their wet edge a little bit longer. This makes it easier to get a smoother finish without lap marks because the wet edges of laps, as you paint back and forth, blend in with one another.

With oil paints you can add a tablespoon of paint thinner per gallon if the paint begins to get too thick.

House Colors

Deciding what color (or colors) to paint the house can be a scary decision. You know that you're going to spend many hours painting the house (or spend lots of money having someone else paint it), and if you don't like the color, you'll be doing the job over again or living with your choice for several years. Here are some things to think about when choosing an exterior color scheme.

First think about the style of your house. Old Victorian homes lend themselves to the use of several colors. A Queen Anne home might look great in pastels. A Cape Cod saltbox is hard to beat when painted gray with white trim. If you have an older home, go to the library and look for books or magazines with homes similar to yours and see what colors they used.

You might also want to drive around your local neighborhoods and look for similar houses and color schemes you like. Take your camera and take pictures of those you like the best. You might even want to stop and ask the homeowner for the exact colors or other information. Most will be very flattered that you liked their job; unless, of course, you live next door and plan to paint your home exactly like theirs!

When picking out the exterior paint colors, you'll need to keep in mind the color of the roof shingles and any brick or stone work on the outside of the house or foundation. You'll want to choose colors that blend or harmonize with those parts of the house.

To make your house look the best, there is a general rule of thumb that painting experts say you should follow: First, choose three colors that blend and contrast with each other. Then paint the body of the house and the foundation in one color. Most of the time you'll want to use the palest shade of your color scheme. Then paint the soffits and other trim, any corner posts, and porches in the deepest color shade. Use the last shade, the medium one (which is usually the brightest), on the front door and window shutters.

You can use color to highlight the best features of your house. That's why a more intense color is often used on the front door or to accent roof peaks or brackets. Don't call attention to things like gutters and down spouts by painting them a bright color. Instead, paint them the same color as the siding or trim so they don't stand out.

Painting the outside of your house is a big job. Do it right, and you won't have to do it again for several years.

Prep it. First check for any small openings that moisture can get into. Caulk small cracks or holes in the siding and around the windows, and replace any rotten siding. Sink any nails that have worked their way up, and fill the nail holes with putty. Replace or repair any deteriorated trim around windows and doors.

Next, wash the exterior of your house and scrape away any loose or peeling paint; then sand the area smooth. When the wood is dry, prime any exposed, bare wooden surfaces before painting.

Good weather, good job. Wait for calm, dry weather. Paint will dry the best when the temperature is between 60° and 70°F. If there's a chance of rain or it's humid outside, hold off on painting.

Cover up. Place drop cloths under where you are painting and over plants, shrubs, sidewalks, and anything else that might catch paint splatters or drips. If you don't have enough drop cloths, old sheets and shower curtains work just as well.

Start at the top. Work your way down from the eaves. Not only will you get the hard part done first, but drips will run onto unpainted surfaces where you can brush them off without smudging.

Brush Basics

When buying a new paintbrush—whether it's of natural hair or synthetic—always look for one that has flagged (frayed) bristles because they hold more paint. An old brush won't hold as much paint as a new one because the flagged ends have worn off.

When you're going to use a new paint brush on a job, remove loose bristles first so that they don't wind up in your paint can or on the newly painted surface. Do this by washing the brush in plain water and combing through it with a hair comb. Then look for loose bristles still on the brush, and pull them out by hand. When working on a paint job that takes a couple of days, save time by thoroughly wrapping brushes in several layers of aluminum foil or plastic wrap and freezing them. You can stick the wrapped brushes right into the freezer section of your refrigerator. Take the brushes out of the freezer and let them thaw out for at least an hour before using them again. Freezing it keeps the paint from drying and getting stuck on the brushes, so you don't have to clean them each day.

Smart Solutions

For best results, use natural-bristle brushes with oil-based paint and synthetic brushes with latex.

Cleaning Brushes

Throwing away brushes after each painting project can get expensive. If you act quickly (before the paint dries), cleaning brushes is not a big deal.

Latex paint. If you've been painting with latex paint, all you'll need to do is hold the brush under an open faucet and rinse out the paint until the water runs clear. Then shake all the water out of the brush.

Oil paint. If you're using oil-based paint, you'll have to use a solvent (paint thinner or turpentine) to clean the brush.

Removing solvent. To get the solvent off a paint brush neatly, place the brush in a plastic bag and use a rubber band to hold the top of the bag around the handle. Then shake the solvent from the brush into the bag.

Hanging a brush. Never let paint brushes rest on their bristles in a can of solvent—they will bend and lose their shape. Instead, put the solvent in an empty coffee can, cut an X in the plastic lid, and push the brush handle up through the slit. By doing this, the brush will hang in the can.

Give clean brushes a pointed edge by hanging the bristles between clamp-type hangers (sold at home improvement stores).

More than one. To clean several brushes at one time, suspend them in the solvent from a piece of wire coat hanger slipped through the holes in the brush handles.

Small brushes. To clean small brushes, poke the handles through a piece of cardboard, then lay the cardboard over the top of a small can of solvent.

Restoring Brushes

When your paint brush is hardened or bent, you shouldn't automatically toss it away. Chances are good you can salvage it.

Hardened latex paint. To rescue a paintbrush that has hardened after it was used with latex paint, hang it in a small bucket with 1 cup of laundry detergent. Fill the bucket with hot water until the bristles are covered. Swish the brush around to mix the water and detergent. Leave the brush to soak for three to four days, agitating the bristles occasionally. Then remove it from the solution and rinse thoroughly with cold water.

When the brush is almost dry, wrap old newspaper around it, leaving about 2 inches of paper extending beyond the bristles. Fold the excess paper back over the brush head, and secure it with rubber bands. When the brush is dry, it will be clean, soft, and almost as good as new.

Hardened oil paint. A paintbrush that's hardened after use in oil paint or varnish can be softened in hot vinegar. Place the brush in a pan, cover it with white or cider vinegar, and simmer on the stove for 10 minutes. Rinse the brush thoroughly. When the brush is almost dry, wrap old newspaper around it, leaving about 2 inches of paper extending beyond the bristles. Fold the excess paper back over the brush head, and secure it with rubber bands.

Bent bristles. To straighten a clean, dry brush that's bent from standing too long in a can of solvent, soak the brush in warm water for an hour or so. This will make the bristles more flexible. Then take two pieces of scrap wood and place one on either side of the bristles; then secure them with a rubber band or a string. Leave the wood on the bristles for two to three days.

Storing Leftover Paint

Inevitably there's some paint left in the bottom of the can at the end a painting job. Here's how to save that paint so you can use it again later.

Preventing paint crust. To prevent a thick film from forming on leftover paint, place a round circle of aluminum foil right on top of the paint surface. To make the circle the correct size, set the can on top of the foil and cut around it.

Keep oil-based paint fresh by adding 4 tablespoons of mineral spirits to the top of the paint. This will form a layer, sealing in the paint below it. Don't mix up the paint and the mineral spirits until you use the paint next time.

No lid splatter. When replacing a lid on a can of paint, drape an old cloth or towel over the lid, then hammer it back on. The cloth will catch any paint that splatters.

Marking old paint. Always mark the paint level and color on the outside of each can before packing it away. You can use your brush dipped in the paint to mark the level of paint inside. This way you can see the level and the color. Make a note of the room or area that you used the paint for (master bedroom, downstairs hallway). Colors can be very similar—and if you make touch-ups with the wrong shade, you'll have to do the job twice.

Storing small amounts. Use empty nail polish or shoe polish bottles for leftover paint. They're excellent for holding enough paint for small touch-up jobs later. Be sure to clean the bottles out thoroughly first, and label them.

> ### Watch Out!
>
> Don't store latex paint some place where it's likely to freeze. Once frozen, it will no longer be usable.

Cleanup Time

The job is done and it's time to clean up. Here are some hints to make this last job easier.

Removing paint from skin. Use cooking oil or baby oil to remove paint from your face or hands. It is much safer and won't burn your skin like turpentine will.

Cleaning roller pans. Put a plastic bag over your roller pan before putting the paint in it. Make sure it's big enough so that you can twist and seal it closed. When you are finished with the job, throw the bag away and you have a clean roller pan. (You can also buy inexpensive molded plastic liners for quick clean-ups.)

Clean oil-based paint from rollers. Fill an empty quart milk carton with solvent, put the roller inside, and crimp the carton ends shut. Give the carton a few shakes, then let the roller soak inside for a few hours before rolling it clean on newspaper.

Cleaning varnish stains from skin. Remove varnish stains from your hands with liquid laundry detergent or prewash (such as Spray 'n' Wash). Rub it on your hands, then wash it off with warm water. In most cases, it will work better than paint thinner or turpentine—and it won't burn your skin.

> ### Bet You Didn't Know
>
> When your spray paint nozzle gets clogged, you can unclog it with paint thinner. Pour some paint thinner or turpentine into a small jar; drop the nozzle into the liquid and let it soak for a few minutes. If necessary, poke a straight pin through the hole in the nozzle.

Wallpaper Solutions

Wallpaper can dress up a room and cover a multitude of sins underneath it like no paint can. Although perhaps daunting at first, with a little practice you can become a whiz at hanging wallpaper. Use these tips to steer you in the right direction.

Choosing Wallpaper

Before buying wallpaper, check the packaging for instructions on how to care for the paper. Most wallpaper manufacturers are now using international symbols to indicate the type of wallpaper and how it should be used. The symbols give you information about cleaning the wallpaper, such as:

➤ Can be sponged
➤ Can be washed
➤ Easily washed
➤ Can be scrubbed

Easy Choices

Washable papers are inexpensive and easy to maintain—and prepasted ones are much easier to hang than those you have to paste yourself.

Smart Solution

Attach several cup hooks or wooden clothes pins to the top of a wooden ladder for hooking on rags so that they'll be handy when you need them.

Watch Out!

Be sure to check the lot numbers on rolls of wallpaper you've ordered before unwrapping them; you'll want all your rolls to be from the same batch (lot number) to make sure the color matches exactly.

Choose easy-to-strip wall coverings if you think you'll want to change the covering at a later date. This is something to think about, especially when papering a nursery or a small child's room. With easy-to-strip wallpaper, you peel off the top layer of the backing and leave the layer below as a lining for the next covering.

Small patterns, big advantage. When hanging wallpaper, you'll need to match the pattern as you hang it. A pattern that is repeated every six or eight inches means a lot less waste per roll than one that's repeated every 24 inches.

Calculating How Much Wallpaper to Buy

When you pick out the wallpaper you plan to use, the back of the sample in the wallpaper book (or the roll itself) will tell you how much area each roll will cover. Most rolls will cover about 36 square feet for a single roll of American wallpaper or about 28 square feet for a single European roll.

The back of the sample will also tell you the repeat, or drop, for a pattern. This tells you how often the pattern repeats itself, and you need to know this because it affects how much paper you will have to waste. For example, if your paper is simply vertical stripes, there will be no drop. If it has a large design, though, you may have to throw away up to 18 inches of each strip to make the repeats line up.

Here's how to calculate how much paper you'll need:

1. Multiply the length of all the walls by the ceiling height.
2. Multiply the height of each door and window by it's width.
3. Add up the window and door totals from #2.
4. Subtract the windows and doors (#3) from #1.
5. Divide this surface area by the coverage area of a roll.

Smart Solution

Keep a few leftover scraps of wallpaper when you finish a job, and staple them to an attic wall. When you need to repair a worn spot, you can grab one of the scraps and it will have faded just like the paper on the wall. If you leave the scraps rolled up, they will not fade as fast as the ones on the wall—and chances are the replacement piece will have more color than the wall.

This will give you the number of rolls you need before calculating for waste.

To calculate the waste, note the width of the wallpaper you have picked out. Take a tape measure and go around the room marking out where each new strip will begin. Add up the strips and multiply this number by the drop. Remember, even if a strip is only a foot or two long, over a door, it still needs a drop. Now add in 2 inches for each strip. This is for trim waste on the non drop end of each strip. If your paper does not have a drop, you'll need to add a total of 4 inches for each strip—2 inches of trim for each end of each strip. The wallpaper book will tell you how long each roll is, so it's an easy matter to add up how many rolls you'll need for drop and trim waste.

Once you have calculated how much wallpaper you will need, add 10 percent for waste. If this is your first wallpaper job, add in another roll after the 10 percent—you are likely to make more mistakes than an experienced paperhanger.

Getting Started

If you haven't wallpapered before, choose a small room or just one wall for your first project. Avoid complex rooms such as bathrooms and kitchens until you build up some confidence.

Wear a carpenter's apron. You can put all the tools you'll need inside the pockets, so when you're up on the ladder the tools are up there with you, within easy reach.

Tear, don't cut, patches. When patching over wallpaper, always tear the patch. A torn edge will be much easier to blend into the wall, but a cut edge will stick out like a sore thumb.

Fixing bumps. When you find a bulge in the wallpaper, slit it with a razor blade. Use a knife to insert a little paste under the paper, then smooth it closed with a wet sponge.

Removing Old Paper

Do not paper over existing wallpaper. Remove all the old material, and make sure the surface is smooth before you begin applying the new covering. This will ensure a neat, professional-looking job. (See above for easy-to-strip papers.)

To remove old wallpaper, mix up a solution of equal parts water and white vinegar. Use a sponge to wet down a section of the wall with the solution, continuing until the wallpaper won't absorb any more water. Let the vinegar-and-water solution sit for at least 15 minutes. Sponge some more of the solution on the wallpaper again, and then peel it off with a wide putty knife. It should come off easily, but if it doesn't, repeat the process and try again.

The Least You Need to Know

➤ No matter how careful you are, painting is a messy job. It's usually easier to protect surfaces than it is to remove paint splatters from them later.

➤ Before painting windows, clean them thoroughly and use soap, newspaper strips, or petroleum jelly to keep paint off the glass.

➤ To ensure a good exterior paint job, prep the surface carefully and wait for good weather.

➤ Take care of good paint brushes by cleaning and storing them properly; they'll last through many jobs.

➤ Prepasted wallpapers are the easiest to hang, and washable ones are best suited for heavy-use areas, such as hallways, kitchens, and children's rooms.

➤ Remove old paper with water and vinegar before putting on the new paper. Special easy-to-strip papers make removal a snap.

Chapter 22

Home Maintenance and Repairs

In This Chapter

➤ Getting ready to tackle simple problems as they come up

➤ Minor plumbing problems you can probably fix yourself

➤ Squeaky floors and steps, sticky doors and windows

➤ Picture and mirror hanging

➤ Garage floors—and doors

➤ Patio furniture

Even with the best preventive maintenance, there will always be things to fix around the house from time to time. Many of them you can do yourself, with a little help. Your local library no doubt has books and videos that can walk you through most any project around the house.

Employees at hardware stores are also great resources. You'd be surprised how knowledgeable many of them are—and how freely they'll give you advice, if you just ask. They can answer your questions and let you know if yours is a project that can easily be done or if you should get someone in to do the job for you.

Getting Started

Being prepared is half the battle. Here are some things to consider before the need for a repair arises.

A Basic Tool Kit

Having an all-purpose tool kit on hand makes home repairs less of a hassle. Here are the basics:

➤ Hammer

➤ Screwdrivers (both regular and Phillips)

➤ Pliers

➤ Scissors

➤ Utility knife

➤ Awl

➤ Steel tape measure

➤ Tapes (electrical, duct, and adhesive)

➤ Lubricating oil, or a spray such as WD-40

Smart Solution

Buy a good basic home repair manual and keep it handy. It will quickly pay for itself. You'll find that with a good illustrated guide, you can do many projects yourself.

Bet You Didn't Know

To remove a broken light bulb from its socket, use a raw potato. First make sure the switch is turned off, then push the potato into the base and twist the bulb out.

You can add to your tool kit as needed. Store it in one location that is easy to reach. You may even want to keep it in the kitchen or a handy closet instead of in the garage or down in the basement.

Know Your House

Learn how to make simple repairs before the breakdown occurs. For example, learn how to re-light pilot lights on everything in your house that runs on gas before you have to do it in the cold or without electricity.

Electrical work. As soon as you move into your new home, locate your circuit breakers or fuse box and figure out how to replace a fuse or reset a tripped circuit breaker. It's a good idea to keep a flashlight in an easy-to-find spot because darkness and tripped breakers or fuses tend to go together.

When doing any type of electrical work, flip off the circuit breaker or remove the fuse for the area you are working on.

Calling In a Pro

If you are faced with a home repair that is over your head, call a qualified service technician. Ask if he'll give you an estimate. Some will give you a free estimate, while others will charge for the estimate but deduct it from the bill if you have the work done by them. Believe it or not, you may have room to negotiate when given a estimate on a repair. You may feel a little awkward about trying to get the price dropped a bit the first time you try it, but what have you got to lose? Use a little tact and maybe you'll be successful.

Ask friends, neighbors, or coworkers for advice on who to call for repairs. They will be happy to tell you about local companies—both good and bad. People always tend to remember excellent —and poor—service.

Premium prices for off hours. Think twice before you call a repair technician to your house on a weekend or evening. You'll probably pay a premium for these hours. Some companies will even charge extra if they start to work on the job before five o'clock and end up working late. Ask when overtime rates kick in to make sure you don't end up paying extra.

Plumbing

Plumbers make house calls for stopped-up toilets and slow kitchen and bathroom drains more than for any other problem. Here are some tips to help keep your pipes and toilets clog-free.

Clogged Drains

Bathroom sinks and tubs are prone to clogging because of the hair, soap bits, and all kinds of goodies that get washed down the drain. Over time, the buildup of hair and gunk causes the drain and pipe openings to get smaller so that water doesn't drain as fast. A slow drain in a bathroom sink may take three minutes to drain; a tub drain, perhaps 10 minutes or more.

Smart Solution

When you need to turn off the power in a certain room and you're not sure which switch to flip in the fuse box, try this: Plug in a portable radio in the room, and turn up the volume so you can hear it at the fuse box. When you flip off the correct switch, the radio will shut off.

Bet You Didn't Know

If you are planning a major home improvement project or working on the outside of your home, check the local zoning laws before you start the project. Subdivisions and other parts of the city can have extensive regulations concerning home additions, sheds, carports, driveways, garages, and porches, to name a few. If you build something that is not allowed, you can be fined and required to tear it down. What a waste of money! Even something as simple as a fence can have regulations about its height, material, and distance from the street.

Watch Out!

Don't fall for home improvement scams. Always take your time when deciding whether to go ahead with a major project. Especially be on the alert when a contractor approaches you and proposes some home improvement job rather than responding to your request for an estimate. Encourage elderly parents or other relatives to check with you or another member of the family before they give anyone money to do home improvement work.

Watch Out!

Don't dispose of cooking oil and grease by pouring it down the drain or garbage disposal. Instead, pour it into a can, put the lid on tightly and put it outside in the trash.

Bleach Drain Cleaner

One of the best ways to keep a sink drain running smoothly is to pour a cup of full-strength bleach down it every two weeks. The bleach will eat the hair so the clog can't get started. It will also help keep the drains smelling fresh. You can quickly do every sink and tub in the house. Simply pour the bleach into the drain and after five minutes turn on the cold water and let it run down the drain. (Always keep bleach away from children and pets.) If the metal part of your drain can be removed (many pop right out), clean out the hair and gunk before adding the bleach.

Homemade Drain Cleaner

This cleaner will remove many drain clogs without harmful chemicals.

1 cup baking soda

1 cup table salt

$1/4$ cup cream of tartar

Mix baking soda, salt, and cream of tartar in a small bowl. Stir thoroughly and pour into a clean, covered jar. When ready to use, just pour a cup down the drain and let sit for several hours.

Unclogging Stopped-up Drains

Clogged drains stop us in our tracks! Here are some hints to unclog them.

Greasy drains. Pour in $1/2$ cup of salt and $1/2$ cup of baking soda, followed by 4 cups of boiling water. Allow to sit overnight, if possible. Greasy drains usually respond to this treatment.

Moderately clogged drains. Pour in $1/2$ cup of baking soda, followed by $1/2$ cup of cider or white vinegar. Caution: The two ingredients will interact, creating foam and fumes, so put the the drain cover or strainer back in place after pouring in the soda and cider. Flush the drain with water after about three hours.

Rock Salt for Clear Toilet Drains

Tree roots can mean big trouble for toilets, especially those in older homes where the trees have had plenty of time to send out roots. Roots will slip inside the smallest crack in the drainage pipe—or can even grow up through the sewer. They'll continue to grow right inside the pipe until it becomes clogged.

This is not a problem you can fix yourself—call a plumber. Sometimes he'll need a special tool to cut the roots out of the pipes if they have been neglected for many years and are dense. It's an expensive job, and in a few short years the tree roots can grow back and clog the pipes again.

To prevent roots from invading your pipes, throw a handful of rock salt down the toilet and flush once every two weeks. Rock salt, used in water softeners and old-fashioned ice cream freezers, can be bought at many supermarkets and hardware stores. Keep some on hand and use it regularly.

Bet You Didn't Know

If a plunger doesn't work when you try to unclog a drain, try using a straightened wire coat hanger, bent at one end to form a small hook. Using the hook, try to loosen or remove the debris that is causing the problem.

When placed into the toilet, the salt dissolves into salt water and will kill the fine ends of the tree roots inside the pipes. You don't have to worry: The salt water will not kill the entire tree, just the roots that have invaded your drain pipe. Everything above ground will look the same. The tree will be as healthy as always, and the root will seek water someplace else because its roots don't like salt water.

Rock salt can be used in the city or the country, with a sewer or septic system.

Taming Other Toilet Trouble

Here are some other precautions to keep in mind for your toilets and drains.

Don't use your toilet as a trash can. Things not intended to be flushed down the toilet can clog it up. Dental floss is one of the worst culprits. Although it's thin and innocuous-looking, the floss gets caught on other things and can quickly give you a major problem.

Paper, bugs, cigarettes, and other trash should be thrown in the garbage instead of the toilet. You'll save water and help keep the drains clear. Unless the package states that the tampons or sanitary napkins are flushable, don't put them down the toilet; just one sanitary napkin can stop it up.

Don't buy the cheapest toilet paper. Sometimes the cheapest product doesn't save you money in the long run. The really cheap toilet papers (you know the kind—those that feel like cardboard paper) don't dissolve quickly and can stop up the toilet.

Instead, buy any of the brands that feel soft to the touch; they'll dissolve quickly and keep your toilet working properly.

I clip coupons and switch between three or four soft brands. I stock up on toilet paper when it is on sale, and I pay less for a better brand than the rough stuff. With a little planning, you can too.

Don't go crazy trying to save water. If you installed some sort of waster-saver in your toilet and then notice that you are having problems with the toilet draining, try taking out the water-saving device and see if the problem clears up. Some older toilets just won't push the toilet paper and waste out of the system without lots of water. If this is the case, you can replace the old toilet with a new water-saving toilet for probably less than $100 at a home improvement store to help you cut back on the water bill.

Toilet Repairs

When a toilet isn't working right, you may be able to roll up your sleeves and fix the problem yourself. Here are some of the more common problems that you may want to tackle.

Nonstop water running. If the water won't stop running, the problem may be with the float ball. Check to see if there is water inside the ball by lifting its arm, unscrewing it, and shaking it. If there's water inside, the ball has a leak and needs to be replaced. It's just a matter of buying a new one at a hardware store or home center and replacing it.

If there isn't any water in the ball, try bending the float arm downward so that the bent arm triggers the water to stop rising when it is slightly less than an inch from the top of the overflow tube.

If neither of the above suggestions get the job done, the problem may be in the float arm assembly. Turn off the shutoff valve underneath the toilet, and dismantle the float arm assembly. Replace the entire assembly with a new one. It's usually sold all together, so you'll probably have to replace the whole unit instead of just the worn or broken part.

Partially filled tanks. If the toilet gurgles or the tank gets only partially filled when you flush, the problem may be with the valve seat (the drain at the bottom of the tank). Check whether the stopper ball that covers it is properly positioned. If not, turn off the water valve and flush the toilet of its water. Then loosen the screw that holds the guide arm (which controls the stopper ball), and reposition the stopper ball. Don't forget to retighten the screw.

Also, check for corrosion on the inside of the valve seat. If it feels rough, smooth it with wet-dry sandpaper. If

Bet You Didn't Know

If your toilet bowl is clogged, flushing it again will only cause the bowl to overflow. Instead, use a plunger to unclog the toilet. For better plunger cup suction, get water from the sink and pour it into your toilet bowl so that the water covers the plunger cup.

neither of these tactics works, you'll probably need to replace the stopper ball with a flapper ball available at hardware stores.

Partial flush. If you're getting only a partial flush from your toilet, then the stopper ball may be falling on the valve seat too quickly. To remedy the problem, raise the guide arm that holds the stopper ball by loosening the thumbscrew and lifting the guide arm so that the stopper ball will float longer.

You can usually get the same results by unhooking the lift wire and shortening it, bending it in the new position, and then rehooking it in the same hole or a different hole.

Checking for silent leak. To check your toilet for a silent leak, pour some food coloring into the tank. Don't flush the toilet for an hour. Then, if any of the colored water from the tank appears in the bowl, seepage has occurred and either you or your plumber should replace the valve.

Garbage Disposals

A garbage disposal has a big job to do, and from time to time you'll have to remove some stuck food or a foreign object from it. Here are some tips to keep your garbage disposal in tip-top shape.

Grease clogs. To clear the unit of greasy food, try putting in a handful of ice cubes and running the disposal. The ice should congeal the fat, allowing the garbage disposal to grind it into small, flushable pieces.

Bad smell. To make your garbage disposal smell sweeter, put a slice of lemon into it. If it has a bad odor that won't go away, remove the rubber splash guard and scrub off any food particles or grime.

Unjamming Garbage Disposals

When the garbage disposal jams, shut off the power to it. Then remove the splash guard and look inside to see how bad the problem is. Remove the obstruction and, if necessary, insert the end of a broom or mop handle into the grinding chamber and push against the turntable until it rotates freely.

If the garbage disposal shuts off while in operation, wait about five to 10 minutes for the motor to cool, then push the reset button on the bottom or side of the disposal. If it won't start, make sure the unit is plugged in and that the fuse or circuit breaker is functioning.

Light Bulb Lingo

Remember when the only choice was a regular light bulb? Now we have quite a variety to choose from. Here are some of the pros and cons of each.

Incandescent. This is the plain old light bulb we're all familiar with. It gives off a warm, flattering light, rich in red and yellow tones. Incandescent bulbs are the least expensive to purchase but the most expensive to operate because they use proportionately more electricity than the others. They come in a wide variety of brightnesses (wattages), shapes, and coatings.

Fluorescent. Fluorescent tubes cost more than light bulbs, but they last longer and are much cheaper to operate since they use less electricity to produce the same amount of light as a standard incandescent light bulb. The older tubes produce a source of light that is rich in blue-green tones. Fluorescent lighting is very common and acceptable for the office, but for years many people objected to using them in the home because of their cool and rather harsh color light. Now newer fluorescent tubes are coated with minerals that enable them to emit a light richer in red—more similar to the light of incandescent bulbs. If you have not replaced a fluorescent tube in your house for several years, try the new warmer tubes. You'll probably notice—and like—difference.

Compact fluorescents. These tubes are folded and twisted to take up about the same amount of space as a standard light bulb. You can buy ones that adapt to standard light fixtures and even recessed fixtures. There are also small units for under cabinets. While they cost much more than regular light bulbs, they last many times longer and will cost less in the long run. And, like other fluorescents, they consume less electricity than incandescent bulbs.

Quartz halogen. These small bulbs produce a very bright, white light that is close in color to daylight. They're used in video recorders and movie cameras, as well as in many stylish light fixtures, such as high-tech track lighting, torchieres, and high-intensity lamps. Halogen lights put out a lot of heat, so they must be used in special fixtures.

Floor Repairs

Floors take a lot of abuse from being walked on every day. You can end up with squeaks, dents, holes, and other little problems that need attention. Even some seemingly big problems can be fixed easily. Here are some solutions to try.

Squeaky floors. Apply cornstarch, talcum powder, or powdered graphite between the floor boards. (You can buy graphite at a hardware store.) This will help lubricate the boards, and many times this will stop the squeak. If none of them work, you will need to nail or screw the board into the joist below.

Squeak under carpet. If you have a squeaky wood floor under tile or carpet, you may be able to eliminate the squeak without removing the floor covering. Try to reset loose boards by pounding a hammer on a block of scrap wood (a driving block) in the area over the squeaky boards. (Don't hammer right into tile; you may crack it.) The pressure may force the loose nails back into place.

Squeaky stairs. Stair squeaks are usually caused by a loose tread rubbing against a riser when someone steps on the stairs. First try lubricating the stairs by forcefully blowing powdered graphite, cornstarch, or talcum powder into the joints where the backs of the treads meet the risers. (You can use fireplace bellows or your mouth to blow in any of these powders.)

If the lubrication does not stop the squeak, remove the trim molding, and use a hammer and driving block to tap small wooden wedges into the space between the tread and the riser. After driving the wedges, cut them flush with the riser, using a utility knife, and replace the molding to hide them.

Smart Solution

Try filling dents in a hardwood floor with clear nail polish or shellac. By using something clear, the floor's color will show through so the dents will not be as noticeable.

Linoleum bulges. Sometimes you can flatten bulges or curled seams in a linoleum floor by placing aluminum foil over the areas and holding a hot steam iron right above the foil. The heat from the iron will soften and reactivate the adhesive. Place some heavy objects, such as a stack of books, over the treated areas to keep them flat until the adhesive has a chance to cool and harden.

Perfect floor patch. Here's how to replace a damaged area of resilient flooring like linoleum: Place the scrap over the damaged area so that it overlaps sufficiently, match up the pattern, if needed, and tape it to hold it in place. Then cut through both layers at the same time to make a patch that will exactly fit. Replace the damaged area with the tightly fitting patch.

Gouge repair. To patch a gouge (not a dent) in a resilient floor, take a scrap of the flooring and grate it with a food grater. Mix the resulting dust with clear nail polish and plug the hole. Once dry, it will blend perfectly.

Hole repair. To camouflage a gouge or hole in a resilient floor, use crayon wax. Choose a crayon that matches the floor color, melt it, fill in the hole or gouge, and then wax the floor.

Drawer Repairs

Here are some ways to make sure your drawers stay in good working order.

Stuck drawers. When a drawer sticks, remove it and look for shiny places on the top or bottom edges or on the sides. Sand down these shiny areas with sandpaper. Try the drawer to see if it slides more easily. If necessary, repeat sanding until it does.

Easy sliding. To make your drawers slide in and out easier, rub the drawer and the frame where they touch with candle wax, paraffin, or a bar of soap. This is especially helpful for frequently used drawers or ones that are filled with heavy items.

Sticky drawers in humid weather. If drawers get stuck only in humid or rainy weather, fix the problem when the weather dries out by coating the unfinished wood with a penetrating sealer or with wax.

Door and Window Repairs

Malfunctioning doors and windows can really be a nuisance, especially when you use them every day. When something goes wrong, try one of these solutions.

Squeaky doors. You can usually stop a door from squeaking by putting a few drops of oil at the top of each hinge. Move the door back and forth to work the oil into the hinge. If the squeaking does not stop, raise the pin and add some more oil. Any oil will do, even baby oil.

Sticky locks. Apply graphite to lubricate problem locks. It the lock is tight or will not turn at all, you can probably also fix it with graphite (see sidebar).

Loose doorknob. To stop a knob from rattling, loosen the set-screw (the one sticking out of the handle beneath the knob), and remove the knob. Then place a small piece of putty or modeling clay in the knob, and put the knob back on. Push it on as far as possible, and then tighten the screw.

Dragging door. If a door is sticking or dragging, there may be a problem with the screws in the hinges. Try tightening them. If the screws are not holding, replace them one at a time with a longer screw, or insert a toothpick or matchstick into the hole and put the old screw back in.

Stuck doors. Wait for cool, dry weather to fix a sticking door. The problem may last only as long as the high humidity does. Otherwise, look for a shiny spot on the door where it sticks. Depending on how bad the problem is, you should either sand the spot down with sandpaper or use a planer. Be careful not to overdo it and take off too much wood, because you want the door to fit snugly.

Painting doors. Always sand the door edges before repainting. Buildup of old paint can cause a door to stick.

Smart Solution

You won't have to worry about oil dripping on the floor if you quiet a squeaky hinge by lubricating its pin with petroleum jelly instead of oil.

Bet You Didn't Know

Graphite from a soft pencil can be used to lubricate a resistant door lock. Rub the key back and forth across the pencil point, and then slide the tip in and out of the lock several times.

Broken window glass. To remove cracked glass from a window without making a big mess, crisscross the pane on both sides with several strips of masking tape, then tap it with a hammer. Most of the pane will be held together by the tape, and it should come out in a few big pieces rather than several shards.

Screen holes. To repair a very small hole in a door or window screen, apply several coats of clear nail polish; wait for each to dry between coats. For larger holes, you'll need a piece of screen to place over the hole. You can either sew on the screen patch or use glue to keep it in place.

Picture This: Hanging Pictures

Hanging pictures, mirrors, and other decorative items on walls is easy if you follow certain procedures and use the right hardware for the job.

Hanging 20 Pounds and Less into Drywall and Plaster

All these options will work for lightweight items; read about them all before you make your choice. If you want to hang something that weighs more than 20 pounds, the only alternative is to find a wall stud and drive a nail or screw into it.

Picture hook. The easiest way to hang a picture on plaster or drywall is to use a picture hook. This is a hook with a brad passing through it at a downward angle. These hooks come in several sizes, rated for different weights.

Cloth hanger. If you absolutely do not want to put nails into the walls, then use a gummed cloth hanger. But keep in mind that this type of hanger will not carry the weight of a heavy picture

Anchor. Another way to hang a lightweight picture is to use a plastic wall anchor. This is a plastic plug that's designed to expand as you drive a screw into it. It's easy to install:

1. Drill a hole slightly smaller than the anchor, then tap the anchor into the wall with your hammer.
2. Drive a screw into the hole in the center of the anchor. The anchor will expand in the wall and lock itself and the screw in place.

Smart Solution

To prevent a plaster wall from cracking when hanging a picture, place a small piece of masking tape on the wall. Then gently drive into the middle of that tape the smallest nail or brad the item's weight will allow.

Hanging Heavier Pictures

Molly bolt. When hanging a heavy picture (about 20 pounds) you'll want to use a Molly bolt. This is a slotted cylinder of thin metal with a screw inside it. The end of the cylinder expands inside the wall when the screw is tightened. Here's how you install it:

1. Drill a hole in the wall—the package will tell you what size the hole needs to be— and fit the Molly into the hole.
2. Tighten the screw until it will no longer turn.

The screw can be removed completely and reinserted, or simply loosened enough to catch the picture wire behind it.

Toggle bolt. A toggle bolt is another type of anchor that is designed to hold heavy (20 pounds and more) pictures. It is similar to the Molly bolt , but unlike the Molly, you can't remove the screw if you want to use the bolt again because the toggle will fall behind the wall. The toggle bolt consists of a long thin bolt with a pair of folding "wings" (the toggle) that spring open behind the wall. Here's how to hang something using a toggle bolt:

1. Drill a hole in the wall large enough to pass the folded toggle through.

2. Insert the screw through whatever you want to secure against the wall, then thread on the toggle. Close the toggle wings flat against the screw and push the whole unit through the hole. The wings will spring open behind the wall. Tighten the bolt. You can keep the toggle from turning inside the wall by pulling back on the bolt while you tighten it.

Taking It Out

Nothing is forever and from time to time you'll want to remove anchors or toggle bolts. Here's what you need to know.

➤ A picture hook can be taken out by gently pulling on the brad holding it in place. Some picture hooks come with a brad that can be unscrewed.

➤ Remove a cloth hanger by moistening it with warm water.

➤ To remove a plastic wall anchor, loosen the screw and pull out the anchor. If it is stuck, drive it through the hole into the wall cavity. Then patch the hole.

➤ To take out a Molly bolt, unscrew the bolt and remove the entire unit.

➤ For a toggle bolt, unscrew the bolt until the toggle falls off behind the wall. Then patch the hole.

Into Brick Walls

A brick wall is pretty impenetrable, but you can drive a nail into it without too much effort to hang a picture. Here's how.

Using a carbide-tipped masonry bit, drill a hole about 1 inch deep. Be certain that you make the hole in a brick, not in the mortar because the mortar will crumble if you drill into it. Use a small wad of steel wool as a "nail anchor." Pack the hole you've drilled with steel wool using a nail set or large nail and hammer. Then drive a nail into the packed steel wool. The steel wool will grip the nail and act as an anchor.

Do not use this trick outside or in a damp area, because the steel wool will rust when it gets wet and can stain the wall.

Hanging an Unframed Mirror

The easiest way to put up a mirror that has no frame around it is to use inexpensive plastic clips. These clips come with screws for mounting on wooden doors. If you want to mount the mirror on a wall, use plastic wall anchors, then follow these steps:

1. With a pencil and a carpenter's level, mark where you want the bottom of the mirror to be.

2. Install two clips (use three if the mirror is over 24 inches wide or is very tall) on this line.

3. Rest the mirror in the bottom clips and install the top clips, using the top of the mirror as a guide for their placement.

4. Install a couple of clips on each side of the mirror for added support.

Patio Furniture Maintenance

Good patio furniture may cost a bit more than the cheap stuff, but as they say, you get what you pay for. Here are some tips for keeping it looking good longer.

Bet You Didn't Know

When hanging a cherished or valuable painting, try to place it in a spot that stays cool and away from any direct heat and light. Don't hang it over a heat register, radiator, or near a fireplace. If you do, the paint may become dry and brittle, and dirt carried by rising warm air will end up on the painting. Direct sunlight and even the light from fluorescent bulbs can fade the painting.

Repairs

Lubricating joints. When folding chairs and chaise lounges are hard to open or close all you need to do is spray the metal joints with a silicone spray such as WD-40.

Replacing webbing. When the plastic webbing of the seat is torn you can easily replace it yourself. Look in the *Yellow Pages* for dealers that sell webbing. During the summer months you can pick it up at your local home improvement store. First, you must figure out how much material you'll need. Measure the webbing on the chair seat and allow for a few extra feet. Rent or buy a heavy stapler. Use the old webbing-weave pattern as your guide. You may want to make a drawing of it, or you can take a picture of it if you have the time. Cut off the old webbing, then weave the new seat following your drawing or photograph, and staple the loose ends together on the underside of the seat.

Cleaning

For best results, wash your patio furniture often. Treat it like you would your car. If you wash your car once a week, the job is easy, quick and your car always looks good. If you don't do it for six months, then it's an ordeal. Here's a quick rundown of the most common types of patio furniture and how to clean each. With a little tender loving care and maintenance, it will last and look good for many years.

Mesh furniture. Mesh furniture is easy to clean: simply hose it off weekly and let dry. For more thorough cleaning every four to six months, clean it with liquid soap detergent and warm water. Use a brush to scrub the soapy water in the furniture, then rinse with the garden hose.

Outdoor wicker. Vacuum the wicker and cushions with a soft brush or an upholstery tool. Both the frame and the wicker can be washed in a mild detergent and water when they become soiled. Use a wet sponge to wipe the soil from the surface, rinse and allow to dry thoroughly.

Acrylic cushions. Spot wash by sponging briskly with soap in lukewarm water. Rinse thoroughly with clean water to remove soap; air dry.

Solution-dyed acrylic does not harbor mildew, but dirt does. If mildew does occur, use a mild solution of one cup bleach plus two cups soap per gallon of water. Spray on the entire area and allow to soak in. If necessary, scrub vigorously with a sponge or clean rag. Rinse thoroughly with clean water and air dry.

Vinyl straps. Protect them with a coating of car wax. Buff to remove the excess. When necessary and before waxing, clean with a mild laundry detergent and warm water. To remove scuff marks, apply white toothpaste or a gentle abrasive. Use a dry cloth and rub gently. To remove mildew, use a solution of warm water, mild laundry detergent and chlorine bleach (no more than one-quarter cup to three gallons of water).

Aluminum frames. Clean them with warm water and mild soap. Protect them with a coat of car wax and buff off the excess.

If the surface is pitted scrub it with steel-wool and detergent or soap. Wipe the surface dry and protect it from further pitting by waxing with a paste wax or even a thin layer of varnish. (Use a spray varnish to get an even, professional-looking finish.)

Wrought iron. Clean with warm, soapy water and rinse.

The Least You Need to Know

➤ Have basic tools ready, and familiarize yourself with your house so that you can do simple emergency jobs easily when they come up (and they will!).

➤ Don't use a toilet as a trash can, and if you've got big trees nearby, flush rock salt down the toilet twice a month to prevent tree roots from growing in your drain pipe. Keep a wastebasket beside each toilet, and encourage everyone to use it.

➤ Dents, gouges, and holes in flooring can be easy to fix with materials you already have around the house.

➤ Just any old hanger won't do—choose the right one for your wall and picture's weight.

➤ Good-quality patio furniture can look good for years with simple repairs and regular cleaning.

Chapter 23

Energy-Saving Solutions

In This Chapter

➤ Ways to save when cooling your house

➤ Heating-bill cutters

➤ Conserving hot water

➤ Energy-efficient use of refrigerators, freezers, and other appliances

➤ Little energy-savers all around the house that can add up

Saving energy means saving money—and preserving natural resources. So feel good when you turn off that light nobody's using, and follow the other tips and strategies in this chapter.

Keep Your Cool

When warm weather rolls around, we crank up the air conditioning and watch our cooling bill rise. Use these tips to keep temperatures—and costs—down.

Out, Bright Sun

Outdoor shading. Close the drapes, blinds, or shades on all windows during the heat of the day. Outside vertical louvers, awnings, or shutters offer even greater blocking power. If you live in a warm, sunny climate, louvers, awnings, or shutters will pay for themselves in saved electricity.

Watch Out!

Don't place lamps or a television set near your air-conditioning thermostat. Heat from these appliances can trick your air conditioning unit into running longer than necessary.

Bet You Didn't Know

Clean or replace air-conditioning filters once a month during hot summers. When the filter is dirty, the fan has to run longer to remove the same amount of air; this takes more electricity.

Bet You Didn't Know

When turning on the air conditioning, don't set your thermostat at a colder setting than normal. It will not cool down the house any faster—it will just cool it to a lower temperature than you need and use more energy than necessary.

Watch the Temperature, Inside and Out

Adjust the thermostat. When you use air conditioning, set your thermostat as high as possible: 78°F is often recommended as a reasonably comfortable and energy-efficient indoor temperature. At 75°F, you spend approximately 20 percent more on electricity, and at 72°F, about 40 percent more than you would at a setting of 78°F.

Keep a thermometer outside near a window so you can watch the outdoor temperature. When it drops to 78°F, turn off the air conditioning, open the windows, and save.

Adjust the fan. Set the window air-conditioning fan speed on high, except in very humid weather. When it's humid, set the fan speed at low; you'll get less cooling, but more moisture will be removed from the air (which will make it feel cooler).

Managing Indoor Space and Activities

Fireplaces. Don't air condition your fireplace opening. In summer, as in the winter, fireplace openings can be a source of lost energy dollars. Close the damper, and check and promptly repair any leaks.

Indoor chores. If possible, do your cooking and clothes drying, and use other heat-generating appliances in the early morning or late evening hours, when it is cooler outside. On hot days, serve uncooked dishes; the cooler food will probably taste better in the heat, too. Use energy-saving appliances such as crockpots, microwaves, and pressure cookers if you have them instead of heating up the house with the oven or stove. You'll stay cooler and cut your energy costs.

Out? Off! Turn off window air conditioners when you leave a room for more than two hours. You'll use less energy cooling the room down later than if you had left the unit running. An inexpensive timer can be used to turn the unit back on a half hour before you get home.

Fan booster. An electric fan used with your window air-conditioning unit can spread the cooled air farther around the house without greatly increasing your power use. Be sure the air conditioner is powerful enough to help cool the additional space.

Attic Fan

Attic fans (sometimes called whole-house fans) can substantially lower your electric bill by reducing the need for expensive air conditioning. Studies show that an attic fan that is properly sized and correctly installed can shorten the amount of time you use air conditioning by 30 to 50 percent without sacrificing comfort.

In the warmer southern climates, this can translate into a savings of $100 to $200 each year. In the cooler northern climates, an attic fan may make it comfortable enough that you won't even have to turn the air conditioning on at all. At low to moderate humidity levels, an attic fan can make your home feel comfortable inside even when it's up to 85°F outdoors.

Saving Big-Time

Every hour you have an attic fan on and the air conditioning off, you save money. If you're paying 8 cents a kilowatt hour for electricity, you can run a 400-watt attic fan for about 3 cents per hour. Compare that to the 34 cents it costs to run a typical 3-ton-capacity air conditioner. An attic fan can be installed for about $250 to $600, depending on its size and quality. If you live in a warm climate, you could save enough money on your electric bills to pay for the unit in less than two years.

Savings on the Ceiling

In the winter we call it a wind chill, but in the summer it's a welcome cool breeze. One of the main ways our bodies stay cool is by evaporation, so anything we can do to speed up evaporation makes us feel cooler.

If you don't have an attic fan, you can get a similar cooling effect from a ceiling fan (on a smaller scale, of course). By moving air around the room, the ceiling fan speeds evaporation and makes you feel cooler. That means you can keep the thermostat set a little higher, resulting in a lower cooling bill. Here's how to get the most savings from your ceiling fan:

➤ A ceiling fan doesn't cool the air or furniture in a room—it only cools you. So only use a ceiling fan when you are in the room. Turn it off when you leave, just as you would a light.

➤ Ceiling fans are most effective when mounted 7 to 8 feet above the floor. In a room with a high ceiling, use an extension rod from the ceiling to lower the fan so that it hangs at the proper height.

➤ When buying a fan, look for one that has a variable speed control so that you can adjust the blade speed to provide the amount of cooling you desire.

Bet You Didn't Know

During the winter, your ceiling fan should rotate counter-clockwise at the lowest speed. This brings the warm air down from the ceiling to make the room feel warmer. During the summer, flip the switch to make your fan rotate clockwise.

Tightwad Tip

Remove window screens and keep your windows sparkling clean in the winter. Doing both (or either!) brings more sunlight and solar heat into the house.

Bet You Didn't Know

In rooms with a high ceiling, keep in mind that hot air rises, so a ceiling fan on low speed can push heat down where you want it without creating cold drafts. The ceiling fan will make the room feel several degrees warmer, and the cost of operating it is minimal.

Heat it Up!

Winter means it's time to turn on the heater. Here are some ways to save energy and reduce your heating bill during the cold winter months.

He who hesitates, saves. Don't turn on your heat until you have to. When the evenings start to get cool, wear warmer clothes and add an extra blanket or two.

Filters. Clean or replace the filter in your forced-air heating system once a month during the heating season. A dirty filter makes your furnace work harder. Write down your filter size in your address book or on a piece of paper in your wallet. You can save yourself a return trip by getting the size right the first time. Cleaning or replacing filters is really worth the effort.

Let the sun shine in. Keep draperies and shades open during sunny days to bring the warming sun rays inside. Close them at night to help keep cold out.

Keep cold out. Look for cracks both inside and out that admit cold air into the house. Likely places are around window and door frames, air conditioning units, vents, and wherever pipes enter the house. Fill the cracks or holes with caulk. You'll probably spend less than $50 in materials and net a savings of about 10 percent on your heating costs each year.

If you have storm doors and windows, by all means take the time to fix them up every winter; they can reduce your heating bill by as much as 15 percent!

Bath water. When you take a hot bath during the cold winter months, don't drain the water immediately; instead, leave the hot water in the tub to cool to room temperature. The extra heat and humidity will warm your house several degrees. (If you have small children or curious pets, put a gate up to keep them out of the water.)

Timing Is Everything

One of the easiest ways to save on your annual heating bill is to set back the thermostat before bedtime and when everyone will be out of the house for several hours. Energy experts estimate that you can save up to 15 percent on your annual heating costs by making a 5-degree setback while your family sleeps.

You can manually do this or invest in a clock thermostat. Clock thermostats are easily installed and cost anywhere from about $30 to more than $300 for a very sophisticated model. A lower-priced model will do the trick and save money because, unlike humans, the clock thermostat won't forget. Another handy feature of the clock thermostat is that you can set it to warm the house back up to the normal temperature before your family gets up in the morning or returns from work or school.

Fireplace Facts

In many homes, fireplaces are net energy losers. But if you follow a few of these tips, you can enjoy the crackling fire without paying a high price for it.

➤ Build small, steady fires instead of large, roaring ones. Smaller fires are more efficient at warming the house and sending less energy up the chimney.

➤ Invest in a glass door for the front of your fireplace and use it. It's a real energy saver.

➤ Once the fire in your fireplace is completely out, close the damper. An open damper can let the warmed air in your house escape through the chimney.

➤ Check your damper to see if there is a gap when it's closed. Some dampers leave a gap of an inch or more that will allow house air to escape through the chimney. Close the gap with insulation or a flue plug when your fireplace is not in use.

Clothing Counts

Your body gives off heat. Dressing for cold weather can make you more comfortable without added energy costs.

➤ Wear closely woven fabrics. They add at least $1/2$ degree in warmth to your body.

➤ Pants are warmer than skirts or dresses by at least 1 degree.

➤ A light long-sleeved sweater adds almost 2 degrees in warmth.

➤ A heavy long-sleeved sweater adds about 4 degrees.

➤ Two lightweight sweaters add about 5 degrees in warmth because the air between them serves as extra insulation to keep in more body heat.

The Little Things

In addition to reducing the cost of heating and cooling, there are many other smaller things you can do to reduce energy consumption; they can really add up.

Home Utility Audit

Before you start to add insulation, caulking, or weather-stripping—and before you upgrade your water heater or furnace—give your local power company a call. You may be surprised at how willing the experts are to help you find ways to save energy. Many local power companies offer a free walk-through audit that checks for air leaks, level of insulation in the walls and the attic, and heating and cooling system performance. Some install water-saving devices such as shower heads and toilet dams at no charge.

Some utility companies even help with the costs of a home energy fix-up through rebates or monthly discount credits—and they may be able to do energy-related home improvements or increase the insulation in your home to the recommended amount for a reduced cost.

If your power company offers a free energy audit, by all means, take them up on it. Even if you think your house is in good shape energy-wise, an audit may find things you didn't. It can be an eye opener and a money saver; taking the time to schedule an energy audit is time well spent.

Tune up and save. To keep your heating system working efficiently, have it serviced regularly: Once a year for oil-fired furnaces, boilers, and water heaters. Once every two years for gas-fired furnaces, boilers, and water heaters. One every two years for central air conditioners and once a year for heat pumps. A professional tune-up can save you as much as 10 percent on your winter fuel bills. Plan ahead and have it serviced before the cold weather sets in. Once the frigid air hits and everyone turns on the heat, service companies may be swamped with emergency repairs.

Let it out! Electrical outlets around the house need to be sealed with inexpensive gaskets to prevent heat loss. You can find these gaskets at any hardware store. This is a simple project that anyone can do.

More Moisture

The humidity level in your house plays a large part in how comfortable the temperature feels. During the winter, if your house is dry, add a house plant or keep a few shallow bowls of water sitting out in inconspicuous places where air circulates freely. The extra humidity will make you feel warmer without turning up the thermostat.

If you have static electricity in your house—or if your family seems to have dry throats and nasal passages—the air is probably too dry and you'll feel warmer with a little added humidity. Installing a humidifier in a forced air system will help, but it's important not to overhumidify, lest you start having condensation problems on windows and walls, and encourage molds and other bionasties to grow. Interesting, one of the best ways to raise the humidity in an older, leaky house is to weatherseal it and reinsulate.

Watch the Windows

Window treatments save energy year-round. They reduce heat loss in the winter and prevent unwanted heat gain in the summer. Here's how the most popular window treatments stack up, in order from worst to best. Window treatment installation is important, too. The insulating savings of blinds, drapes, and shades depends more on the tightness of fit and seal around the window than it does the material.

Window Treatment Ratings

Sheer curtains   Worst

Metal mini-blinds

Vertical blinds

Unlined draperies

Lined draperies

Window shades

Wood shutters without a lining

Aluminized pleated shades

Wood shutters with a lining

Window quilts with lining   Best

Heating Water

Heating water accounts for about 15 percent of all the energy we use in our homes—don't waste it. Do as much household cleaning as possible with cold water. And when turning off faucets and showerheads, get in the habit of turning off the hot water before the cold. As I've said before, little things add up.

Check hot water temperature. Most water heaters are preset at 140°F, but a setting of 120°F can provide adequate hot water for most families. If you reduce the setting from 140°F to 120°F, you can save 18 percent of your water heating costs. Even reducing the setting 10°F (to 130°F) will save you more than 6 percent. The

Tightwad Tip

Turn off your water heater when you take an out-of-town trip. Any time you'll be away for more than two days, you'll save money by turning it off. Reheating the water when you get home is much cheaper than keeping it hot.

lower temperature also makes scalding less likely, which is a serious problem with infants and the elderly.

Garbage disposal. Use cold water rather than hot to operate your food disposal. This saves the energy needed to heat the water and aids in getting rid of grease. Grease solidifies in cold water and can be ground up and washed away.

Tightwad Tip

Use energy-intensive appliances such as dishwashers, clothes washers and dryers, and electric ovens in the early morning or late evening hours to help reduce peak load energy use. Many utilities offer lower rates during the off-peak hours. Find out when your utility company offers the lowest rate, and take advantage of the savings.

Bet You Didn't Know

Heated waterbeds use more electricity than any other home appliance. If you own one, keep blankets and a comforter on top to help retain heat, and insulate the sides by tucking blankets in all the way around.

Lights and Appliances

Lighting, cooking, and running other appliances account for 24 percent of all the energy we use in our homes.

Kitchen and bath fans. Use kitchen, bath, and other ventilating fans wisely. In just one hour, these fans can blow away a house-full of warmed or cooled air. Be sure to turn them off as soon as they have done their job.

Cooking. In the kitchen, keep range-top burners and reflectors clean. They will reflect the heat better, and you will save energy. When you have a choice, use the range-top rather than the oven. When it makes sense, use small electric pans or ovens for small meals rather than the kitchen range or oven—they use much less energy. Microwaves and pressure cookers can also save energy because they cook at a much faster rate.

Faucet aerators. Install a water-saving device (an aerator) in your kitchen sink faucet. These are inexpensive to buy, and some utility companies will even give them to you free of charge. By reducing the amount of water in the flow, you use less hot water and save the energy that would have been required to heat it. The lower flow pressure is hardly noticeable.

Cold rinse. If you need to rinse dishes before putting them in the dishwasher, use cold water. Keep in mind that with many newer-model dishwashers, there's no need to rinse dishes before washing; just scrape off the food and load them.

Low suds. Don't use too much detergent when washing clothes. Oversudsing not only wastes detergent, but it also makes your washing machine work harder and use more energy. Presoak heavily soiled garments. You'll avoid two washings and save energy.

Lint control. Most of us know to keep the lint screen in the clothes dryer clean, but you also need to keep the outside exhaust of your clothes dryer clean. Check it regularly. A clogged exhaust lengthens drying time and increases the amount of energy used.

Steam wrinkles away. Save energy needed for ironing by hanging clothes in the bathroom while you're bathing or showering. Many times, the steam will remove the wrinkles, especially in knits, so you won't have to use the iron.

Clean lights. Always keep lamps and light fixtures clean. Clean fixtures will give off more light and save energy.

Energy-efficient appliances. When you buy a new appliance, look for the highest Energy Efficiency Rating (EER). The higher the number, the less it will cost you to operate. Buying an energy-efficient appliance may cost a bit more initially, but that expense will usually be recouped in reduced operating costs over the life of the appliance.

Bet You Didn't Know

When decorating, you can save energy by using light colors for walls, rugs, draperies, and furniture. They reflect light and therefore reduce the amount of artificial light required. (Light walls also make a room seem larger.)

Cold Storage

Refrigerators and freezers account for 15 percent of all the energy we use in our homes. When you are forced to replace these items, shop for an energy-efficient model.

Tight seal. Make sure your refrigerator door seals are airtight. Test them by closing the door over a dollar bill so it is half in and half out of the refrigerator. If you can pull out the dollar easily, the latch may need adjustment or the seal may need replacing.

Best temperatures. Don't keep your refrigerator or freezer too cold. Efficient temperatures are 38°F to 40°F for the fresh food compartment of the refrigerator, and 5°F for the freezer section. If you have a deep freezer for long-term storage, it should be set at 0°F; setting it at -10°F instead will increase its energy use by up to 20 percent.

Bet You Didn't Know

Think twice before you keep an old refrigerator around as a spare. Older models are energy hogs. Unless you really need the additional refrigerator space, it probably will cost more energy to keep it around than it's worth.

Defrost. Regularly defrost refrigerators and freezers. Frost buildup increases the amount of energy needed to keep the engine running. Never allow frost to build up more than a quarter of an inch thick.

Humidity down. To keep humidity under control in the refrigerator, liquids should always be covered. Keep drinks in covered pitchers or bottles with lids on them.

Close it. Keep the refrigerator door closed as much as possible. Opening it frequently or for long periods of time causes your refrigerator to work much harder. Keep milk and other frequently used items in the front of the refrigerator so your family can quickly get what they need without wasting energy.

Fill 'er up! A half-empty freezer uses much more energy to keep cold. To fill up the space, store ice cubes and make large blocks of ice in clean plastic milk cartons. The ice will come in handy for use in coolers and for backyard barbecues in summertime.

The Least You Need to Know

➤ Heating and air conditioning are big energy items; concentrate on reducing these first.

➤ Window treatments and what you wear around the house can have a big impact on how warm or cold you feel. Dress yourself and your windows for the season.

➤ An energy audit is the best way to find out what you need to do to conserve energy around your house. Some local utilities will be happy to do the audit for you.

➤ Refrigerators and freezers account for 15 percent of energy consumed; making them efficient will reap big rewards.

Chapter 24

Chapter 24

Pesky Pests

In This Chapter

- Nontoxic ways to eliminate ants, cockroaches, flies, and other nasty indoor insects
- Discouraging deer, rabbits, and gophers from raiding your garden
- Homemade people-safe insect repellents and fly traps
- Quick relief from insect bites
- Dealing with not-so-nice mice, moles, mosquitoes, and moths
- Snubbing skunks, silverfish, and slugs

To keep pests from making your home their home, make sure you don't inadvertently provide them with food, water, and shelter. Here are some tips for keeping them from taking up residence in your house—and for getting rid of them, should they do so.

Mothballs. This is an inexpensive, widely available deterrent to many pests. Several types of insects, and mice, raccoons and even visiting cats and dogs are put off by the smell. However, mothballs are also potentially very dangerous to children and pets, so you should use extreme caution or avoid using them if you have two- or four-legged little ones around.

Don't just scatter mothballs here and there. Instead put them in a plastic container (a margarine tub works perfectly) and punch holes in the lid so the smell can escape. Place the mothball containers behind stoves, refrigerators and beds, and near the doors to outside.

Smart Solution

Keep ants away from the food on your picnic table by placing each table leg into a bucket or plastic bowl of water. The ants cannot swim, so they will leave your picnic food alone! This strategy also works to keep ants out of baby's playpen when outside.

Annoying Ants

To keep ants away, the best defense is to not leave food where they might get it. Keep any crumbs or other small pieces of food wiped up, and keep pantry items in well-sealed storage jars and containers. If ants can't find food in your house, they'll look elsewhere.

Block their path. Ants enter your house in search of food. When they find food, they establish a path that leads back to their nest outside. Follow the trail to the point of entry into the house, and seal it off, if you can, with caulk.

Outdoor ant hills can be destroyed by pouring boiling water down each opening.

To keep ants from coming inside your house, plant mint or tansy around the house foundations. Or try sprinkling any of these outside near doors and around windows and the house foundation—and anywhere else that ants travel:

➤ A mixture of 2 cups of borax and 1 to 2 cups of powdered sugar
➤ Used coffee grounds
➤ Equal parts of red pepper and sugar
➤ Talcum powder
➤ Cream of tartar
➤ Bay leaves
➤ Cinnamon
➤ Oil of cloves

Vinegar. A fairly effective ant stopper for inside the house is ordinary white vinegar. Wash down any areas where you see ants with full-strength vinegar, and let the area air dry. Don't forget to wipe down around the windows in the kitchen, too.

Cinnamon. Place a cucumber on kitchen shelves and sprinkle a little cinnamon on it, or leave out a few sticks of cinnamon gum to keep ants off your shelves of food.

Bay leaves. To keep ants out of your flour and sugar containers, place a couple of bay leaves inside the containers. Replace them once a month.

Soap and water. To kill ants that are already in the house, spray them with a solution of water and 1 tablespoon of liquid soap in a spray bottle.

Ant Traps

These are safe and nonpoisonous.

$1/4$ cup sugar

$1/4$ cup baking yeast

$1/2$ cup molasses

3×5-inch small index cards

Mix sugar, yeast, and molasses in a small bowl, and smear a thin layer of the mixture on index cards with a spatula. Place the cards, syrup side up, in areas where ants travel.

Aphids

Wash aphids off house plants in the sink under a gentle flow of water. Spray a large group with a solution of mild detergent in water, or dab the leaves with a cotton ball dipped in alcohol after you have rinsed them off with water.

Cockroaches

Cockroaches can be the toughest of all pests to get rid of, and sometimes they seem worse than other pests. To clear them out of your house, try these solutions.

Boric acid. Dust all the cracks and crevices in the kitchen (especially under appliances, moldings, and cupboards) and any other areas where you see roaches with boric acid powder. Don't forget to dust under sinks and any other dark places they can hide. Keep the boric acid away from children and pets.

Boric acid will not kill roaches as fast as some pesticides, but it will have a long-lasting effect. This is because if roaches don't pick up a toxic dose of another pesticide the first time, they learn to stay clear. But with boric acid, they keep going back into it until they die. (Boric acid works on ants, too.)

Smart Solution

You can buy boric acid powder at drug, hardware, or grocery stores.

Get them drunk. Another way to do in roaches is to fill a large bowl with wine and set it under the kitchen sink, or wherever they tend to congregate. The roaches will drink the wine, become disoriented, fall into the bowl, and drown.

Cement 'em. Place a bowl of dry cement next to a bowl of water. Roaches are curious—they will walk through both bowls, and when they do, their legs will become cemented.

Cockroach Bait

This bait is very effective for cockroaches. They simply can't refuse it. An added bonus is ants like it, too!

> 1 teaspoon boric acid powder
>
> 2 1/2 ounces corn syrup

Mix the boric acid powder with the corn syrup in a pan. Heat together over warm heat on the stove until the boric acid powder completely dissolves. Cool and dilute the mixture with equal parts of water. Now you've got yourself a sugary, sticky ant and roach bait.

Use a spoon or an eye dropper to fill bottle caps (or other small containers) with the bait. Place the bottle caps where you know roaches or ants have been. You can also use the eye dropper to squeeze the bait into cracks around the foundation of the house inside and outside. Be sure to keep this bait out of the reach of children or pets.

Cockroach Balls

You can make a batch of these cockroach balls and use some now and save the rest for later. They aren't hard to make and the cockroaches are really attracted to them. You'll see the cockroach population decrease quickly when you use this recipe.

> 1 cup borax
>
> 1/4 cup sugar
>
> 1/4 cup chopped onion
>
> 1 tablespoon water

Make a paste of the ingredients, and roll it into about 50 little balls. Place two or three balls into small (sandwich-size) plastic bags, and leave the tops open. Place the bags anywhere you have a roach problem. (Be careful to hide the bags where small children and pets cannot get to them.) The roaches will eat the balls and carry some back to their home. The active ingredient, borax, clogs their breathing passages. The onion scent draws them in to eat.

With this method, you probably won't see many dead roaches because they will die where they live, out of sight.

Deer

Deer are beautiful animals, but they have big appetites. If you don't quickly find a remedy to keep them away from your garden, you won't see a harvest. Here are some ideas to try.

Deer Repellent #1

This repellent will not hurt the deer; it'll just scare them away from your garden or flowers.

> 1 old sheet or a yard of thin cotton or muslin
>
> ¹/₄ cup blood meal
>
> 1 cup hair clippings
>
> String or rubber bands

Cut the fabric into about 20 small squares (about 4 inches by 4 inches). Mix the blood meal and hair together, and place about 1 tablespoon into the center of each square. Bring up the ends and secure them with string or a rubber band.

Smart Solution

If you don't trim your hair at home, ask your barber or beautician if you can sweep up your hair and take it home to repel deer and rabbits.

Hang these packets from the branches of the trees and shrubs where deer are a problem. Deer will avoid the area as soon as you hang up the packets.

Deer Repellent #2

This recipe works great because deer don't like the smell or taste of blood meal—but your plants, trees, and shrubs love the blood meal.

> 1 teaspoon blood meal
>
> 1 gallon warm water

Mix together the blood meal and water. Spray the mixture on and around the shrubs, trees, and plants the deer like to eat.

Deer Repellent #3

The scent of this repellant will send deer elsewhere for a meal.

> 1 cup milk
>
> 2 eggs
>
> 2 tablespoons liquid soap
>
> 2 tablespoons cooking oil
>
> 2 gallons water

Mix together and spray your plants with it. The scent offends deer.

Other Deer Detractors

This list will give you plenty of other things you can try to keep those deer away from your garden. Keep in mind that sprays and powders need to be reapplied after a soaking rain.

➤ Spray trees, shrubs, and around the perimeter of your garden with a mixture of 1 teaspoon dishwashing detergent, 1 egg, and 1 quart water. The soap smell and/or taste keeps them away.

➤ Fix a cord around the garden about 3 feet high, and tie pieces of white cloth along the cord every 2 feet. The flash of white at tail height means danger to deer.

For other deer-repellent techniques, see Chapter 7, "The Lawn and Garden."

Bet You Didn't Know

If stray dogs, raccoons, deer, or other animals are attacking your garbage, sprinkle full-strength ammonia over the garbage bags before placing them in the cans. The ammonia will not only discourage animals, but it will also keep away most insects.

Fleas

These little insects are no fun. You'll need to go into red alert mode when you find them in the house and on your pets.

Comb your pet frequently with a flea comb to remove adult fleas and eggs. Bathe the animal in a mixture of orange oil and shampoo. If you cannot find orange oil, buy a shampoo containing some citrus extract.

Get—and keep—fleas out of the house by steam-cleaning all rugs and pet bedding. Be sure to wash the pet bedding with hot water. Vacuum the furniture, rugs, all people bedding, and all the baseboards.

Flies

To kill flying insects such as flies, wasps, and bees, use hair spray. Most insect sprays will only infuriate wasps and bees, but the hair spray will harden their wings so they cannot fly. They will literally drop like flies!

You can use herbs to get rid of flies, too. Put sprigs of elder, lavender, or mint in vases, or hang them up; rub the leaves frequently so that the scent is released.

To prevent flies from swarming around the garbage cans, see sidebar, above, or wash the cans out with the garden hose and allow them to dry in the sun. Then sprinkle some powdered laundry detergent in them.

Fly Paper

This is an old-fashioned solution and isn't very pretty to look at, but it does work well and you can see the results. For out-of-the-way areas, this may be just the solution you're looking for.

> 2 cups milk
>
> 2 tablespoons black pepper
>
> 2 tablespoons white sugar
>
> 2 tablespoons brown sugar
>
> Brown paper bags, cut into strips

Boil the milk, pepper, and sugar together for five minutes. Simmer uncovered for five minutes more, or until thickened. Let cool. Roll the brown paper strips into a tight ball, and drop them into the milk mixture. Let them become completely saturated, then unroll the strips gently and let them air-dry on a cookie sheet. The strips are ready to hang when they are slightly sticky to the touch.

When ready to use, suspend the strips up and out of the way wherever flies are a problem. Keep the strips away from young children, especially when they are covered with flies. The fly paper can look pretty ugly when full of flies, but it is quite effective.

Fly Repellent

In areas where you don't want to look at fly paper, try this fly repellent instead.

> 4 tablespoons crushed bay leaves
>
> 3 tablespoons ground cloves
>
> 3 tablespoons eucalyptus leaves
>
> 1 tablespoon eucalyptus oil
>
> 1 yard loosely woven fabric, cut into 10 4-inch squares
>
> 8-inch lengths of string or ribbon

Mix all the spices and oil in a glass or an enamel bowl. Place about 1 tablespoon in the center of a square of fabric, bring up the four sides of the square, and tie with a string or ribbon to secure. You should have enough to make 10 bags. Hang the bags up and out of the way in doorways or other areas where flies are a problem.

Smart Solution

In the spring, moving leftover firewood away from the house will help discourage insects that may nest in the wood from infesting your house.

Fruit Flies

Fruit flies grow and thrive in decaying fruit. When possible, refrigerate your fruit to prevent it from attracting them.

Basil repellent. A few sprigs of fresh basil in the fruit bowl will also repel fruit flies. If you keep a small pot of basil growing in your kitchen, you probably won't have to worry about fruit flies. It's a good idea to grow basil in pots right outside the door. The pots look pretty, you can use the basil in cooking, and they will help keep fruit flies away.

Fruit fly trap. Place a piece of cut-up ripe fruit in the bottom of a small bottle or jar. Roll a piece of paper into a funnel shape; leave the large funnel opening at the top and the narrow end at the bottom. Pour a little beer or vinegar in the bottom of the jar over the fruit. Fruit flies will fly into the trap to get the fruit and be unable to get out. The beer or vinegar will drown them.

Gnats

To keep the gnats away while you're outside, rub a thin layer of baby oil on all exposed skin—or dab a little vanilla extract on your skin.

Gophers

Place a large rock or patio stone at least 12 inches in diameter in the middle of the lawn. Take a shovel with a straight wooden handle, and pound it on the stone for two to three minutes twice a day for at least three days. The vibration will scare the gophers and drive them away. This is the method old farmers swear by.

If you are using a gopher trap (made of metal screening, similar to a crab trap), bait it with peanut butter.

Treating Insect Bites

Any of these remedies will relieve itching and minimize inflammation due to insect bites:

➤ Apply a paste of either cornstarch or baking soda, mixed with a little vinegar, fresh lemon juice, or witch hazel.

➤ Apply a paste made of meat tenderizer and water.

➤ Rub bites with a wet bar of soap.

➤ Rub a dab of white toothpaste over the spot.

Researchers have found that garlic is an effective, safe, and cheap insecticide for most all kinds of indoor and outdoor insect pests. In studies, garlic insecticide killed up to 95 percent of common pests such as mosquitoes, slugs, crickets, houseflies, and weevils. Garlic works as an insecticide because it contains allicin, which stops protein synthesis in many bugs.

Home-Brewed Garlic Insecticide

This is simple to make and is also nontoxic. Spray on your plants, flowers, bushes, trees, or anywhere, inside or out, that you see pests. This formula will kill the un-wanted pests but will not harm your pets.

> 3 ounces of finely chopped garlic
>
> 2 teaspoons of mineral oil
>
> 1 pint of water
>
> 1 tablespoon of liquid soap

Soak the garlic in mineral oil for 24 hours or longer. Then slowly add a pint of water in which the soap has been added. Stir well. Strain the liquid, and store it in a glass jar or plastic container. To prevent a reaction, do not store the garlic insecticide in any type of metal container.

This homemade insecticide is highly concentrated. For the first application, dilute one part garlic insecticide in 20 parts of water. After the first application, use one part garlic brew to 100 parts water.

Pantry Bugs

Mealworms. These little pests that you usually don't see, which are attracted to open packages of macaroni, noodles, and spaghetti—they will eat through the package to get inside the noodles—are repelled by the smell of spearmint. You won't be bothered by these pests if you place a few sticks of wrapped spearmint chewing gum in or near the packages. Be sure to leave the gum wrapped so that it won't dry out and lose its spearmint scent.

Weevils and moths. To deter weevils and food moths from laying eggs in flour, rice, dried beans, and grains, place a bay leaf in each of the containers.

Tiny insect eggs can travel with grains through harvesting, processing, and packaging. Prevent bugs from hatching in wholegrain flour and other grains by freezing unopened packages for 24 hours. Freezing kills any eggs that might be in the bag.

Smart Solution

Soak pieces of paper in vinegar and put them around the edges of the garden. This will keep cats, dogs, rabbits, and other animals away from your garden. Replace the vinegar-soaked paper once a week.

Mice

There are few things that send us screaming on top of chairs or tables, but mice can really drive us crazy. Whether you are scared to death of them or just think they need to go, here are some ideas to eliminate them.

Mint. Keep a pot of peppermint growing in your kitchen window, and keep some sprigs of fresh mint in your kitchen cabinets and on the counters to keep mice away. Rub the plants often to release their scent. You can also saturate a piece of cardboard with oil of peppermint, available at most drugstores.

Bet You Didn't Know

Plants and herbs can do a better job of repelling insects if you lightly rub the fresh or dry leaves to release the scent.

No more mouse holes. Plug up mouse holes wherever you see them. Steel wool does a good job.

Yummy peanut butter. Bait traps with peanut butter. The smell will bring the mice running.

Keep a cat. Cat scent alone is many times enough to discourage mice and keep them away.

Moles

Pinwheels placed around the lawn will scare away moles. Flooding their tunnels with water from the garden hose will also work, but it may take a while because moles love to tunnel and probably have miles of them around your property.

Mosquitoes

Not only are mosquitoes pesky, they also want to have us for lunch. You need to launch an all-out attack on them quickly.

Eliminate breeding sites. Cover rain gutters if they have puddles of water, and try to eliminate all puddles and any other standing water near the house. Mosquitoes breed in water and multiply quickly.

If you have saucers of water under plants, change the water often to keep mosquitoes from breeding.

If your shed or barn has a flat roof, drop a little oil (any type of oil is fine) in any puddles that accumulate. The oil will discourage mosquitoes from setting there.

Lights. Colored lights will attract fewer insects and mosquitoes than white or clear lights. Hang Christmas lights on the patio for illumination. When the bulbs burn out, replace them with yellow or amber-colored bulbs. You'll get more light and fewer bugs.

Keep Them Away!

Mosquitoes just seem to like some people more than others. To make yourself less attractive to them, try these ideas:

➤ Eat less sugar. Mosquitoes love to attack people who eat lots of it.

➤ Rub a little chamomile or vinegar on your skin. Drinking chamomile tea also will help keep them away.

➤ Gently rub a sheet of fabric softener on your skin to drive away the mosquitoes.

➤ Eat more garlic or take garlic pills.

➤ Rub cucumber ice cubes on your face and hands. To make them, peel and strain cucumbers and freeze the liquid in an ice cube tray.

Moths

Moth holes ruin clothes. Here are some ways to keep moths away from them.

Cedar. If you can't stand the smell of mothballs, use cedar in your closets and drawers instead. Cedar is nonpoisonous and comes in chips, blocks of wood, hangers, and even drawer liners.

Rosemary. Large sprigs of fresh rosemary are good for keeping moths away. Lay a few sprigs on the closet shelf, and keep the door shut so the fragrance can fill the closet.

Sachets. Make homemade moth-repellent sachets. Fill cheesecloth bags, clean socks, or nylon stockings with any combination of the following: cedar chips, dried lavender, dried mint, dried rosemary, whole peppercorns, or aromatic pipe tobacco.

Rabbits

Rabbits can and will eat almost anything green. Even flowers with stickers (such as rose bushes) aren't safe from these greedy little creatures! To keep them from making a meal out of your flowers and garden, give these a try:

➤ Scatter human hair clippings around the garden or flower bed. You can put the hair into pieces of fabric or use old panty hose to hold the hair. (See deer repellents, earlier in the chapter.)

➤ Plant horseradish throughout your vegetable patch, since rabbits don't like the smell.

For more rabbit-repellent techniques, see Chapter 7, "Lawn and Garden."

Smart Solution

To keep squirrels out of a bird feeder, cut a hole in the bottom of a small plastic wastebasket, and slide it upside down on the pole that holds the feeder.

Silverfish

Silverfish breed in high humidity, so you may see them in the bathrooms. They also love to get in books. Vacuum the area where you see silverfish, and do your best to lower the humidity in the room, either by using a dehumidifier or turning on the air conditioner instead of leaving your wondows open when it's humid outside. Sprinkle the area with cloves or Epsom salts.

You can also sprinkle a mixture of boric acid powder and sugar on affected areas. Do not use boric acid on any areas that children or pets can get into.

Skunks

Can you believe that skunks hate strong odors? It's true! So, to keep skunks from making your barn, garage, or shed their home, hang a bar of strong-smelling soap or a room deodorizer in the building.

Slugs

Slugs are just plain ugly! The creepy trail of slime they leave on sidewalks is enough to make you want to get rid of them, but they also like to munch on your flowers and vegetables. Here's how to get rid of them.

Ginger. Sprinkle ginger around the plants that slugs prey on to keep them away.

Salt. To discourage slugs from slithering under a door, pour a line of salt across the outside of the doorway. Slugs are mostly water, so the salt will dehydrate them immediately. You can also sprinkle salt on slugs to kill them. (But if they're not bothering you, then don't bother them.)

Beer. To eliminate slugs, fill a small bowl about half full with beer, and put it on the ground or sidewalk near the plants where slugs like to eat. The slugs will be attracted by the yeasty smell, fall in the bowl, and drown.

Slug Cocktail

If you don't have any beer on hand, here's another "cocktail" the slugs love.

> 2 tablespoons flour
>
> 1 teaspoon sugar
>
> 1 teaspoon baker's yeast
>
> 2 cups warm water

Mix all together and pour into a bowl. Set the bowl on the ground or sidewalk near the plants where slugs like to eat. This works just like the beer: The slugs will be attracted by the yeast, fall in the bowl and drown.

Snails

You probably don't see as many snails as slugs, but when you do, you will want to eliminate them because they are just as troublesome.

Ginger. Sprinkle ginger around the plants where you see snails, since they don't like the smell.

Eggshells. Crush pieces of eggshells around newly planted vegetables or flowers to keep snails away. They won't climb over the rough shell pieces.

Spiders

Even though spiders help us out by eating flies that bother us, most of us don't like living with them. Use these tips to keep the spiders out of your house:

➤ Leave soap scraps and the last little bit of stick deodorant in places where you see spiders. The smell will deter them.

➤ To keep spiders from entering the house through windows, leave hedge apples on the windowsills.

➤ Dust spiderwebs out of corners often. Where there is a spiderweb, there is a spider.

➤ Spray cotton with pennyroyal (a variety of mint, from the garden shop or health food store), and place it where spiders enter the house.

➤ Rub the inside and outside of windowsills with rubbing alcohol or insect spray.

The Least You Need to Know

➤ Mothballs will keep many types of pests at bay—but keep them away from pets and children because they're toxic.

➤ Ants dislike cinnamon, tansy, mint, cloves, and powder; place these in their paths.

➤ Boric acid powder is the secret ingredient in your war on cockroaches.

➤ Human hair and blood meal around the garden discourage deer and rabbits from feasting on your veggies.

➤ Make yourself unappealing to mosquitoes with vinegar, garlic, chamomile, or cucumbers.

➤ Protect grains in your pantry with spearmint or bay leaves.

➤ Rub windowsills and other places spiders hang out with sticks of deodorant or cotton balls dipped in pennyroyal, rubbing alcohol, or common insect repellent.

This for That: Substitutions for Common Ingredients

Allspice 1 teaspoon = 1 teaspoon cinnamon plus $1/8$ teaspoon ground cloves.

Arrowroot 1 tablespoon = 2 tablespoons all-purpose flour or 1 tablespoon corn-starch.

Baking powder 1 teaspoon = $1/4$ teaspoon baking soda plus $1/2$ teaspoon cream of tartar.

Beef stock 1 cup = 1 cup water plus 2 teaspoons soy sauce; or 1 cup water plus a bouillon cube or instant bouillon.

Bread crumbs 1 cup = 1 cup crushed corn flakes or $3/4$ cup cracker crumbs.

Broth, chicken or beef 1 cup = 1 bouillon cube or 1 envelope instant broth dissolved in 1 cup boiling water.

Brown sugar, light 1 cup = $1/2$ cup dark brown sugar plus $1/2$ cup granulated sugar.

Butter 1 cup = 1 cup vegetable shortening plus $1/2$ teaspoon salt.

Buttermilk 1 cup = 1 cup plain yogurt; or 1 cup whole milk plus 1 tablespoon lemon juice or white vinegar (let stand 5 minutes for lemon juice and 10 minutes for vinegar); or $1/2$ cup plain nonfat yogurt mixed with $1/2$ cup skim milk.

Cayenne $1/8$ teaspoon = 3 to 4 drops of pepper sauce or Tabasco sauce.

Celery seed Use the same amount of finely chopped celery leaves.

Chili sauce 1 cup = 1 cup tomato sauce plus 2 tablespoons sugar, 1 tablespoon vinegar, and $1/8$ teaspoon ground cloves.

Chocolate (unsweetened) 1 square (1 ounce) = 3 tablespoons cocoa plus 1 tablespoon butter or shortening.

Corn syrup, dark 1 cup = $3/4$ cup light corn syrup plus $1/4$ cup light molasses; or $11/4$ cups packed brown sugar plus $1/4$ cup water.

Corn syrup, light 1 cup = 1 $1/4$ cups granulated sugar plus $1/4$ cup water.

Cornstarch for thickening 1 tablespoon = 2 tablespoons all-purpose flour or 1 tablespoon arrowroot powder.

Cracker crumbs, fine $3/4$ cup = 1 cup fine dry bread crumbs.

Cream, heavy (for cooking and baking, but not for whipping) 1 cup = $3/4$ cup milk plus $1/3$ cup melted butter.

Cream, whipping 1 cup = $2/3$ cup well-chilled evaporated milk, whipped; or 1 cup nonfat dry milk powder whipped with 1 cup ice water.

Cream, light 1 cup = $7/8$ cup milk plus 3 tablespoons melted butter.

Cream, sour 1 cup = $7/8$ cup buttermilk or plain yogurt plus 3 tablespoons melted butter.

Cream, sour, for dip 1 cup = 1 cup plain nonfat yogurt.

Creamer for coffee Use instant nonfat powdered milk.

Egg, whole for baking 1 = 2 egg whites plus 1 tablespoon cooking oil and 1 $1/3$ tablespoon liquid to make up for the fat in the egg yolk. Or for baking cookies: 2 egg yolks plus 1 tablespoon water.

Flour, all-purpose 1 cup = $11/8$ cups cake flour; or 1 cup fine cornmeal.

Flour, self-rising 1 cup = 1 cup all-purpose flour plus $1/3$ teaspoon baking powder plus $1/4$ teaspoon salt; or 1 cup all-purpose flour plus 1 teaspoon baking soda plus 2 teaspoons cream of tartar.

Fruit juice 1 cup for cooking = 1 cup brewed spicy herb tea

Garlic 1 small clove = $1/8$ teaspoon garlic powder or instant minced garlic

Gravy browner Use strong coffee or instant coffee granules.

Half and half, for cooking or baking 1 cup = $7/8$ cup milk plus $11/2$ tablespoons melted butter.

Herbs, dried 1 teaspoon = 1 tablespoon fresh, minced, and packed.

Herbs, fresh 1 tablespoon = 1 teaspoon dried herbs.

Honey 1 cup = $11/4$ cups sugar plus $1/4$ cup water.

Ketchup 1 cup = 1 cup tomato sauce plus 2 tablespoons sugar, 1 tablespoon vinegar, and $1/8$ teaspoon ground cloves.

Lemon juice 1 teaspoon = 2 teaspoons vinegar. (This can be substituted when making jams, preserves, pie crusts—almost anything except a lemon pie.)

Lemon rind, grated 1 teaspoon = $1/2$ teaspoon lemon extract.

Mace Use the same amount of nutmeg.

Marshmallows 1 large one = 10 small ones.

Milk, skim 1 cup = $1/3$ cup instant nonfat dry milk plus $3/4$ cup water.

Milk, whole 1 cup = $1/2$ cup evaporated milk plus $1/2$ cup water; or 1 cup water, $1/3$ cup instant nonfat dry milk, and 2 teaspoons melted butter; or 1 cup skim milk plus 2 teaspoons melted butter.

Mustard, prepared 1 teaspoon = $1/4$ teaspoon dry mustard plus $3/4$ teaspoon vinegar.

Nonstick cooking spray Mix 5 ounces vegetable oil and 1 ounce vodka in a spray bottle (shake well before using).

Oil for baking Use the same amount of applesauce.

Onion, chopped 1 small = 1 tablespoon instant minced onion; or 1 teaspoon onion powder; or $1/4$ cup frozen chopped onions.

Parsley Use the same amount of celery leaves.

Red pepper sauce 3 to 4 drops = $1/8$ teaspoon cayenne pepper.

Saffron Substitute turmeric.

Shortening 1 cup = 1 cup plus 2 tablespoons butter or margarine; or use $2/3$ cup oil for baking.

Steak sauce Mix equal parts of Worcestershire sauce and ketchup.

Sugar 1 cup = 1 cup firmly packed brown sugar; or $1 3/4$ cups confectioner's sugar (do not substitute in baking); or 2 cups corn syrup.

Sugar, brown 1 cup = 1 cup granulated sugar mixed with 2 to 4 tablespoons dark molasses (use 2 tablespoons molasses for light brown sugar or 4 tablespoons for dark). Mix thoroughly with a fork to distribute molasses.

Sugar, confectioner's 1 cup = 1 cup granulated sugar plus 1 tablespoon cornstarch. Blend several minutes at high speed.

Sugar, refined or superfine, for baking Blend small batches of granulated sugar in a blender at high speed.

Tabasco sauce 3 to 4 drops = $1/8$ teaspoon cayenne pepper.

Tomato juice 1 cup = $1/2$ cup tomato sauce plus $1/2$ cup water plus a dash each of salt and sugar; or $1/4$ cup tomato paste plus $3/4$ cup water plus a dash each of salt and sugar.

Tomato ketchup 1 cup = 1 cup tomato sauce plus 2 tablespoons sugar, 1 tablespoon vinegar, and $1/8$ teaspoon ground cloves.

Tomato paste 1 tablespoon = 1 tablespoon ketchup; or stir and heat to the bubbly stage 1 teaspoon flour mixed with 6 tablespoons tomato sauce.

Tomato puree 1 cup = $1/2$ cup tomato paste plus $1/2$ cup water.

Tomato soup 1 can ($10^{1}/2$ ounces) = 1 cup tomato sauce plus $1/4$ cup water.

Tomatoes, canned 1 cup = $1/2$ cup tomato sauce plus $1/2$ cup water; or $1^{1}/3$ cups chopped fresh tomatoes, simmered.

Vanilla 1-inch bean = 1 teaspoon vanilla extract.

Vinegar, white 1 teaspoon = 2 teaspoons lemon juice.

Wine, dry white $1/4$ cup = $1/3$ cup dry white vermouth; or use chicken broth for savory dishes and apple, pineapple, or orange juice for sweet foods or desserts.

Worcestershire sauce Diluted steak sauce (half steak sauce, half water); or plain soy sauce.

Yeast 1 cake ($^{3}/4$ ounce) = 1 package active dried yeast or 2 teaspoons granulated baking yeast.

Useful Weights and Measures

Measures and Equivalents

Tablespoon—Teaspoon

1 tablespoon	=	3 teaspoons
$7/8$ tablespoon	=	$2 1/2$ teaspoons
$3/4$ tablespoon	=	$2 1/4$ teaspoons
$2/3$ tablespoon	=	2 teaspoons
$5/8$ tablespoon	=	$1 7/8$ teaspoons
$1/2$ tablespoon	=	$1 1/2$ teaspoons
$3/8$ tablespoon	=	$1 1/8$ teaspoons
$1/3$ tablespoon	=	1 teaspoon
$1/4$ tablespoon	=	$3/4$ teaspoon

Cup—Tablespoon

1 cup	=	16 tablespoons
$7/8$ cup	=	14 tablespoons
$3/4$ cup	=	12 tablespoons
$2/3$ cup	=	$10 2/3$ tablespoons
$5/8$ cup	=	10 tablespoons

$^1/_2$ cup = 8 tablespoons

$^3/_8$ cup = 6 tablespoons

$^1/_3$ cup = 5$^1/_3$ tablespoons

$^1/_4$ cup = 4 tablespoons

$^1/_8$ cup = 2 tablespoons

$^1/_{16}$ cup = 1 tablespoon

Pint—Cup

1 pint = 2 cups

$^7/_8$ pint = 1$^3/_4$ cups

$^3/_4$ pint = 1$^1/_2$ cups

$^2/_3$ pint = 1$^1/_3$ cups

$^5/_8$ pint = 1$^1/_4$ cups

$^1/_2$ pint = 1 cup

$^3/_8$ pint = $^3/_4$ cup

$^1/_3$ pint = $^2/_3$ cup

$^1/_4$ pint = $^1/_2$ cup

$^1/_8$ pint = $^1/_4$ cup

$^1/_{16}$ pint = $^1/_8$ cup

Quart—Pint—Cup

1 quart = 2 pints

$^7/_8$ quart = 3$^1/_2$ cups

$^3/_4$ quart = 3 cups

$^2/_3$ quart = 2$^2/_3$ cups

$^5/_8$ quart = 2$^1/_2$ cups

$^1/_2$ quart = 1 pint

$^3/_8$ quart = 1$^1/_2$ cups

$^1/_3$ quart = 1$^1/_3$ cups

$^1/_4$ quart = 1 cup

$^1/_8$ quart = $^1/_2$ cup

$^1/_{16}$ quart = $^1/_4$ cup

Gallon—Quart—Pint—Cup

1 gallon = 4 quarts

$^7/_8$ gallon = $3^1/_2$ quarts

$^3/_4$ gallon = 3 quarts

$^2/_3$ gallon = $10^2/_3$ cups

$^5/_8$ gallons = 5 pints

$^1/_2$ gallon = 2 quarts

$^3/_8$ gallon = 3 pints

$^1/_3$ gallon = $5^1/_3$ cups

$^1/_4$ gallon = 1 quart

$^1/_8$ gallon = 1 pint

$^1/_{16}$ gallon = 1 cup

Pound—Ounces

1 pound = 16 ounces

$^7/_8$ pound = 14 ounces

$^3/_4$ pound = 12 ounces

$^2/_3$ pound = $10^2/_3$ ounces

$^5/_8$ pound = 10 ounces

$^1/_2$ pound = 8 ounces

$^3/_8$ pound = 6 ounces

$^1/_3$ pound = $5^1/_3$ ounces

$^1/_4$ pound = 4 ounces

$^1/_8$ pound = 2 ounces

$^1/_{16}$ pound = 1 ounce

Oven Temperatures

250°F to 275°F = Very slow oven

300°F to 325°F = Slow oven

350°F to 375°F = Moderate oven

400°F to 425°F = Hot oven

450°F to 475°F = Very hot oven

500°F to 525°F = Extremely hot oven

Linear Measurements

1 hand = 4 inches

1 link = 7.92 inches

1 span = 9 inches

1 foot = 12 inches

1 yard = 3 feet

1 fathom = 2 yards; 6 feet

1 rod = $5^{1}/_{2}$ yards

1 chain = 100 links; 22 yards; 66 feet

1 furlong = $^{1}/_{8}$ mile; 40 rods; 220 yards; 660 feet

1 statute mile = 8 furlongs; 320 rods; 1,760 yards; 5,280 feet

1 international nautical mile = 1,852 kilometers; 6,076.115 feet

1 knot = 1 nautical mile per hour

1 league = 3 miles; 24 furlongs

Metric Measurements

Acre = 4,840 square yards; 43,560 square feet; 0.4047 hectare; 4,047 square meters

Are = 100 square meters; 119.60 square yards

Bushel = 4 pecks; 2,150.42 cubic inches; 35.239 liters

Centigram = 0.01 gram; 0.154 grain

Centiliter = 0.01 liter; 0.61 cubic inch; 0.338 fluid ounce

Centimeter = 0.01 meter; 0.39 inch

Cubic centimeter = 0.0000001 cubic meter; 0.061 cubic inch

Cubic decimeter = 0.001 cubic meter; 61.023 cubic inches; 0.908 dry quart; 1.057 liquid quarts

Cubic inch = 0.00058 cubic foot; 16,387 cubic centimeters

Cubic foot = 1,728 cubic inches; 0.0370 cubic yard; 0.028 cubic meter

Cubic meter = 1.307 cubic yards

Cubic yard = 27 cubic feet; 46,656 cubic inches; 0.765 cubic meter

Decigram = 0.10 gram; 1/543 grains

Deciliter = 0.10 liter; 6.1 cubic inches; 0.18 dry pint; 0.21 liquid pint

Decimeter = 0.10 meter; 3.95 inches

Dekagram = 10 grams; 0.353 ounce

Dekaliter = 10 liters; .35 cubic feet; 2.64 gallons

Dekameter = 10 meters; 32.81 feet

Dram = 27.344 grains; 0.0625 ounce; 1.772 grams

Fluid ounce = 8 fluidrams; 29,573 milliliters

Fluidram = $1/8$ fluid ounce; $3/4$ teaspoon; 3,697 milliliters

Foot = 12 inches; 0.333 yard; 30.48 centimeters

Gill = 5 fluid ounces; 8.669 cubic inches; 142.066 cubic centimeters

Grain = 0.037 dram; 0.002286 ounce; 0.0648 gram

Gram = 1,000 milligrams; 0.035 ounce

Hectare = 10,000 square meters; 2.47 acres

Hectogram = 100 grams; 3,527 ounces

Hectoliter = 100 liters; 3.53 cubic feet; 2.84 bushels

Hectometer = 100 meters; 109.36 yards

Hundredweight = 100 pounds; 112 British pounds; 45.36 kilograms

Inch = 0.12 foot; 0.36 yard; 2.54 centimeters

Kilogram = 1,000 grams; 2.2046 pounds

Kilometer = 1,000 meters; 0.62 mile

Liter = 1,000 milliliters; 61.02 cubic inches; 0.908 dry quart; 1.057 liquid quarts

Meter = 0.1000 kilometer; 39.37 inches

Metric ton = 1,000,000 gram; 1.102 short tons

Mile (see Statute Mile)

Milligram = 0.001 gram; 0.015 grain

Milliliter = 0.001 liter; 0.061 cubic inch; 0.27 fluidram

Millimeter = 0.001 meter; 0.039 inch

Ounce = 16 drams; 4,375 grains; 28.350 grams

Peck = 8 quarts; 537.605 cubic inches; 8.810 liters

Pint = 0.5 quart; 16 ounces; 33.600 cubic inches; 0.551 liter

Pound = 16 ounces; 7,000 grains; 453.59 grams

Rod = 5.5 yards; 16.5 feet; 5.029 meters

Square centimeter = 0.0001 square meter; 0.155 square inch

Square foot = 144 square inches; 0.111 square yard; 0.093 square meter

Square kilometer = 1,000,000 square meters; 0.3861 square mile

Square meter = 1.20 square yards

Square mile = 640 acres

Square rod = 30.25 square yards; 25.293 square meters

Square yard = 1,296 square inches; 9 square feet; 0.836 square meter

Statute mile = 1,760 yards; 1.6093 kilometers

Ton, short = 20 short hundredweight; 2,000 pounds; 0.907 metric tons; 907.18 kilograms

Ton, long = 20 long hundredweight; 2,240 pounds; 1.016 metric tons; 1.017 kilograms

Yard = 3 feet; 36 inches; 0.9144 meter

Conversions

Celsius to Fahrenheit: Multiply by 9, divide by 5, add 32.

Centimeters to inches: Multiply by .394.

Cubic feet to inches: Multiply length times width times height, then multiply by 1,728.

Cubic feet to cubic meters: Multiply by .0283.

Cubic meters to cubic feet: Divide by .0283.

Fahrenheit to Celsius: Deduct 32, multiply by 5, divide by 9.

Fluid ounces to liters: Multiply by .0296.

Gammas (micrograms) to milligrams: Divide by 1,000.

Grams to pounds: Multiply by .0022.

Inches to cubic feet: Multiply length times width times height, and then divide by 1,728.

Kilograms to pounds: Divide by 2.2046.

Liters to fluid ounces: Multiply by 33.81.

Liters to quarts: Multiply by 1.057.

Milligrams to gammas (micrograms): Multiply by 1,000.

Milligrams to grams: Divide by 1,000.

Ounces to grams: Multiply by 28.35.

Pounds to kilos: Multiply by 2.2046.

Measuring off the Cuff

Centimeter = a little more than the width of a paper clip (about 0.4 inch)

Gram = a little more than the weight of a paper clip

Hectare = about 2.5 acres

Kilometer = somewhat more than $1/2$ mile (about .6 mile)

Liter = a little larger than a quart (about 1.06 quarts)

Meter = a little longer than a yard (about 1.1 yards)

Metric ton = about 1 ton (which is 2,500 pounds)

Millimeter = about the diameter of a paper clip wire

Canned Food Size Numbers

Occasionally recipes will call for cans by the numbers instead of ounces. Here's what the numbers mean:

No. 1 can	10 to 12 ounces
No. 300 can	14 to 16 ounces
No. 1 1/2 can	1 pound, 17 ounces
No. 303 can	1 pound, 17 ounces (same as No. 1 1/2 can)
No. 2 can	1 pound, 12 ounces to 1 pound, 14 ounces
No. 3 can	3 pounds, 3 ounces or 1 quart, 14 ounces
No. 10 can	6 pounds, 2 ounces or 7 pounds, 5 ounces (A no. 10 can can be either 6 pounds, 2 ounces or 7 pounds, 5 ounces.)

Index

C

U-V